Illicit Money

Illicit Money

Financing Terrorism in the Twenty-First Century

Jessica Davis

LYNNE
RIENNER
PUBLISHERS

BOULDER
LONDON

Published in the United States of America in 2021 by
Lynne Rienner Publishers, Inc.
1800 30th Street, Suite 314, Boulder, Colorado 80301
www.rienner.com

and in the United Kingdom by
Lynne Rienner Publishers, Inc.
Gray's Inn House, 127 Clerkenwell Road, London EC1 5DB

Library of Congress Cataloging-in-Publication Data
Names: Davis, Jessica, 1980– author.
Title: Illicit money : financing terrorism in the twenty-first century /
    Jessica Davis.
Description: Boulder, Colorado : Lynne Rienner Publishers, Inc., [2021] |
    Includes bibliographical references and index. | Summary: "Dissects how
    terrorists raise, use, and hide funds and explores means to counter
    these illicit activities"— Provided by publisher.
Identifiers: LCCN 2021016760 (print) | LCCN 2021016761 (ebook) | ISBN
    9781626379824 (hardcover) | ISBN 9781626379930 (ebook)
Subjects: LCSH: Terrorism—Finance.
Classification: LCC HV6431 .D295 2021 (print) | LCC HV6431 (ebook) | DDC
    363.325068/1—dc23
LC record available at https://lccn.loc.gov/2021016760
LC ebook record available at https://lccn.loc.gov/2021016761

British Cataloguing in Publication Data
A Cataloguing in Publication record for this book
is available from the British Library.

Printed and bound in the United States of America

∞   The paper used in this publication meets the requirements
     of the American National Standard for Permanence of
     Paper for Printed Library Materials Z39.48-1992.

5 4 3 2 1

Contents

Part 3 New Frontiers

Tables and Figures

Tables

Figures

Acknowledgments

This book was a long time in the making. The initial seeds of it were planted while I was still working at the Canadian Security Intelligence Service (CSIS), although my interest in financial matters and terrorism can more properly be traced back to my time at FINTRAC, Canada's financial intelligence unit, and perhaps even further, to my work on the G7 (then the G8) file at Global Affairs Canada. In fact, the financial component of terrorism has touched every aspect of my career, including my work with the Canadian Forces supporting the military deployment in Afghanistan. This is probably true of most counterterrorism practitioners, because money is one of the main underlying enablers of terrorist activity. To that end, I owe a great deal of thanks to all my former and current colleagues for encouraging and challenging me.

Illicit Money would not have come about without the support and encouragement of my husband, Ross Cameron; my family, Jennifer, Tamara, Donna, and Steve Davis; and of course, our beloved dog, Nugget.

I owe a debt of gratitude to Stephanie Carvin for providing early advice on the book proposal and insisting that I focus on the "so what?" of the argument. Danielle Cotter and Tracey Durner provided robust and in-depth comments on an early draft, and Graham Myres offered extensive comments on several aspects of the book. His critical eye significantly improved the manuscript.

I thank all my former colleagues who reviewed papers, pushed back on ideas, and encouraged flickers of insight. Although they have to remain nameless, I hope they accept my unending gratitude for taking the time to give feedback that made me a better analyst and, ultimately, a better writer.

I also thank the CSIS managers who supported this project while I still worked there. They demonstrated a great deal of trust in me when they allowed me to undertake this book (and my previous one, *Women in Modern Terrorism*), and I can only hope the book rewards that trust.

The gang at Intrepid Podcast also deserve my thanks, particularly for listening to my early morning rants about terrorist financing and for demonstrating unparalleled levels of enthusiasm for this project—even when my own was lagging.

I also owe thanks to my anonymous reviewers and particularly to Phil Williams for taking significant time with the manuscript, drawing my attention to missing resources, pointing out flaws in my logic or arguments, and also providing supportive comments. Those kind words were little sparks of joy during the editing process.

And last but most definitely not least, I thank Jillian Hunchak, who provided extensive research for portions of this book (particularly the section on kidnapping for ransom); Lucas Tersigni for his help pulling it all together; my copyeditor, Melanie Stafford; and my wonderful editor at Lynne Rienner Publishers, Marie-Claire Antoine. This is our second time working together on a book, and I hope it won't be our last.

Of course, all the errors, omissions, and oversights in this book are mine alone.

1

Financing Terrorism

Terrorist financing in the twenty-first century is a complex affair.
Terrorists use a wide variety of methods to raise funds; procure weapons
and goods; and conduct both inexpensive, low-complexity attacks and complex, expensive operations. This complexity is compounded by a superficial
public understanding of terrorist financing. Analysis of terrorist financing
has long been considered a niche area, with only a few scholars willing to
undertake work in the field. Among practitioners, the same is largely true;
understanding and countering terrorist financing is seen as a critical, if eso-
teric, area of specialization.

This state of affairs is unfortunate because money is fundamental to
terrorism, enabling organizational and operational activities. As we have
learned from the civil war literature, grievances might be the underlying
motivation for conflicts (including those that involve terrorism), but they
do not escalate into violent conflict without the economic means to do
so.[1] Of course, understanding grievances is critical to understanding terrorism, but grievances taken alone tend to overpredict conflict.[2] Understanding and assessing the feasibility of violence is foundational to understanding when rebellion and violence will occur. Terrorism occurs when
it is financially viable and is limited in scope and scale by the resources
to which terrorists have access.[3]

Although the literature on terrorist motivations (including radicalization)
can fill entire libraries, the literature on terrorist financing is far less developed. This is in part because of the lack of primary source data. Terrorists
tend to consider financial information of the utmost privacy and sensitivity
and go to great lengths to protect it. People also lack general comfort with

1

information of a financial nature, including in academia and among counter-terrorism practitioners.[4] As a result, although we know much about what motivates terrorists (although, as Sageman points out, this does little to help us identify who will become a terrorist), we know far less about the mechanism that underpins all of their activities and plans: financing.[5]

The main purpose of this book is to guide academics and practitioners in understanding terrorist financing. Beyond facilitating basic knowledge, this book also serves as a framework for analysts of terrorist financing by providing a theory from which to predict how terrorist groups, cells, and individuals will finance their activities. Scholars will recognize an effort to develop both normative and descriptive theories of terrorist financing that define and explain choices terrorists make, while simultaneously hypothesizing about the future of terrorist financing. Practitioners will recognize this theory as a method for structuring analysis, categorizing information, and predicting future terrorist financing methods. Ultimately, in this book I seek to further develop concepts of terrorist financing and identify patterns of activity that have emerged over time to deepen our understanding of past financing and to guide predictions of future activity.

Although I do not start from scratch in developing an analytic framework and theory of terrorist financing, only a handful of scholars have done work in this area. As Horgan and Taylor noted in 1999, terrorist financing is "a set of activities that have, to say the least, traditionally not received much attention in the terrorism literature, except by way of anecdotal evidence or black propaganda. Admittedly, little is actually known by way of empirical research about terrorist fund-raising as a whole."[6] Although the literature has advanced somewhat since 1999, our actual knowledge of terrorist financing remains limited.

Terrorist financing is a set of dynamic processes shaped by globalization, technological changes, and counterterrorist financing pressures. In response, terrorist groups seek to establish diversified portfolios, and many groups are eschewing overreliance on state sponsorship or wealthy donors.[7] For instance, al-Qaeda was much more fiscally "autonomous than its late-twentieth-century state-sponsored predecessors."[8] Increasingly, we need to understand this autonomy and diversification in order to design effective counterterrorism financing mechanisms and practices.

Methods, Analytical Frameworks, and Levels of Analysis

In this book I attempt to bring empiricism to the study of terrorist financing, building on previous cases and analyses. Whereas prior works were hamstrung by a limited amount of literature on terrorist financing, the increased number of analyses on this topic—combined with literature on rebel governance and civil war and insurgent financing—allows for more robust analysis as well as the development of typologies to explain current financing methods, tools, and techniques and what can be done to stop them. I build on a number of foundational studies, including the following.

Colin Clarke's *Terrorism, Inc.*, makes a significant contribution by differentiating between the gray and dark economies of terrorist financing, drawing distinctions between organizational and operational financing and highlighting key differences between kinetic and nonkinetic responses to terrorist financing.[9]

Timothy Wittig's *Understanding Terrorist Finance* provides a framework that supports systematic analysis of terrorist financing as he seeks to understand all the economic activities of terrorist actors. He moves beyond simple questions about terrorist financing to explore the sociopolitical meaning of terrorist financing activity, and he questions the utility of counterterrorist financing regimes for different groups.[10]

Jodi Vittori's *Terrorist Financing and Resourcing*, which provides a compelling overview of strategic financial choices terrorist groups face, provides a more expansive analysis by incorporating the concept of resourcing (moving beyond just financing) along with a typology of terrorist organizations that serves as a useful analytic framework for understanding financing/resourcing strategies of terrorist actors.[11]

The framework I propose here builds on these foundational studies. It is intended to be a tool that provides the ability to accurately categorize the observed financial activities of terrorist actors (how they raise, use, move, store, manage, and obscure funds), identifies the level of the actor (organization, cell, or individual), and determines if the activity is operational or organizational financing. I draw on the levels-of-analysis approach common in international relations.[12] Frameworks developed from a levels-of-analysis approach are analytic constructions designed to help make sense of the world.[13] This framework facilitates both qualitative and quantitative analysis of terrorist financing and provides a structure upon which to map empirical data. Ultimately in this book I aim to support the development of evidence-based policymaking in the counterterrorism financing space through the use of structured analysis and research methods. The creation of a comprehensive framework backed by data (even if tentative or preliminary) for understanding terrorist financing is critical for the field to move beyond its current state. The framework also proposes a common lexicon to describe the full range of activities in which terrorists engage in terms of financing. Fundamentally, clearly articulating the full spectrum of activities and behaviors in which terrorist engage, how often, and why will help to create a better understanding of the phenomenon of terrorist financing and enhance our ability to detect and deter the activity.

My framework draws on, solidifies, and modestly expands existing frameworks of terrorist financing. For instance, Dean C. Alexander writes about how terrorists interact with economic systems through companies and individuals that knowingly or unknowingly aid terrorists (what I call support networks), what products terrorists use (such as weapons), and the types of services they acquire (such as rental vehicles, flight schools, accountants, etc.).[14] In 2011, Michael Freeman proposed a compelling normative theory of terrorist financing, focusing specifically on how terrorists acquire funds. He reviewed the advantages and disadvantages of four primary types of terrorist fund-raising (state sponsorship, illegal activity, legal activity, and popular support). He argued that terrorists assess these sources of funds based on their quantity, legitimacy, security, reliability, control, and simplicity of implementation. Freeman noted that no two terrorist groups will have the same funding profile, and as a result, no single strategy exists to counter terrorist financing.[15]

Rudner identified four core elements of terrorist financing:

> "(a) the evolving Islamicist terror threat; (b) the pattern of terrorist activities and operations and their financing requirements; (c) terrorist economic management and the supply of funding to meet operational demands; and (d) counterterrorist institutional responses and interventions by governments and international organizations to staunch the flow of financial resources to terror groups, activities, and operations."[16]

Rudner also contrasted terrorist financing and counterterrorist financing, a distinction too infrequently made in the literature on both topics.

What most frameworks or theories regarding terrorist financing lack is a full description of financing mechanisms; many restrict themselves to only a few of the most common. For example, the Financial Action Task Force (FATF) defines terrorist financing as how funds are raised, moved, and used.[17] The Australian Financial Intelligence Unit (AUSTRAC) conceptualizes terrorist financing as the raising, transferring, and usage of funds for terrorist purposes.[18] Levitt and Jacobson describe a straightforward framework for understanding terrorist financing: the raising, laundering, storing, and accessing funds.[19] In practice, terrorist financing encompasses a broader range of activity than most models suggest.

The mechanisms involved in terrorist financing are often confused with the specific methods and tactics of financing. For instance, Dion-Schwartz, Manheim, and Johnston note five categories of terrorist financing activities. These include fund-raising, illegal drugs/arms trafficking, remittance/transfer, attack funding, and operational funding (which includes communications as well as organizational and financial management).[20] This categorization conflates mechanisms (e.g., how funds are raised or managed) with the method or technique of financing (e.g., trafficking weapons to raise funds).

Although this distinction might seem like a pedantic concern, articulating a descriptive theory of terrorist financing with clearly identified mechanisms of how terrorist actors finance their activities is key to designing effective counterterrorist financing efforts. Without this clarity, policymakers can be confused about the actual processes involved in terrorist financing, which in turn might result in confused policy responses or lead to no response whatsoever. In practice, if policymakers cannot succinctly describe terrorist financing methods, they cannot articulate an argument to enact policy, legislation, or regulation to counter a specific financing tool, technique, or method.

Although the theory of terrorist financing presented in this work is largely descriptive, it also has normative elements that suggest terrorists, as Michael Kenney notes, will adapt to counterterrorist initiatives (including financial ones), that they will act based on the tools available in the jurisdictions where they are based and where they have (or want to have) operations, that they will seek to hide their activities from authorities, and that they will adopt new technologies.[21] This is by no means a revolutionary theory; however, it does provide analytic structure for predicting how terrorist actors will finance themselves and, in the absence of information, helps develop investigative leads.

One of my levels of analysis involves reflecting on the difference between organizational and operational financing; that is, the financing of terrorist groups versus the financing of terrorist attacks and plots.[22] Organizational and operational financing generally employ many of the same methods and techniques for raising, using, storing, moving, managing, and obscuring funds but differ in scope and scale.[23] The distinction between organizational and operational financing exists in some of the literature, but it is rarely used as a level of analysis to develop further insights. For instance, Basile makes a distinction between organizational and operational funding, and Horgan and Taylor also made an early contribution to our understanding of terrorist financing and the distinction between organizational and operational funds.[24] Their research found that the Provisional Irish Republican Army (PIRA) had funds centralized for operational use and organizational survival, and they highlighted that the group sought to ensure that its funding activities did not enrich individual members for nonoperational reasons.[25] Ridley also makes a distinction between operational and organizational financing.[26]

However, much of the literature lacks either these distinctions or in-depth analysis of the implications of such distinctions. This in turn leads to imprecise or off-the-mark criticisms of counterterrorist financing strategies. For instance, one critique is that counterterrorist financing efforts have failed to thwart a single terrorist attack.[27] Although this might be true (there is no way to either verify or falsify this claim, given the extent to which information to support or refute this assertion remains classified), it is equally possible that counterterrorist financing initiatives might have decreased organizational capabilities of terrorist groups or reduced the scale of operational activity. Analyzing different levels of terrorist financing through a lens of organizational and operational activity leads to more precise counterterrorist financing initiatives, goals, objectives, and critiques.

At the operational level, it is also useful to differentiate between how terrorist cells and individuals finance their activities. Cells are often spawned from terrorist organizations or their ideology, whereas individuals can be failed cell members or lone actors in a broader terrorist organization or movement. Fundamentally, this level of analysis is meant to identify how these specific actors finance their activities with a view to potential financial disruption or areas in which financial intelligence might identify critical aspects of the terrorist activity. Without these distinctions, our understanding of terrorist financing mechanisms, techniques, and methods is incomplete, and our approaches to countering terrorism and terrorist financing will be imprecise.

The purpose of conducting analysis in this manner (differentiating between organizational and operational financing and between cells and individuals) is not to demonstrate how distinct these actors are; instead, it is to demonstrate the similarities between the ways they go about financing their activities—to demonstrate that even small-scale terrorist activity conducted by an individual has financial elements, and that the main differences exist in scope and scale of activity rather than the actual mechanisms.

Sources and Analysis

To undertake this study of terrorist financing, I gathered data on fifty-five terrorist organizations, eighteen plots, and thirty-two attacks. I collected these data to review the existing material on terrorist financing and to categorize the financing activities of organizations, cells, and individuals. These data provide a preliminary baseline of which financing activities are the most prevalent in organizational and operational terrorist activity. These findings also form the basis for counterterrorism financing policy prescriptions (Chapter 10) and the forecasts on the future of terrorist financing (Chapter 11).

The main method I use in this book is the case study, looking at terrorist organizations over time and specific attacks (or plots; i.e., attempted attacks). In order to organize the data from which terrorist financing can be qualified and quantified, I created case studies of the groups to identify how they finance their activities. The same is true of terrorist plots and attacks: I compiled case studies to outline how the activity was financed and to identify knowledge gaps in those data. These cases constitute the sample for this research. Within these cases, I identified methods of financing, then recorded them in a table to create preliminary data on the basic methods and trends in terrorist financing. Throughout this process, I kept in mind the limitations of the literature, information on terrorist financing writ large, and missing data. The sources of information for this study include government documents (including reports from financial intelligence units) and research published by multilateral agencies such as UN sanctions monitoring reports and Financial Action Task Force reports and evaluations. Other sources include media reporting and academic studies.

Although my quantification of qualitative data within the sample is by no means exhaustive, my analysis of this data provides basic descriptive statistics on how terrorist organizations finance their activities. The qualitative data in this book also provides nuance and context for considering terrorist constraints and opportunities. Some of the issues I encountered in collecting this data involved a lack of temporal information on when a group started using a particular technique and if or when they stopped using it. The scope and scale of the activity was likewise difficult, if not impossible, to identify, quantify, and categorize. As such, the information presented on the analysis of terrorist organization financing demonstrates a baseline as well as a method of building and expanding data collection, which can also inform counterterrorist financing investigations and policy at both the national and international levels.

To analyze operational activity, I undertook similar in-depth case studies to establish a full accounting of a terrorist cell or individual's activities. I developed full profiles of how attacks were financed, which included detailing how the individuals raised funds, what they used their money to purchase, how they moved money to cell members or to people assisting the plot, and so forth. I also sought to determine if they stored and managed funds in a particular way and if they employed any financial tradecraft (operational security measures aimed directly at the financial components) to hide the source, destination, or use of funds.[28]

The development of these profiles (or cases) was challenging because only partial information is available for most plots or attacks. Much of this information has to be collated piecemeal from court reports, inquiries, and media reporting. Much of the information related to analysis of terrorist financing activity is not released publicly as part of trials or following a successful terrorist attack. Even in classified material, the financing component is not always fully analyzed, understood, and disseminated because of lack of time, analytic capability, or interest.[29]

I also encountered other challenges in terms of analyzing plots (disrupted attacks). For terrorist plots, much of the planning remains hypothetical, as opposed to attacks, in which the planning has been implemented. Terrorist plots are also less likely to get a full public accounting compared to successful attacks. Although the details of terrorist attacks are not always publicly disclosed, the level of certainty in assessing terrorist plots is lower because the activity was incomplete.[30]

In some cases, there is little information about the financing of plots because they were disrupted before any acquisition of material took place or concrete plans emerged. This is true of one of the plots in the dataset, a 2013 plot in Montreal that involved a conspiracy to disrupt or destroy trains operating on Canada's national railway service, Via Rail Canada.[31] In that instance, the perpetrators had two loosely defined plans and had determined some of the material they would need to perpetrate one of their attacks but had not taken any concrete steps to raise or use funds.[32]

Of course, as a former intelligence analyst, I am also compelled to note that my research and analyses are based exclusively on unclassified, open sources and are therefore not complete reviews of terrorist financing. However, one of the benefits of this book is I use a strategic, comparative, actor-based analysis; few intelligence agencies have the sustained interest or resources to undertake this type of analysis given that they are consumed with immediate operational requirements. Although I remain keenly aware of the limitations of these data and the analytic findings based on them, my work is intended to provide a strategic perspective on terrorist financing and start a conversation based on the evidence regarding terrorist financing and the practice of countering it.

Definitions

For the purposes of this book, I have used some basic definitions. A terrorist organization is defined as the main or central body leading a terrorist ideology and is treated as synonymous with a group.[33] Such organizations are easily identified by their formal names, such as al-Qaeda, the Islamic State in Iraq and the Levant (ISIL), Lashkar e-Taiba (LeT), and so forth. They usually comprise a wide variety of people and can range from a handful of core members to several hundred or thousand adherents. The organizations are generally focused on strategic-level initiatives, such as ideology, propaganda, and state building (when they are able to control territory), but they might also engage in attacks to further their objectives.

A terrorist attack is defined as one involving a group or individual with religious or political objectives that inflicts harm on people with the intent of terrorizing the audience. The attackers can be identified as members of an organization; espouse the same political views as a terrorist organization; have pledged allegiance to an organization or ideology; or have received operational, logistical, or ideological support from an organization or drawn inspiration from it. A terrorist plot is defined as an attack for which planning was underway, but that was disrupted by law enforcement or security services.

Terrorist plots and attacks are usually conducted by terrorist cells. These cells comprised fewer people than a terrorist organization and are focused on a specific terrorist plot or action. A cell has two or more people, with the largest plots or attacks involving cells of more than twenty people. These cell members are focused on a tactical objective, and they usually disperse (or are killed) following the attack. Cells might also be surrounded by supporters not directly involved in the plot who might provide financing or other logistical help. Sometimes, these facilitators are the wives and girlfriends of male terrorists or are friends or criminal associates of cell members.

Individual terrorists are sometimes (erroneously) called "lone actors," or worse, "lone wolves." These are individuals who, for the purposes of the specific attack, act alone. However, as has been amply demonstrated, individuals rarely act in isolation.[34] Instead, they get support (both in terms of logistics and encouragement) from members of a broader terrorist organization or movement. Individuals usually conduct relatively simple attacks but have also been known to engage in more sophisticated terrorist attacks; the size of the cell or the number of individuals involved in the action are not a reliable determinant of its complexity and lethality but might point to particular capabilities (or lack thereof) of the group.

About the Book

A robust evidence base is increasingly important to the study of terrorist financing and counterterrorist financing. The tools, techniques, and methods terrorists use to finance their activities have proliferated to an astonishing extent and include a variety of new technologies. This proliferation has left terrorist financing analysis in a state of disarray, with a lack of clear definitions and descriptive language, ultimately leading to a muddled understanding of how terrorists finance their activities and deploy those techniques, tools, and methods. In this book, I seek to clarify this understanding of terrorist financing and consider the various actor levels and how these levels affect traditional and new trends, methods, and techniques.

There are three parts to this book. Part 1 focuses on how terrorist organizations, cells, and individuals raise money. Chapters in this section outline the main categories of terrorist fund-raising: from donors and their networks, through setting up various types of organizations, and by engaging in criminal activity such as kidnapping for ransom and more.

Part 2 focuses on some of the less studied elements of terrorist financing—namely, how terrorists use, store, manage, move, and obscure their funds. This section opens with an introduction of how terrorists use funds, followed by a description of how terrorists store, manage, and invest their money. Subsequent chapters outline how terrorist actors move their money and discuss terrorist financial tradecraft, or how terrorists hide the sources and destinations of their funds.

Part 3 offers a strategic analysis of past terrorist financing methods and emerging tactics, such as cybercrime, social media, and financial technologies. The final chapter connects known terrorist financing methods, techniques, and activities with counterterrorist financing options. This last chapter considers disruption opportunities or ways to counter terrorist financing; it takes into consideration levels of analysis and methods, trends, and activities. The counterterrorist financing approaches correspond directly to the financing activity of groups, cells, and individuals. Often, countering terrorist financing is viewed as the purview of the police and the national-level financial intelligence unit. As a counterpoint, I suggest that significantly more actors and approaches are involved in this activity, and their respective capabilities and roles should be understood, articulated, and deployed to effectively counter terrorist financing.

Notes

1. Collier, "Economic Causes of Civil Conflict."
2. Levy and Thompson, "Civil War," 194.
3. Collier, Hoeffler, and Rohner, "Beyond Greed and Grievance."
4. Anthes, "Financial Illiteracy in America."
5. Sageman, *Understanding Terror Networks*, 69.
6. Horgan and Taylor, "Playing the 'Green Card': Part 1."
7. Gunaratna and Acharya, "Terrorist Finance and the Criminal Underground."
8. Cronin, "How Al-Qaida Ends."
9. Clarke, *Terrorism, Inc.*
10. Wittig, *Understanding Terrorist Finance.*
11. Vittori, *Terrorist Financing and Resourcing.*
12. Levy and Thompson, "Civil War," 200.
13. Ibid., 201.
14. D. C. Alexander, *Business Confronts Terrorism*, 56.
15. M. Freeman, "Sources of Terrorist Financing," 471.
16. Rudner, "Using Financial Intelligence Against the Funding of Terrorism," 32.
17. Financial Action Task Force, *Financing of the Terrorist Organization ISIL.*
18. Australian Financial Intelligence Unit (AUSTRAC), "Terrorism Financing in Australia 2014."
19. Levitt and Jacobson, "U.S. Campaign to Squeeze Terrorists' Financing."
20. Dion-Schwarz, Manheim, and Johnston, *Terrorist Use of Cryptocurrencies*, 14–15.
21. Kenney, *From Pablo to Osama*, 162.
22. M. Freeman, "Sources of Terrorist Financing," 461.
23. Australian Financial Intelligence Unit (AUSTRAC), "Terrorism Financing Regional Risk Assessment for South-East Asia 2016."
24. Basile, "Going to the Source."
25. Horgan and Taylor, "Playing the 'Green Card': Part 2," 39.
26. Ridley, *Terrorist Financing*, 1.
27. Neumann, "Don't Follow the Money," 93.
28. Schuurman et al., "Lone Actor Terrorist Attack Planning and Preparation," 1191–1200; Davis, "Financing the Toronto 18."
29. Ibid.
30. Ibid.
31. Bell, "Massive RCMP Probe."
32. *R. v Esseghaier.*
33. Phillips, "What Is a Terrorist Group?" 227.
34. Schuurman et al., "End of the Lone Wolf," 771–778.

PART 1

Raising Money

2
Finding Donors

Terrorists need money to buy weapons, conduct attacks, and sustain their organizations (among other needs), and they raise some of this money from donations from state sponsors, wealthy individuals, and support networks. Terrorists also receive donations from members—cells and individuals donate personal funds to support the group, cell, or activity (self-financing). Terrorist organizations obtain donations from a diverse spectrum of supporters; these donations form the backbone of many groups' funding strategies and are often the first type of funding these groups generate as they set up their terrorist organizations.[1] The various categories of donors are not always distinct. For instance, a wealthy donor might be part of a broader support network or might also be within a government taking part in state sponsorship of terrorism. Despite this overlap, these categorizations remain useful because they provide a typology to explain the mechanisms through which terrorists obtain funds. This understanding assists in designing effective measures to counter terrorist financing.

Donations alone rarely suffice to support a terrorist organization for long. Terrorist organizations might receive some of their initial funding from donations, be they from state sponsors, wealthy individuals, support networks, or self-financing, but their fund-raising methods diversify quickly. Terrorist actors seek to diversify their sources of funds and enhance their resilience to counterterrorist financing efforts, while at the same time ensuring they are not beholden to any particular donor. The type of terrorist entity matters in terms of donations: organizations receive all types of donations, whereas terrorist cells and individuals primarily benefit from self-financing.

13

There are no structural impediments to cells and individuals receiving state sponsorship or support from a donor network, but in practice this is rare.

State Sponsorship

For decades, states have been known to sponsor terrorist and insurgent groups, and research on this topic predates the use of the term *terrorism* in much of the literature. States have provided funds and other types of support to a variety of insurgencies. Writing in 2001, Byman et al. found that since 1991, 59 percent of insurgencies have received state support significant or critical to the survival and success of the movement.[2] Michael Freeman also argues that state sponsorship is one of the main mechanisms terrorist organizations use to raise funds (along with illegal activities, legal activities, and popular support).[3] A number of states have directly sponsored terrorist activity, whereas several others have provided more passive support, including most recently for White nationalist extremism.

States fund terrorist groups for a variety of reasons, most of which involve the security dilemma.[4] They might fund terrorists to increase their internal and external stability, to decrease the stability of a neighboring state (by extension, increasing their own stability), to gain wealth, and to support ethnic or religious groups. Terrorist groups accept state sponsorship because it offers access to a level of funding difficult to achieve and sustain otherwise. But state sponsors are not entirely beneficial to terrorists because they place demands on these organizations and can be unsustainable sources of funds if subjected to international sanctions. For instance, Iran's support for Hizballah, a Shia Islamist group, has varied significantly over time because sanctions and economic pressures have reduced Iran's ability to fund the terrorist group. Terrorists are likely to accept state offers of support out of sheer economic necessity. However, this support can create internal divisions within the group and foster corruption among members, while simultaneously enhancing the terrorists' ability to achieve their objectives.

The vast majority of state sponsorship of terrorism is provided to organizations, and evidence of direct support for terrorist operations by states is rare. However, terrorist groups can and do allocate their funds for operational purposes, so although tying state funding directly to an attack is difficult, funds provided to a terrorist group can provide overall support and enhance their operational posture.

Who Funds Terrorism?

Over the past sixty years (if not longer), more than a dozen states have funded terrorist or insurgent organizations. The list of state sponsors of terrorism has included, at one time or another, Cuba, Eritrea, India, Iran, Iraq, Italy, Libya, North Korea, Pakistan, Qatar, Russia, Saudi Arabia, Sudan,

Syria, the Union of Soviet Socialist Republics (USSR, or Soviet Union), the United States, and Yemen. Some of the most flagrant state sponsors of terrorism have historically included Cuba, Iran, Iraq, Libya, North Korea, Sudan, Syria, and Yemen.[5] As recently as 2018, the United States accused Qatar of openly financing Hamas and supporting extremist groups in Syria.[6] These states have all been publicly named state sponsors of terrorism or, at the least, passive sponsors of terrorism. The groups these countries have supported span the ideological spectrum and include ethnonationalist groups, Islamist extremist organizations, left-wing terrorist organizations, and White supremacist groups. The strategy of funding these groups works to the advantage of state sponsors in a variety of ways as these groups can be a useful tool for shaping the international environment to the funders' advantage.

In the 1970s and 1980s, state sponsors of terrorism used a variety of tools to provide terrorist and insurgent organizations training and equipment, enhance their ability to conduct attacks, and increase their overall lethality. State sponsors used their embassies, intelligence services, and state airlines to provide support. For instance, the Kurdistan Workers' Party (PKK), a revolutionary socialist and nationalist group, received support from the Soviet Union.[7] Cuba and Libya provided funds to the Euskadi Ta Askatasuna (ETA [Basque Homeland and Liberty]), a nationalist separatist group. ETA also received funds from the government of Spain (although not necessarily wittingly); this included as much as 50 percent of its annual budget from grants sponsored by Spain and the European Union (EU) to further Basque cultural and language activities that the group managed to divert, likely through its support networks.[8]

From the 1970s until fairly recently, Libya contributed an estimated $35 million to various insurgent and terrorist organizations. In the early 1970s, Libya gave funds to the Moro National Liberation Front (MNLF), a separatist group in the Philippines, to support training fighters. The Provisional Irish Republican Army (PIRA), a paramilitary organization, also secured approximately $3.5 million in 1972 ($21.6 million in 2020 dollars) from Libyan leader Muammar Qaddafi.[9] Libya also provided Abu Sayyaf (a jihadist militant group operating in the Philippines) an estimated $6 million in 1991 ($11.3 million in 2020 dollars).[10]

Iran has also provided sponsorship to various terrorist organizations for more than thirty years. In March 1982, following the Iranian revolution, that country's leaders met in Tehran and agreed to establish terrorist training camps and provide an immediate $100 million ($267.5 million in 2020 dollars) to support revolutionary activities. They also agreed to provide $50 million ($134 million in 2020 dollars) in ongoing funding. In addition, the Iranian Revolutionary Guards provided training to a number of groups in terrorist training camps.[11] Today, Iran primarily funds two terrorist organizations: the previously mentioned Hizballah, and Hamas, a Palestinian nationalist and

Islamic organization. Estimates of the amount of money Iran provides vary widely over time. Historically, Iran is estimated to have given approximately $200 million annually to Hizballah. In 2017, Iran was reported to have boosted its financial support to Hizballah to $800 million per year ($842 million in 2020 dollars).[12] In addition to funds, Hizballah also receives aid and logistical support from Iran and Syria.[13] The Armed Islamic Group of Algeria (GIA) is also believed to have received funds from Iran and Sudan.[14]

A note of caution is required about changes in state support for terrorism over time, because analyses rarely account for inflationary effects. Iranian support for Hamas illustrates this point well. As of January 1993, Iran was budgeting $30 million ($54 million in 2020 dollars) annually for Hamas.[15] As of 2018, Hamas was believed to have a budget of around $70 million ($72 million in 2020 dollars) per year, of which approximately 85 percent (or $60 million) was believed to come from state and private donations or through various international financing schemes.[16] The increase from $22 million to $60–70 million might appear significant, but inflation accounts for a large portion of the increase.

Although Iran and Libya are notorious funders of terrorist groups, they are far from the only ones. Other terrorist groups have also raised money from state sponsors, including the Liberation Tigers of Tamil Eelam (LTTE), an ethnonationalist separatist group in Sri Lanka; right-wing extremist groups; the Taliban, in Afghanistan; and Al-Shabaab, a jihadist group operating primarily in Somalia. During its early years, the LTTE received direct support from the Indian government; the Research and Analysis Wing, its foreign intelligence agency, provided support to the LTTE as early as 1981. This support included training and weapons, as well as the salaries of several LTTE leaders. This support ended in 1987 with the signing of the Indo–Sri Lankan Accord.[17]

A rather unique example of state sponsorship for terrorism is the case of the Taliban, which has witnessed aid morph into state sponsorship. Prior to 9/11 and its international recognition as a terrorist entity, the Taliban received significant aid from sponsors such as Pakistan and Saudi Arabia. Pakistan also provided the group political recognition and was a significant contributor of members, guns, and money. Between 1997 and 1998, Pakistan provided the Taliban $30 million in aid ($48 million in 2020 dollars), of which $6 million was earmarked to pay the salaries of the group's leadership.[18] In 2001, the US government awarded the Taliban government a grant of $43 million ($63 million in 2020 dollars) for its successful efforts to reduce opium production.[19] Following its listing as a terrorist entity, the Taliban has continued to receive funds and other support from state sponsors. Since at least 2006, Iran has arranged a frequent shipment of small arms, ammunition, rocket-propelled grenades, mortar rounds, 107 mm rockets, plastic explosives, and man-pad systems to the Taliban. In October 2007, Iran's Islamic Revolutionary Guards Corps–Quds Force (IRGC-QF) provided the Taliban weapons and financial support.[20] As of 2018, reports suggested that the Taliban might be receiving as much as $500 million ($514 million in 2020 dollars) in donations and foreign funding each year.[21] When funds are dubbed "aid," state sponsorship is a matter of perspective, as the case of the Taliban demonstrates.

Al-Shabaab, a terrorist group better known for its control of territory and taxation schemes, has also benefited from state sponsorship. Eritrea is alleged to have given support to the group in the form of financial and military assistance, providing, at one point, between $40,000 and $60,000 per month via Eritrean embassy couriers between 2006 and 2011.[22] This support might have totaled as much as $4.3 million (around $5 million in 2020 dollars) over that period. This monthly support likely allowed Al-Shabaab to recruit and consolidate its forces, control territory, and provide a consistent base of funding the group could use to expand its activities. In recent years, Al-Shabaab has likely accepted some funds and support from Gulf countries. In mid-May 2019, Al-Shabaab carried out a bombing in Bosaso that media claimed was to "advance Qatar's interests" in the region by driving out its rival, the United Arab Emirates (UAE). Both countries are believed to support various extremist groups in Somalia and use them as proxies to advance their interests.[23]

Right-wing extremist organizations have also benefitted from state sponsors. In Italy, right-wing terrorists received support from members of the Italian intelligence service. In Turkey, the Grey Wolves, a right-wing extremist organization established in the 1960s, is also thought to have received support from state security services.[24] In these cases, it is unclear whether the Italian or Turkish governments are supportive of the groups or whether individuals within those governments decided independently to provide these groups funds and assistance. More recently, Russia has been found to be supporting numerous far-right groups in Europe and the United States, in some cases through the direct contribution of grants and loans.[25]

White supremacist groups also benefit from passive support from the United States. Byman calls the United States the "Saudi Arabia" of the White power movement. He argues that the United States permits incitement and tolerates it when US citizens nurture and promote their racist ideas. Byman also notes that US free speech laws enable the production of propaganda and paraphernalia, and that US-domiciled technology companies are also important conduits for propaganda distribution, fund-raising, and recruiting.[26] There is also historical precedent for this issue—the US was a vibrant source of funds for the PIRA. The United States is far from alone on the issue of passive support for terrorism, either; many other states have failed to take action on the White supremacist threat.

States are almost never onetime sponsors of terrorism. Their sponsorship usually occurs over a prolonged period, but the beginning and ending dates for this activity are rarely explicit. Over time, states are likely to increase or decrease their funding in a way that correlates with their economic capacity as well as their political will. Understanding the nuances of this ebb and flow of state sponsorship is beneficial for counterterrorism practitioners because this could potentially point to inducements or punishments that could be used to decrease state sponsorship.

In the 2000s, Gunaratna and Acharya argued that the end of the Cold War marked a decline in the state funding of terrorism.[27] Indeed, in the early 2010s, state sponsorship of terrorism appeared to be on the decline. Many of the "axis of evil" countries were no longer in a position to fund terrorist groups, and international action against state sponsors of terrorism was at an all-time high. In more recent years, more covert methods of funding terrorist groups have emerged, and state sponsors might be increasingly emboldened to support their proxies. The rise of White supremacist terrorism is of particular concern—groups and individuals associated with the broader movement have been making recruiting gains internationally and are increasingly emboldened to conduct attacks. At the same time, deciphering how state sponsorship of the movement affects and enables the actions of small cells or individuals is an important analytic task required to spur states to act against this threat.

Why Do States Fund Terrorism?

States choose to sponsor terrorist groups for a variety of reasons. Byman and colleagues outline a comprehensive list in their work on outside support for insurgencies, which applies equally to terrorist organizations. States provide support to gain regional influence and best a rival, to destabilize neighbors, to support regime change, to enact payback, to ensure influence within the opposition, to enhance their internal security, to gain prestige, and to support coreligionists and people of similar ideologies. Sometimes they do it out of pure irredentism or to benefit financially from the conflict.[28] Essentially, states provide external aid to rebel groups to meet their foreign policy objectives.[29]

States use terrorist organizations as proxies to achieve their political ends or to stymie the political objectives of their adversaries. They also support terrorist organizations to avoid directly implicating themselves in whatever nefarious activity they want undertaken. States can choose one or more terrorist or insurgent groups to support to achieve these objectives or simply to serve as a thorn in the side of their adversaries. They can also delegate kinetic action to terrorist or insurgent groups to take advantage of technical skill sets offered by terrorist actors, particularly in the realm of unconventional tactics.[30]

Even though there is an important link between states and terrorist actors, the financing states do not control every aspect of a terrorist organization or, in some cases, many (or any) of their actions.[31] As a result, although terrorist actors might serve as a proxy for their state sponsors, this is not always the case, and sometimes, the terrorists themselves might outright reject proposed action by the states as being too high risk or not in their immediate interests. For states, "investing" in terrorist actors as a means of augmenting their kinetic capabilities can be a risky strategy.

The risks of sponsoring terrorist groups are largely expressed at the international level through sanctions (economic, financial, or political). Terrorist organizations rarely seek retribution against a state sponsor. However, a state ending support for a terrorist organization might increase the possibility of its government being subjected to terrorist attacks by that (or other) group(s). This hypothesis is difficult to evaluate because most terrorist organizations that have accepted state sponsorship continue to do so or no longer exist.

State sponsorship of terrorism is often presented as monolithic support by a government for a terrorist or insurgent group, but this is not always the case. In some instances, so-called state sponsorship actually represents the diversion of funds (often, from state coffers) by individuals within the government to terrorist organizations without the government's knowledge or permission.

Determining the level of support within any government for a terrorist organization can be challenging. The sponsorship of the terrorist group might be sanctioned or condoned by the government leaders as a whole or might be supported by a faction within the government. In other instances, a small group of people, usually within the government's security or intelligence agencies, might choose to supply funding to a terrorist organization. For instance, Inter-Services Intelligence (ISI), Pakistan's intelligence service, spent $50 million annually to support groups that included Lashkar-e-Tayyiba (LeT), a Pakistani-based Sunni Islamist extremist organization that aims to unite Indian-administered Kashmir with Pakistan under an extreme interpretation of Islamic law; Hizb-ul-Mujahideen, a separatist group active in Jammu and Kashmir that seeks integration with Pakistan; and Jaish-e-Mohammed (JeM), a jihadist group active in Kashmir that also supports integration with India.[32] At various times throughout the past several decades, the Pakistani government has likely tolerated this expenditure. At least it does not appear that the government has completely "clamped down" on the ISI's support for the militants. Indeed, Pakistan supports some terrorists and fights others.

Byman notes that some states passively support terrorist groups, such as knowingly allowing them to raise money, enjoy sanctuary, and recruit new members.[33] He also notes that sponsorship can be provided by political parties, wealthy merchants, and other actors with no formal affiliation with the government.[34] Byman argues that states provide passive support because there might be public sympathy for a terrorist organization or the sense that the group poses little threat to the host government. There might be a relatively low cost to inaction or, in some cases, a direct benefit to passive sponsorship.[35] All of these actions constitute state sponsorship of terrorism but might respond to different counterterrorist financing approaches, inducements, and punishments. These nuances have important implications for counterterrorism policies designed to target state sponsorship of terrorism. Efforts to sanction governments writ large might prove ineffective if a government lacks control over some of its constituents.

States choose to sponsor terrorist organizations to ensure or enhance domestic stability, undermine rivals, destabilize their adversaries, and benefit financially from the turmoil. Which groups they choose to fund and how they provide money (and other resources) to those groups depend on the geographical and political context in which they are operating. Sponsoring a terrorist organization is not without cost, however; international sanctions can have devastating consequences on economies and can isolate a state politically.

Why Do Terrorists Accept State Funds?

Terrorists can be described as consumers of state funds—but there is not necessarily unfettered demand for state sponsorship. Although states can provide important sources of funds and other resources, they do not confer those benefits without obligation. States can seek to control or influence the activities and directions of a terrorist organization and use financial resources as a lever to do so. Such pressures notwithstanding, the lure of state resources is a temptation few terrorist groups can ignore.

State funding of terrorist organizations comes with strings attached but remains an attractive source of funds for terrorist groups. Finding a state patron can be beneficial for a terrorist organization because it can provide a significant influx of cash as well as longer-term stability to grow the organization and support operational activities. That support can transcend basic finances and can include safe haven, political support, and direct military support.[36] State sponsors of terrorism might also provide recruits to the terrorist or insurgent organization.[37] For example, Arab states gave the Algerian National Liberation Front (FLN), an anticolonial nationalist group, both political aid and sanctuary.[38] Although this aid might not have involved a significant (or any) transfer of funds, sanctuary allows terrorist organizations to conduct a variety of financing activities, including raising funds, but just as importantly storing and managing funds.

For terrorist organizations, state sponsorship is not always a winning proposition. State support and the proportionally larger sums of money it usually involves can lead to corruption, feuding, and internal discord.[39] States might also seek to create divisions within an insurgency to better control it.[40] In contrast, outside support can, as Byman puts it, tar a group with a foreign brush, which in turn might decrease the group's legitimacy.[41]

There are some significant gaps in our understanding of state sponsorship. In particular, the specific mechanisms involved in the provision of state funds to terrorist organizations are worthy of further investigation. So, too, is the idea that terrorist groups might decline state sponsorship depending on particular criteria. Certainly, much is made of terrorist groups (and states) that have a client-sponsor relationship. But it stands to reason that some groups have turned down offers of support. Understanding the mechanisms and situations in which this occurs could have useful implications for countering terrorist financing through state sponsors.

There are pros and cons to state sponsorship from the perspectives of terrorists, but few groups are known to have turned down offers of funds from states. Some might rebel against their funders or deny them the influence they seek to purchase, but few will say no to the money outright. Terrorist groups cannot always afford to be picky when it comes to donations. Although they do seek to diversify their funding sources, when one appears (often worth millions, if not billions), they take advantage of it. State sponsorship might come with some expectations on the part of the sponsor, but it also provides terrorist organizations a significant influx of cash (few states fund terrorist organizations for less than millions of dollars) and ongoing financial stability that can allow a terrorist group to grow, expand, and plan in a way other funding sources do not support.

Organizational Versus Operational Funding
Generally speaking, state sponsors provide funds to terrorist organizations, and examples of cells and individuals receiving funds from states to conduct terrorist activity are rare, although Libya has been accused of funding the Lockerbie bombing.[42] The fifty plots and attacks upon which my research is based did not have any direct indication of state funding. Of course, terrorist organizations provide inspiration for such attacks and might go much further and provide advice, direction, and funding, meaning that state sponsorship can both indirectly and directly fund terrorist cells and individuals. Even though states sponsor terrorist groups, tying those funds to their attacks is difficult. Most terrorist groups fund operations from their general or operational budgets rather than seeking out dedicated funding from state sponsors.

Of the more than fifty terrorist organizations I studied for this research, at least twenty-five received some form of state funding. These terrorist organizations were not constrained to one region geographically or one ideology or religion, and they had a wide range of sponsors, some of which changed over time. State sponsorship did not preclude these organizations from engaging in other terrorist fund-raising activities either—they all engaged in a variety of activities to raise funds. All but two of the organizations that received state sponsorship continue to operate today.

Although state sponsorship is a desirable source of funds for most (if not all) terrorist groups, these groups do not rely solely on this means for funding. Terrorist organizations diversify their funding sources, even when the bulk of those funds come from a state patron. This enables the groups to create financial resilience, a particularly important skill set when the sponsor is under international sanctions or experiences an economic setback.

Wealthy Donors

It is common in the terrorist financing literature to find reference to "wealthy donors" who provide funding to terrorists. In particular, Gulf-based donors are frequently cited as important terrorist financiers, and even terrorist groups with many other sources of income obtain some funding from so-called wealthy donors. Perhaps because of their suscepti-bility to being identified and sanctioned, somewhat disproportionate atten-tion has been paid to these donors in terms of their importance for group fund-raising efforts.

Many terrorist organizations have benefited from donations by wealthy patrons over time, such as Abu Sayyaf, Hamas, Al-Shabaab, the LTTE, the Taliban, al-Qaeda, National Action (a neo-Nazi terrorist group), LeT, and Hayat Tahrir al-sham (an al-Qaeda-affiliated group in Syria).[43] Wealthy donors transcend the ideological spectrum and provide groups startup money, onetime influxes of funds, and in some cases ongoing support.

Al-Shabaab has benefited from wealthy donors able to provide signifi-cant amounts of funds at one time, specifically Qatar-based 'Umayr Al-Nu'aymi, believed to have channeled funding to a range of jihadi causes, including $250,000 ($279,000 in 2020 dollars) to Al-Shabaab in 2012.[44] Wealthy patrons were also a key part of the LTTE financing strategy. In the United States, a portion of the LTTE's money came from a small number of wealthy individuals.[45] One such donor was Shad Sunder, a wealthy Tamil living in California, who donated as much as $4 million (roughly $6 million in 2020 dollars) to the LTTE in the 2000s.[46] In other diaspora communities, the LTTE raised money much more incrementally from a broader support network of less well-off individuals and through taxation and extortion.

Funds from wealthy donors have also played, and likely continue to play, a significant role in Taliban fund-raising. In 2009, donations from the Persian Gulf constituted more than the Taliban's estimated revenue from Helmand Province, the heart of its drug-supply revenue-generating activities, and were estimated to be in the hundreds of millions of dollars.[47] These donations helped to stabilize the group's finances when variations in revenues from other sources such as opium production and extortion activities occurred.

Many terrorist organizations benefit at least in part from individuals able to provide an influx of funds, usually in the high hundreds of thousands or millions of dollars. These individuals are distinguishable from other supporters or donors by the scope and scale of their donations. They are usually high net worth individuals and enjoy significant political influence (and protection) because of their sizable wealth and business connections in the countries in which they operate. In recent years, wealthy donors have primarily come from the Gulf countries and supported Sunni Islamist extremist terrorism. In the past, other types of terrorist organizations have also benefited from these types of benefactors. For instance, anarchists in the late nineteenth and early twentieth centuries also had wealthy patrons.[48]

Al-Qaeda stands out as one of the most iconic terrorist groups to benefit from wealthy donors, although this has also been overstated as a source of persistent revenue for the group. Osama bin Laden was widely reported to have contributed much of his personal wealth to the group, but the 9/11 Commission found that al-Qaeda was primarily funded through donations, not through bin Laden's personal fortune.[49] As of 2014, al-Qaeda's reduced but ongoing presence in Pakistan was still believed to be funded in part from "deep-pocket" donors, including Gulf-based sympathizers and supporters in Pakistan and Turkey.[50]

Other al-Qaeda affiliates also employed this fund-raising strategy, such as al-Qaeda in Iraq and subsequently the Islamic State in Iraq and the Levant (ISIL, or the Islamic State). Between 2013 and 2014, the Islamic State in Iraq accumulated up to $40 million ($44 million in 2020 dollars) from donors in Kuwait, Qatar, and Saudi Arabia.[51] This practice is believed to have continued with the emergence of ISIL.[52] These donations positioned the group for later financial success, allowing it to recruit fighters, pay salaries, and ultimately control territory. Even when ISIL did not need the funds, it received a steady provision of financial contributions from wealthy individuals throughout the Persian Gulf.[53] Even for groups that obtain more money from other sources, donations from wealthy patrons demonstrate support and allow for diversification of their fund-raising schemes.

Terrorist groups, cells, and individuals draw significant benefits from wealthy donors who have more to offer than simply funds. Access to logistics can also play a valuable role in helping a terrorist group raise funds, recruit and train supporters, and for cells and individuals to conduct terrorist attacks. For instance, the LeT is believed to have received some initial "seed" funding from Dawood Ibrahim, the leader of a large Mumbai-based criminal organization. Ibrahim's companies might have also been used by the group to lure recruits to training camps, and he might have allowed LeT operatives use of his smuggling routes.[54] Another example of a terrorist organization receiving initial seed money is National Action, a proscribed right-wing terrorist organization in the United Kingdom. The group is believed to be well-financed by the founders of the organization, who might have bankrolled it with an inheritance from 2015.[55] This money would have counted both as a donation from wealthy individuals and as a form of self-financing undertaken by the founders of the group.

Internationally, a number of wealthy donors from the Gulf states have been named and sanctioned by the United States and/or the United Nations. One such example was Omar al-Qatari, who provided broad support to Jabhat al Nusra/Nusra Front, a Salafist jihadist organization in Syria that more recently adopted the name Hayat Tahrir al-sham. In 2011 and 2012, he worked with associates in Iran, Lebanon, Qatar, Syria, and Turkey to raise and move funds and weapons and enable the travel of fighters and financial facilitators.[56]

Wealthy donors play a critical role in providing terrorist organizations necessary seed money for their activities. They can also be counted on in times of financial crisis to augment a terrorist group's funding streams. These donors are often influential individuals with extensive business and philanthropic networks; it is relatively easy for them to use their political power and influence to move funds to terrorist groups without being detected.

Donations from wealthy individuals might have as much to do with a desire to support the group as a response to other organizational needs and building legitimacy. For instance, Gulf-based donors sent enough funds to ISIL that the group had to set up a *hawala*-based network to manage the donations from the Gulf, even though there is ample evidence that the group did not suffer from a shortage of revenue.[57] Although the group did solicit funds from supporters (wealthy and otherwise), these calls for donations might have been meant to expand the ISIL brand and give supporters a means of engaging in the fight without joining the group itself.

Organizational and Operational Differences in Wealthy Donor Support

Of the terrorist organizations I studied, 27 percent received some of their money from wealthy donors. Of course, other terrorist organizations probably received funds from wealthy donors as well. Over time, terrorist organizations are likely to attract wealthy donors with a well-developed ideology and spectacular attacks. Wealthy donors likely provide funds to terrorist organizations to meet their own political or religious objectives but also in lieu of joining the organization directly.

The terrorist entities that most frequently receive funds from wealthy donors are the organizations, although operational cells can occasionally receive direct funding. For instance, according to Basile, the 9/11 attacks were underwritten by twenty key financiers who donated $500,000 for the attacks. The money was transferred to the hijackers in a large number of small installments over time and through different financial channels.[58] The scope and scale of the plan might have provided sufficient impetus for the donors to risk funding the attack directly, and the cost of the attack itself might have been sufficient to cause al-Qaeda to seek external funders rather than to fund the attack from its existing resources. Despite this example, if terrorist plotters require additional funds, they generally seek those funds from a terrorist group patron or through various self-financing schemes, including criminal activity, rather than from wealthy donors. Most operational-level terrorists lack the necessary networks to access these wealthy individuals, although they might find willing donors if presented with opportunities to "pitch" them on particular attacks. Donors might be disinclined to provide funding directly for a terrorist attack out of fear that those funds could be traced back to them or expose them politically. Donating funds to a broader terrorist organization, or even better, a charitable front, provides some distance between the donor and the terrorists. That distance is only a matter of perspective, though, because terrorist organizations provide funds to operational cells and individuals.

Identity-Based Support Networks

For every individual who joins a terrorist organization or engages in terrorist activity, many others lack the will or ability to take such steps but still support the organization or broader movement by providing money. Many of these individuals are not wealthy and do not have significant resources at their disposal, but together they can form a support network for a terrorist organization (or operational cells and individuals). Terrorist support networks are individuals or groups who seek to raise funds for terrorist organizations (rarely cells or individuals directly, although funds sent to terrorist groups can make their way to operational activities). These networks may be loose or formal with strong or weak affiliation to a terrorist group, and they might be ad hoc, self-initiated, or encouraged or established by the terrorist organization to raise funds. Generally, terrorist support networks are constructed or emerge along some sort of social identity originating in geography, culture, language, ideology, ethnicity, grievance, or religion shared with the terrorist organization or movement.

Terrorist support networks provide funds in two ways: through voluntary donations and through extortion and protection rackets. In the first instance, donations are voluntary and are given with the knowledge that they are financing a terrorist organization.[59] In the second, identity groups can be extorted for their funds, a topic I examine in more detail in Chapter 3, although the lines between these two types of funding are not always sharp. Above and beyond financial support, these donations can provide a terrorist group a sense of broader support, identifying individuals sympathetic to its cause who might be amenable to offering other types of support, such as safe haven, logistical support, and so forth.

Support networks are also frequently described as diaspora financing when a terrorist group has a geographical or ethnic affiliation with a diaspora group from which it receives funding.[60] This term is misleading, though, because diaspora financing is in fact a nonspecific way of referring to several separate methods of fund-raising. Methods of diaspora financing can include soliciting donations from a community through extortion or taxation (see Chapter 3), but calling this diaspora financing implies a willingness on the part of the individuals to provide funds. A separate method of raising funds from a diaspora community involves soliciting funds from like-minded individuals who happen to be members of the diaspora. In this case, the term wrongly implies that the entire diaspora supports the terrorist organization, when in fact only a small number of supporters willingly donate funds as part of a support network. Finally, diaspora remittances (another element conflated with diaspora funding) might be taxed by a terrorist group, but in this case this is far from voluntary, and describing it as diaspora financing omits the nuance of what is actually happening—the taxation of the remittances. To illustrate this point, we can consider Al-Shabaab and the Somali diaspora. Some support networks have developed to support the terrorist organization, and the taxation of remittances has also occurred. It is incorrect, however, to refer to Al-Shabaab as being financed by the Somali diaspora writ large because many Somali diaspora community members do not support the group ideologically.

Support networks are often drawn from communities (including those outside a specific diaspora group) that have an identity connection or ideological affinity to the terrorist organization. For instance, the PIRA obtained economic support from the Irish diaspora, and their supporters in various countries provided money, weapons, and volunteers.[61] In some cases, the donations came directly from individuals associated with or in support of the cause, in the form of cash or through other monetary instruments. These donations generally ranged between £100 and £150 ($140–$220).[62]

The LTTE's support network illustrates how extensive these networks can be. The group had representatives in at least fifty-four countries around the world, and in some locations it collected a baseline "tax" from Tamils. The Tamil diaspora was a significant source of funds; the number of Sri Lankan Tamils living outside of Sri Lanka ranges from 800,000 to 1.6 million, with the most significant populations in Canada, India, the United Kingdom, and Germany. These populations were the basis for significant fund-raising activities. The LTTE employed a mixed approach of voluntary contributions, coercion, and diverting funds from legitimate charities and government programs.[63] Some people subjected to the tax paid it willingly, whereas others had to be coerced, which illustrates how muddy the water can be between support and extortion networks.[64]

Sometimes, terrorist groups can tap into support networks that have little to do with race, ethnicity, or language and have more to do with ideology. For instance, Hayat Tahrir al-Sham might have received donations from supporters abroad who agreed with their broader objectives but were not necessarily individuals ethnically or culturally aligned with elements of the group.[65]

ISIL also benefited from external donations and support networks. In 2018, French officials identified 416 people who gave money to ISIL. The funds were transferred through Libya and Turkey via financial facilitators.[66] ISIL was not alone in this initiative—many of the groups that operated in Iraq and Syria in the mid-2010s received donations from supporters abroad. Some of the funds sent to jihadists in Syria were from family members or friends and might have been sent as some form of familial support. In other cases the money was intended specifically to fund terrorist activities. Although much of this activity went undetected and unprosecuted, in some cases terrorist financing prosecutions were obtained. For example, in 2019, Abdurahman Kaabar of Sheffield, England, was found guilty of terrorist financing for sending hundreds of pounds to his brother in Syria.[67] The funds were likely provided as familial support (actual kinship ties as opposed to the contrived kinship ties many people espouse for terrorist movements) or to support the terrorist organization writ large.

Terrorist organizations do not always solicit (or indeed, want) money from supporters, but they might lack the ability to completely control the provision of funds, and individual members might accept funds on behalf of the organization. Some of these funds might be provided by supporters in lieu of joining the group itself. For instance, despite no evidence to suggest that the group had solicited funds, a forty-year-old woman from Sydney, Australia, who worked for the federal government was accused of sending $24,000 to ISIL in 2015 ($26,300 in 2020 dollars).[68] In a separate case from the same year, Ali Shukri Amin was sentenced to eleven years in prison for a variety of offenses, including conspiring to provide material support to ISIL. He used Twitter to provide advice and encouragement to ISIL and its supporters. He provided advice on how to use Bitcoin to mask the provision of funds to ISIL and to facilitate ISIL supporters' travel to ISIL-controlled territory.[69] In 2016, two others were arrested (a sixteen-year-old female student and her twenty-year-old male friend) for helping to raise money for ISIL in Australia.[70] These supporters do not appear to be part of widespread networks of broad ISIL support but instead represent relatively isolated supporters largely devoid of any broader connections. These donations also demonstrate the various actor levels present in donor networks, from the organizations to the cells and individuals, and how money may serve as a proxy for membership.

External factors such as cultural and religious holidays affect organizational fund-raising and support networks. For instance, Hizballah relies on its support network for funds and can expect increased donations during holidays and for special events or occasions. During Ramadan, Hizballah can earn as much as $2 million per night from donations from its international support network, including from supporters in Canada.[71] These donations support Hizballah's broader objectives and activities (as opposed to solely terrorist activity) and might be intended (at least in part) for their humanitarian, political, and social services. Other external factors also affect donations, including campaigns. Donations to Al-Shabaab have been affected by the group's activities and international counterterrorism actions. The Ethiopian intervention in Somalia (2006–2009) is reported to have spurred an increase in donations from external support networks to the group. Conversely, the unpopular Kampala attacks by Al-Shabaab are reported to have discouraged donations to the group.[72] Although the premise that unpopular terrorist attacks decrease popular support and donations to terrorist organizations is logically sound, conclusively establishing the link between international counterterrorism activities, terrorist initiatives, and support network financing requires additional data beyond these anecdotes. Monitoring support networks for increases (or decreases) in funding levels around important events might provide insight into some of the key financiers in the network as well as the general level of support enjoyed by the terrorist group.

Support networks for terrorist fund-raising do not have to exist exclusively outside the territory a terrorist group controls or influences. For instance, in Somalia, some of the donations for Al-Shabaab have come from within the group's territory. Women in Kismayo, key fund-raisers for Al-Shabaab, convinced men and women to donate money or goods such as jewelry to help support the group.[73] Donor support networks native to the area in which a terrorist organization is operating can be particularly challenging to tackle from a counterterrorism financing perspective because of lack of rule of law or the ability to limit the activities of terrorist actors.

Although soliciting funds from potential support networks is an old terrorist financing method, social media and new technologies such as crowdfunding make it easier for terrorist actors to reach their prospective audience and receive donations. For instance, Hajjaj Fahd al-Ajmi, a Kuwaiti national with alleged ties to al-Qaeda, had a robust and active presence on Instagram and used the platform to solicit funds.[74] Al-Shabaab has also used social media to solicit funds from its support networks outside of Somalia. In 2016, two women led a support network of fifteen women in fund-raising for Al-Shabaab. The money was used to finance military operations and warehouses in Somalia. The women solicited money in a chatroom and sent that money, likely through hawala, or money services businesses (MSBs), to financiers of Al-Shabaab. The group of women included supporters from Canada, Egypt, Kenya, the Netherlands, Somalia, Sweden, and the United Kingdom as well as the United States (Minneapolis).[75]

Many other terrorists have also solicited funds through social media. For some, the calls are explicit, whereas for others, it is unclear where the money is going, and it is plausible to assume that not all donors know the money is being directed toward terrorist activities. After the original call for funds is made, donors are often redirected via Skype or Telegram or other direct messaging applications in which account information and transaction information is provided. Funds are sent via wire transfer, MSBs, or hawala, although social media platforms are increasingly developing the ability to transfer funds between users.[76]

Although recent terrorist financing schemes using crowdfunding websites have drawn significant attention, this is not a new technique. In 2002, a Hamas website solicited donations for the purchase of AK-47s. The website indicated that a $2,000 donation could purchase an AK-47 for a fighter. Dynamite could be "donated" for a price of $100 per kg, and bullets were $3 each. The website provided donors instructions on how to transfer money to Gaza-based bank accounts.[77] The premise employed in 2002 is the same as today—websites, often crowdfunding sites, advertise the purchase of goods, supplies, or weapons for terrorists (or using a cover story), and donors can provide the funds. But today, the transactions can occur in near real time and can be made more anonymous by combining social media, financial technologies, and cryptocurrencies. This method is not only the purview of terrorist organizations. Individual terrorists (specifically foreign fighters) have also solicited funds in recent years through crowdfunding or individual calls.

Support networks do not only provide support for organizational financing; there is a long history of support networks providing funds for individuals traveling to engage in jihad. Indeed, the concept of Tajheez al-Ghazi—fitting or arming a soldier—has been extended to include support for individuals traveling for jihad.[78] Those costs are generally in the thousands of dollars: in Bosnia, it cost $3,000–$4,000; in Afghanistan $2,000; and for individuals joining jihadist groups in Chechnya, more than $15,000 because of the difficulty of entering the conflict zone.[79] Small fund-raising cells organized and collected funds.[80]

Support networks can also be mobilized to provide financial assistance to detained terrorists. For instance, ISIS suspects in Syria, specifically women detained in camp for ISIS families, raised thousands of British pounds through online campaigns. Two such campaigns explicitly aimed to raise funds to pay smugglers to help them escape from their detention camps. They solicited the funds through Telegram chats and directed supporters to provide funds through PayPal Money Pool accounts.[81] One of these campaigns raised more than £2,600 (around $3,500). The supporters used coded messages to disguise the aim of fund-raising to prevent PayPal from taking down the accounts. Another similar campaign was launched by al-Qaeda supporters in Idlib and ultimately succeeded in freeing four women from a camp. In 2019, the going rate to secure the "full release of a sister" was $8,000.[82]

Support networks for terrorist organizations or movements form in a variety of identity-based communities, but these communities are unlikely to, as a whole, be as extreme as the terrorist actors. Instead, the support network members are likely less committed or extreme than the individuals who joined the terrorist group. Alternatively, they were prevented from doing so through some barrier to entry such as familial obligations, lack of direct connection in the group, or structural barriers such as geographical location.

At least 27 percent of the terrorist organizations I examined had identifiable support networks from which they raised money. The actual percentage of terrorist organizations and movements that benefit from identity-based support networks is likely higher. At the same time, establishing support networks might require investments in operational security as well as a supportive population. As such, this avenue of fund-raising might not be a major source of funds for the majority of terrorist organizations. However, most terrorist organizations likely have some support networks, even if small.

Operationally, 16 percent of the terrorist attacks and plots raised money from support networks for their operational activity. Of the groups that pulled off successful attacks, the vast majority solicited funds from close associates also involved in terrorist activity. In many cases, the donors were related to the attackers. Of the plots, funds were raised from a broader set of individuals, which might account for some of the disruption of these plots, because funds transferring across borders into or out of terrorist suspects' accounts might indicate to authorities that terrorist activity is imminent or occurring or provide them the grounds on which to arrest the individuals. Based on the data available for this study, terrorist activity funded by support networks is more likely to be disrupted than activity funded by other mechanisms.

Terrorist support networks provide funds to terrorist organizations and, to a much lesser extent, cells and individuals. These networks can be organized or directed by the terrorist organization or simply be motivated to provide support to a terrorist organization. Generally, support networks develop along identity lines with the terrorist organization, such as geography, culture, language, religion, ideology, ethnicity, or grievance. This type of fund-raising for terrorist groups can be initiated by the group or by individuals and tends to easily adapt to new technologies. Although support networks have mostly funded terrorist organizations, they are also exploited to fund cells, individuals, and specific operational activities.

Self-Financing

Terrorist organizations, cells, and individuals all engage in some form of self-financing: members or individual terrorists donate personal funds to the cause, either in support of the terrorist organization or to provide for the specific operational needs of their plots. This method of raising funds for terrorist activity is increasingly popular, perhaps reflecting a trend toward less-sophisticated (and therefore lower-cost) attacks as well as increased awareness by potential terrorists about the perils of other forms of fund-raising. In fact, self-financing is a key trend in twenty-first-century terrorist financing, although its origins as a fund-raising mechanism date back to twentieth-century terrorism. At the operational level, terrorist cells and individuals increasingly self-finance their activities through personal savings or the diversion of funds from jobs or other sources of employment to the terrorist group or cell. This might be a result of terrorist organizations' concerns about transferring funds internationally for terrorist operations or, in some cases, because of a lack of funds for these activities.

Some terrorist organizations request donations from members when they join, but the amount of funds this generates is rarely significant. For instance, members of PIRA in its early years were required to contribute dues.[83] For terrorist organizations, this money can help recruits demonstrate their seriousness by committing financial resources, and it might have the additional benefit of reassuring the terrorist organization that the individual is not a spy; terrorist groups often assume most counterterrorist actors will not knowingly or willingly finance terrorist activity.

For operational activities, terrorists often rely on self-financing to raise the funds required for their plots; they augment their personal funds by engaging in external activities such as criminal business models (covered in Chapters 4 and 5). One example of self-financing for a terrorist plot was the 2005 Sydney/Melbourne plot, in which twenty-two people were arrested (nine in Sydney and thirteen in Melbourne) on suspicion of planning a terrorist attack. The Sydney plotters engaged in military-style training and purchased materials they planned to use to manufacture explosives. In this case, the cell members primarily relied on their own incomes to fund their activities.[84] Another example was the Toronto 18 plot in Canada. In that instance, one of the main terrorist conspirators self-financed the plot using approximately $30,000 (Canadian) of personal money from savings, student loans, and credit cards.[85] In some cases, self-financing can be a limiting factor and restrict the scope and scale of terrorist activity. In other cases, when terrorists have personal funds to dedicate to an attack, it can impede law enforcement or security services' ability to detect the financial activity around the attack preparations because there are fewer (if any) international financial transfers and much of the money can be withdrawn in cash, enhancing operational security.

Many successful terrorist attacks have also been self-funded. At the time of the 2005 terrorist attack in London, three of the perpetrators (Khan, Lindsay, and Tanweer) were all unemployed. Khan provided most of the funds for the attack using his existing credit and bank accounts by withdrawing small amounts over a protracted period from these accounts, specifically a £10,000 personal loan.[86] The terrorist attacks of 2019 in Sri Lanka also appear to have been financed in large part from their personal wealth. This wealth allowed for a large, spectacular plot to develop and likely increased the terrorists' ability to use effective operational security measures (purchasing equipment to support that), as well as to avoid detection that might have occurred if they had engaged in petty criminal activity to raise funds. Of course, the attack was not entirely undetected because several allies of Sri Lanka provided advance warning of the plot.[87]

The rise of the Incel movement (a loose network of individuals who consider themselves involuntarily celibate), and the terrorist violence associated with it, adheres to the trend of self-financing. As of 2021, all of the attacks perpetrated by individuals motivated by this movement have been entirely self-financed and of low-level complexity. For instance, the perpetrator of the Toronto van attack in 2018 rented a van (reserved approximately one month prior to the attack),[88] a rental that he funded from his part-time job.[89] In a similar move, the perpetrator of the 2014 Isla Vista killings purchased the three handguns he used in the attack with money saved from gifts from his grandparents and the $500 per month his father sent him. He purchased the guns for approximately $1,450–$2,450.[90]

In many cases, terrorists do not have enough money on hand for their desired operational activities and turn to personal debt to fund them. This includes applying for and receiving a loan just days before an attack, as the perpetrators of the San Bernardino attack did in 2015.[91] They might have used some of these funds to provide for their child after their attack because they transferred much of the money to one of the perpetrator's mothers. They used the rest to purchase components for the twelve pipe bombs found at their residence and more than 4,500 rounds of ammunition, in addition to the ammunition used during the attack.[92] The loan was provided by Prosper Marketplace, a financial technology company that provides peer-to-peer lending for $28,500 ($31,000 in 2020 dollars).[93] Student loans and credit card debt have also been used to fund terrorist travel, another form of operational terrorist activity generally undertaken by individuals.

Napoleoni notes that self-funding has been successful because the unit cost of terrorist attacks has declined sharply and because there has been a shift from transnational attacks to national ones, which are cheaper.[94] However, the causal relationship here is not clear. Have terrorist attacks gotten cheaper because counterterrorist financing efforts have restricted financing? Or did terrorists seek to conduct lower-cost attacks for reasons other than those imposed by counterterrorism financing measures? Analysis of attacks and plots might shed light on this chicken-and-egg problem.

Few terrorist organizations rely on self-funding (particularly in the form of membership dues or fees) to generate funds for the organization. Only 7 percent of organizations in my study could be identified as having derived funds in this way. However, many more terrorist organizations likely benefit from self-funding to some extent; it is entirely plausible that individuals who join terrorist organizations are required to provide their pocket money to the organization prior to admission into the group. However, the amount of money they provide would likely be quite small, with a few notable exceptions. This point is well-illustrated in a study of US supporters of ISIL who had a small financial footprint and modest financial needs (mostly related to travel to join the group).[95] In several cases, individuals provided much more significant sums of money to ISIL. For instance, Mohamed Amin Ali Roble reportedly used a legal settlement (part of $91,654) to travel to join ISIL and fund some of the group's activities.[96] Regardless, self-funding is a limited means of raising funds for a terrorist organization.

In contrast, 36 percent of the plots and attacks I studied were partly self-financed, and this is likely an underestimation. Self-financing is not a new method of terrorist funding, either; many PIRA units were required to self-fund.[97] In all likelihood, most terrorist attacks are funded in part from funds acquired by the cell members or the individual(s) involved. Certainly, purchasing small goods and equipment for the attack occurs with some regularity, even if the bulk of the funds comes from another source. However, self-funding of terrorist attacks and plots is far less newsworthy than funding from international donors or charities, meaning that these small amounts of money are likely underreported in media accounts of terrorist incidents.

Generally speaking, self-funding of terrorist organizations, cells, or individuals is limited in its ability to generate funds, with a few notable exceptions. Although Gunaratna and Acharya argue that it is possible for small groups and private individuals to fund terrorism at similar levels to state sponsors, terrorists have few personal resources that they can dedicate to the terrorist organization, cell, or plot.[98] However, in the age of small-scale, relatively simple terrorist activity, even these small amounts of funds can mean the difference between a successful terrorist attack and a foiled plot.

Conclusion

Terrorist organizations, cells, and individuals use all means at their disposal to raise funds, including donations from state sponsors, wealthy donors, support networks, and self-funding. Determining which groups have used specific methods can help us to assess how diversified their fund-raising methods are and where their financial vulnerabilities lie; this might assist in

prioritizing counterterrorist financing activities. Identifying terrorist donation sources can also provide critical leads for counterterrorist financing
investigations and actions. For terrorist organizations, state sponsors are the
top source of donations, followed by wealthy donors. Identity-based support networks are also important for organizations, whereas self-financing
is less of a factor (trends are illustrated in Figure 2.1).

Figure 2.1 illustrates the percentage of groups that receive donations
and from which category. However, this figure illustrates only how often a
funding mechanism was used; it does not address the quantity of funds
donated through each method. The actual amount generated is important to
understanding the relative significance of funding sources for an organization's strategy, but accurate estimates of how much terrorist organizations
raise from these activities are hindered by lack of data.

Operationally, the importance of these funding sources is entirely
reversed. Self-financing is the most important source of donations for plots
and attacks, followed by identity-based support networks, illustrated in Figure
2.2. Wealthy donors and state sponsors are far less important for operational financing. However, the same caveat holds true for operational
financing through donations as for organizational financing. If terrorist
cells or individuals are able to find state sponsors or wealthy donors to fund
specific attacks, those sources of funds are likely to be more lucrative and
enable a more spectacular attack.

The differences between the importance of various sources of donations
for terrorist organizations, cells, and individuals demonstrated in this chapter
have important implications for counterterrorist financing. Beyond the specific counterterrorist financing policies and practices (discussed in detail in
Chapter 10), these findings illustrate a lot of difference in how terrorist
organizations and terrorist operations are funded and suggest that our understanding of operational and organizational financing should be disaggre-

**Figure 2.1 Terrorist Groups That Obtain Funding from Donors,
by Method**

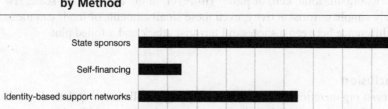

Figure 2.2 Terrorist Plots and Attacks That Obtain Funding from Donors, by Method

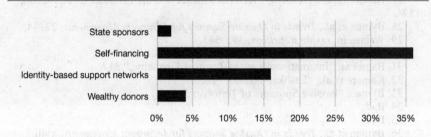

gated to better design counterterrorism financing strategies. These strategies, in turn, will be dictated by the specific types of activities each group undertakes and the nature of the jurisdiction in which that activity occurs.

Notes

1. Rider, "Weapons of War—Part 1," 18.
2. Byman et al., *Trends in Outside Support for Insurgent Movements*, 2.
3. M. Freeman, "Sources of Terrorist Financing," 461–475.
4. Jervis, "Cooperation Under the Security Dilemma," 167–214.
5. Thachuk, "The Gangsterization of Terrorism," 13.
6. US Department of the Treasury, "Remarks of Under Secretary for Terrorism."
7. Hyland, "Many Faces of the PKK."
8. Johnsson and Svante Cornell, "Countering Terrorist Financing," 72.
9. Clarke, *Terrorism, Inc.*, 35.
10. Germann et al., "Terrorist Financing in the Philippines," 150.
11. All dollar amounts are in US dollars. Vittori, *Terrorist Financing and Resourcing*, 102.
12. Aronheim, "ICYMI."
13. Vittori, *Terrorist Financing and Resourcing*, 102.
14. Lia and Kjøk, "Islamist Insurgencies, Diasporic Support Networks, and Their Host States," 26.
15. Darshan-Leitner and Katz, *Harpoon*, 14.
16. Vittori, *Terrorist Financing and Resourcing*, 73.
17. Corley, "Liberation Tigers of Tamil Eelam," 116.
18. Reese, "Financing the Taliban," 97.
19. Ibid., 98.
20. Ibid., 99.
21. Azami, "How Does the Taliban Make Money?"
22. Keatinge, "Role of Finance in Defeating Al Shabaab," 15; Fanusie and Entz, *Al-Shabaab Financial Assessment*.
23. Bergman and Kirkpatrick, "With Guns, Cash and Terrorism."
24. Shelley, *Dirty Entanglements*, 109.
25. Butt and Byman, "Right-Wing Extremism," 139.

26. Byman, "Understanding, and Misunderstanding, State Sponsorship of Terrorism," 12.

27. Gunaratna and Acharya, "Terrorist Finance and the Criminal Underground," 1594.

28. Byman et al., *Trends in Outside Support for Insurgent Movements*, 22–44.

29. Weinstein, *Inside Rebellion*, 342–343.

30. Byman and Kreps, "Agents of Destruction?," 3.

31. Bantekas, "International Law of Terrorist Financing," 317.

32. Kamere et al., "Lashkar-e-Taiba," 76.

33. Byman, "Passive Sponsors of Terrorism," 117.

34. Ibid.

35. Ibid.

36. Byman et al., *Trends in Outside Support for Insurgent Movements*, xviii.

37. Byman, "Outside Support for Insurgent Movements," 982.

38. Vittori, *Terrorist Financing and Resourcing*, 54.

39. Byman et al., *Trends in Outside Support for Insurgent Movements*, xviii.

40. Byman, "Outside Support for Insurgent Movements," 986.

41. Ibid., 987.

42. Bantekas, "International Law of Terrorist Financing," 316.

43. Oakley, "Abu Sayyaf Group," 173; Vittori, *Terrorist Financing and Resourcing*, 73.

44. UN Security Council, "'Abd al-Rahman bin 'Umayr al-Nu'aymi."

45. Corley, "Liberation Tigers of Tamil Eelam," 118.

46. Vittori, *Terrorist Financing and Resourcing*, 39.

47. K. McGrath, *Confronting Al-Qaeda*, 76.

48. Vittori, *Terrorist Financing and Resourcing*, 53.

49. National Commission on Terrorist Attacks upon the United States, *Final Report*.

50. US Department of the Treasury, "Remarks of Under Secretary for Terrorism."

51. Humud, Rosen, and Pirog, "Islamic State Financing and US Policy Approaches," 3–11.

52. Financial Action Task Force, *Emerging Terrorist Financing Risks*.

53. Clarke, *Terrorism, Inc.*, 135.

54. Shelley, *Dirty Entanglements*, 49.

55. Keatinge, Keen, and Izenman, "Fundraising for Right-Wing Extremist Movements," 16.

56. Bauer and Levitt, "How Al-Qaeda Survived Drones, Uprisings, and the Islamic State."

57. US Department of the Treasury, "Treasury Designates Key Nodes."

58. Basile, "Going to the Source," 172.

59. McCoy, "Is ISIS Being Partly Funded by Anonymous Bitcoin Donations?"

60. Byman et al., *Trends in Outside Support for Insurgent Movements*, xv; Hess, "Substantiating the Nexus."

61. Clarke, *Terrorism, Inc.*, 28; Vittori, *Terrorist Financing and Resourcing*, 55.

62. Horgan and Taylor, "Playing the 'Green Card'—Part 1," 8.

63. Corley, "Liberation Tigers of Tamil Eelam," 117.

64. Vittori, *Terrorist Financing and Resourcing*, 39.

65. UN Security Council, "Twenty-Second Report."

66. "416 Who Gave Money to ISIS Identified in France."

67. *BBC News*, "Sheffield Men Jailed for Funding Jihadists in Syria"; Rodger, "Dental Student Abdurahman Kaabar Jailed."

68. Baidawi, "Ex-Federal Worker in Australia Accused."

69. Financial Action Task Force, *Emerging Terrorist Financing Risks*.

70. Baidawi, "Ex-Federal Worker in Australia Accused."

71. Vittori, *Terrorist Financing and Resourcing*, 105; Financial Transactions and Reports Analysis Centre of Canada (FINTRAC), "Terrorist Financing Assessment: 2018," 29.

72. Keatinge, "Role of Finance in Defeating Al Shabaab," 6.

73. Donnelly, "Women in Al-Shabaab."

74. UN Security Council, "Hajjaj bin Fahd Al Ajmi."

75. Whitcomb, "Two Women Convicted in U.S."

76. Yuen, "It's Not Just Russia."

77. Vittori, *Terrorist Financing and Resourcing*, 61.

78. Dean, "Draining the Ocean to Catch One Type of Fish," 18.

79. Ibid., 63.

80. Ibid.

81. PayPal money pool accounts allow users to easily collect funds from friends for shared expenses, holidays, or weddings. PayPal, "What Is a PayPal Money Pool?"

82. Hall, "ISIS Suspects Raise Thousands."

83. Vittori, *Terrorist Financing and Resourcing*, 68.

84. Australian Financial Intelligence Unit (AUSTRAC), "Terrorism Financing in Australia 2014."

85. Davis, "Financing the Toronto 18."

86. House of Commons, *Report of the Official Account*, 14, 15, 18, 23.

87. Jayasinghe and Hookway, "U.S., India Warned Sri Lanka."

88. Herhalt, "Minassian Described Planning."

89. Casey, "Van Attack Suspect Alek Minassian."

90. Duke, "Elliot Rodger's Family Struggled with Money."

91. ComplyAdvantage, "Money in Terrorist Hands."

92. *BBC News*, "San Bernardino Shooting."

93. M. McGrath, "Why It Would Have Been Perfectly Legal."

94. Napoleoni, "Evolution of Terrorist Financing Since 9/11," 20–22.

95. Vidino, Lewis, and Mines, "Dollars for Daesh."

96. Ibid., 26.

97. Horgan and Taylor, "Playing the 'Green Card'—Part 2," 47.

98. Gunaratna and Acharya, "Terrorist Finance and the Criminal Underground," 1628.

3

Using and Abusing Organizations

As part of their strategy of diversification, terrorist groups, cells, and individuals raise money by exploiting various types of organizations and organizational structures. Terrorists divert funds from legitimate and criminal enterprises including other terrorist groups (through patronage), nonprofit organizations including charities and charitable causes writ large, businesses and investments, and cultural activities and groups. The use and abuse of these organizational structures facilitates terrorist fund-raising through the provision or diversion of funds and obscures the sources and destinations of funds for both operational and organizational purposes.

Terrorist Patrons
Terrorist groups seek to spread terror, and one of the ways they do this is by helping other groups get established. In some cases, this involves providing other terrorist groups seed or startup money to help them conduct initial operations and gain recruits. Some terrorist groups that have patronized other groups include Hizballah, al-Qaeda, and the Islamic State in Iraq and the Levant (ISIL), although many more examples likely exist. At the operational level, terrorist group financial support for attacks is often assumed but is much less frequently clearly identified. Over time, cells and individuals have tended to move away from organizational support for their activities, potentially in response to counterterrorism financing pressures.

Organizational Patronage
Many terrorist organizations receive seed or startup money from other terrorist groups that use their wealth to help smaller groups gain a foothold.

These funds help terrorist organizations establish themselves while they figure out a sustainable fund-raising strategy.[1] Although terrorist patronage is a relatively common practice, how it affects terrorist actor capabilities is understudied in the literature on terrorist financing.

In addition to funds, terrorist patrons also provide operational support, guidance, training, and weapons to other groups as well as cells and individuals. The financing mechanisms involved in operational support and how often direct terrorist operational support occurs have implications for counterterrorism practice.

Terrorist organizations throughout history have provided other groups with an initial influx of money or support for operational activities. For instance, Hizballah's Unit 1800 was established with the specific intent of providing Tanzim, the militant faction of Fatah, money and training for suicide attacks against Israel.[2] Al-Qaeda also engaged in patronage of some of its affiliated groups. The Moro Islamic Liberation Front (MILF) received financial help from al-Qaeda as early as 1988. Osama bin Laden sent Mohammed Jamal Khalifa, his brother-in-law, to the Philippines to establish the financial infrastructure for the network, following which Khalifa began to covertly channel money to the group.[3] In other instances, affiliates might have sent funds to support the main organization, such as al-Qaeda in Iraq sending funds to al-Qaeda leadership in Pakistan.[4]

In recent years, ISIL frequently patronized other terrorist groups. ISIL and its various *wilayat* (provinces) have moved money between themselves, helping other nascent groups establish a foothold or mount operations. For example, according to the Philippine military, ISIL sent more than $1.9 million to finance the siege of the city of Marawi.[5] These funds were transferred via Western Union in increments of $10,000.[6]

Even smaller groups can patronize other terrorist organizations. ISIL in Libya, although not a rich terrorist organization compared with ISIL in Syria and Iraq, provided financial support to Ansar Bait al-Maqdis, a group operating in the Sinai Peninsula.[7] The latter group eventually pledged allegiance to ISIL, becoming ISIL in Sinai. In a more conventional form of terrorist patronage, as of 2018, Islamist militant groups in West Africa's Sahel region were also receiving support from al-Qaeda and ISIL to enhance cooperation and carry out sophisticated attacks. These groups operated from Mali and Nigeria, and the financial support likely came through Libya.[8] On the other side of Africa, ISIL in Somalia has received some financial support from ISIL in Yemen.[9]

Some groups move funds between affiliates or aligned groups to support attacks in parts of the world where they might have no infrastructure or to facilitate covert movement of money. For instance, ISIL's outpost in Libya served as a financing hub for the wider region. Funds have been channeled there from the ISIL core and subsequently on to Somalia to support the establishment of a new ISIL affiliate.[10]

Not all terrorist patronage involves terrorist groups providing the money directly to another organization; instead, it might involve providing the beneficiary group access to existing funding sources. According to Jacob Zenn, one of the founders of Boko Haram met one of bin Laden's "lieutenants" in Sudan. After this meeting, his Nigerian fighters received money from al-Qaeda's Saudi financial networks to establish the jihadist movement in Nigeria.[11] This might be less of a case of al-Qaeda patronizing Boko Haram than an indication of al-Qaeda providing access to its donor network.

Operational Patronage

Terrorist patrons provide funds to more than just other groups; they also fund cells and individuals' operational activities. There are a number of examples of terrorist organizations funding the terrorist activities of individuals outside their immediate area of operations or territorial control. Most of these examples go without mention because it is obvious that terrorist organizations funded the attacks. However, with the rise of self-financing of terrorist attacks, the actual provision of funds by terrorist groups to operational cells and individuals might be significantly reduced from historic levels and is worth closer scrutiny.

One of the most notorious examples of a terrorist group funding an attack is, of course, al-Qaeda and the 9/11 attacks on the United States. In this instance, al-Qaeda recruited the individuals for the attack through the organization and provided the funding and plans. Also, ISIL might have directly funded the 2015 Paris attacks and likely had a significant hand in planning them.[12] In other cases, organizational command and control is not always clear. For instance, Tunisians in Libya associated with ISIL facilitated the attacks in Sousse, Tunisia, in 2015 and Bardo, Tunisia, in 2016 with financial and logistical support, but the actual command and control ISIL exerted is debatable.[13]

Operational patronage of many terrorist attacks is often assumed but the actual mechanisms behind this provision of funds are not always known. At the same time, the increased focus on countering terrorist financing internationally has likely restricted terrorist group patronage of attacks, assuming (rightly, in many cases) that funds provided to operational actors would raise the suspicions of law enforcement and security services. The rise of self-financing of operational activity has likely been a response to increased counterterrorist financing efforts.

The trend toward self-financing also mirrors other trends in twenty-first-century terrorism: namely, the demise of the terrorist organization and the rise of the terrorist or extremist movement. In many cases, particularly in right-wing extremism, there is no identifiable terrorist organization per se. Instead, extremist ideas circulate among a few ideologues or promoters of these ideas, but many individuals taking violent action on them (and thus, moving from extremist to terrorist) have little if any connection to these individuals and almost certainly no logistical or financial support (see Chapter 2).

Although most cells and individuals (and nascent terrorist organizations) accept the patronage of a terrorist group when it is offered, this is not always the case. For example, al-Qaeda offered to finance Mohammed Merah's shooting plot in France in March 2012, but he refused the offer.[14] He likely had ample money for the simple, inexpensive plot, which he obtained through his criminal activity and other funding sources. He might have also refused funds in order to maintain control and operational security because funds transferred from one of al-Qaeda's fronts might have triggered international scrutiny of the financial transaction. Alternatively, he might have struggled to find acceptable methods of receiving the funds from al-Qaeda that would not compromise his identity or his plans.

Approximately 27 percent of the terrorist organizations studied received money from a terrorist patron (another terrorist group). The majority of these terrorist organizations belonged to one of the "families" of terrorist groups—al-Qaeda or ISIL—that spawned many affiliated groups. For terrorist patrons, money they send to other groups allows for the expansion of their brand and operational reach and increases relational ties between geographically separate groups and militants. These patrons are usually in ideological or strategic alignment with their client organizations, although junior partners in these relationships might fear that their autonomy is eroded by these relationships and that they might become dependent on the terrorist patron.[15]

Approximately 30 percent of the operational activity of terrorist groups I studied was funded by a terrorist patron. Of course, this amount does not necessarily reflect the full scope of support and activity provided to cells and individuals by terrorist groups and likely underrepresents that support, as evidence of direct forms of financial support from terrorist patrons might have eluded investigators' inquiries. However, it also demonstrates the increasing tendency toward self-financing for terrorist plots and attacks.

The Charitable Sector

The charitable sector, broadly defined here, includes all types of charitable organizations, causes, and activities. This includes formal (often registered) charities, nonprofit organizations, religious entities or organizations, and fund-raising calls for anything that can broadly be considered charitable. I consider this broadly because there are significant differences across jurisdictions in terms of what is "charitable," but also in how groups, cells, and individuals actually use the sector to raise funds for terrorism. Based on a review of operational and organizational fund-raising mechanisms, I developed a typology of seven methods of charitable exploitation. Understanding the differences between these methods is critical for informing effective counterterrorist financing activities, including legislation, regulations, disruption, and prosecutions.

The charitable sector is much maligned in terms of terrorist financing; it is often said to be particularly vulnerable to abuse by terrorist actors. Part of this concern is historical: in the early years of the global war on terror, there were arrests, prosecutions, and publicity around charities used to finance al-Qaeda (or were suspected to). In retrospect, some of those concerns appear to have been overblown or without merit, yet still cast a pall over the entire sector. At the same time, terrorist organizations, cells, and individuals do use charitable organizations and activities to raise funds for terrorist purposes. Charities help terrorist groups "move personnel, funds, and materiel to and from high-risk areas under the cover of charity work" and provide terrorists jobs that offer both a salary and cover.[16] These activities and organizations provide all levels of terrorist actors the ability to generate money as well as avenues through which to move and obscure those funds. In order to understand the risk posed by the charitable sector, a robust understanding of how terrorist actors have abused it is required.

The charitable sector can include charities (sometimes registered with local authorities and with tax-exempt status, depending on the jurisdiction), nonprofit organizations (also sometimes registered with tax-exempt status), and aid organizations. It also consists of the informal charitable sector, which can include pop-up charitable activities, such as crowdfunding campaigns, door-to-door collections not conducted by a formal charitable organization, and many other activities ostensibly for charitable purposes.

One such charitable activity is Zakat, the religious duty of Muslims to donate a portion of their wealth for charitable purposes, which has been tied to terrorist financing.[17] For instance, Raphaeli points to charities and *hawala* as particular sources of terrorist financing and singles out Zakat as a principal source for charitable organizations and, by extension, terrorist groups.[18] This 2003 analysis of terrorist financing failed to distinguish between the variation in types of charitable abuse, including between the level of actors. Of course, Zakat features prominently in the charitable sector for Muslims but in and of itself is not a source of terrorist financing.

There has also been a tendency to conflate mosques with terrorist financing. According to Napoleoni, in response to the war on terror, a decentralized, loosely connected, and often self-financed mosque network funded terrorist activities and received funding from Gulf region donors.[19] However, little evidence has emerged to support the assertion of this mosque network and its role in fund-raising for terrorism. Although some charitable organizations have funded terrorist groups (and mosques often fall into the category of charitable organizations), the nuance of how those activities occurred is lost in such a description, and a more nuanced typology of charitable abuses is required.

Typology of Terrorist Exploitation of the Charitable Sector

Determining the actual level of complicity of a charitable organization with a terrorist group can be extremely difficult, and it can be tempting, for simplicity's sake, to paint the entire organization as a terrorist front. It remains imperative, however, to fully and carefully articulate the extent to which the organization was involved in the terrorism financing activity, which members were involved or aware, and how much money was actually diverted to terrorist causes or activities.

Charities are an attractive target for terrorists for a number of reasons, in part because countries have historically been reluctant to scrutinize their activities, which makes them subject to a wide variety of charitable abuses.[20] Raphaeli also points to charities as fulfilling different aspects of terrorist financing. He notes that charitable organizations can use their own money to finance terrorist organizations but might also serve as a conduit for the transfer for money.[21] He also notes that sometimes charities are fronts or fraudulent organizations.[22]

There are several types of charities and nonprofit organizations used by terrorist organizations to fund-raise:

- wholly owned organizations that are fully complicit and aware of their activities
- those that occupy more of a gray zone, in that they probably have a good idea of where the funds are going but have plausible deniability (even if that deniability is met with significant skepticism)
- those that are more or less legitimate but have an officer or person in a position of control or influence that can divert funds to different terrorist groups or cells
- those used by outsiders without any internal knowledge or awareness

Effectively, individuals working in the sector might have different levels of complicity or responsibility in terms of financing terrorist activity.

For instance, Basile argues that al-Qaeda has been funded by charities and nongovernmental organizations, and although organizations like the Muslim World League, Benevolence International Foundation, and Qatar Charitable Society were not specifically created to fund the group, they have become supportive of its cause. Basile further argues that the Benevolence International Foundation "skimmed" 10 percent of its charitable projects and physically passed the proceeds to al-Qaeda operatives for deposit into their accounts or provided them to operational cells.[23]

Of course, there is significant overlap in some of the ways charities and related organizations and entities are used and abused by terrorist groups, cells, and individuals. In each type of terrorist charitable exploitation, the organization's level of complicity as well as that of the donors is considered. There are seven main ways the charitable sector is used and abused by terrorists:

Type 1: The charity, nonprofit, or organization is a terrorist front, and this is known to its donors.

Type 2: The charity, nonprofit, or organization is a terrorist front, and this is *not* known to its donors.

Type 3: The charity, nonprofit, or organization is a partial terrorist front, and this is known to its donors.

Type 4: The charity, nonprofit, or organization is a partial terrorist front, and this is *not* known to its donors.

Type 5: The charity, nonprofit, or organization is not a terrorist front, but an individual in a position of control or influence is diverting funds to a terrorist cause.

Type 6: The charity, nonprofit, or organization is not a terrorist front, but its activities are being taxed by a terrorist entity.

Type 7: No charity or nonprofit organization is involved, but a terrorist or extremist uses its cause to raise funds. Not all donors are aware, but some might be.

In these scenarios of terrorist fund-raising activities, Types 1 and 2 involve charities, nonprofit organizations, or other entities that are full terrorist fronts. Their purpose is to support terrorist organizations, cells, or individuals. Some charitable organizations are formed with the specific purpose of funding terrorist organizations, whereas others are coerced into diverting funds to terrorist purposes.[24] The difference between Type 1 and Type 2 is that the donors are aware (Type 1), or the nature of the organization (being a terrorist front) is hidden from donors (Type 2). This distinction is important to clarify when terrorists have broader public support or when support for a charitable activity or cause is being misappropriated or diverted.

In Type 1 exploitation of the sector (a known terrorist front), and as part of a broader support network, charities can be established with the direct purpose of raising funds for terrorist organizations, with few other (if any) purposes. Examples of a full-fledged terrorist charity or nonprofit organization are rare in a Western context but more common in areas closer to where terrorist organizations operate or control territory. Being able to prove a charity was established for this purpose might also be challenging, and uncertainty might exist about whether a charity represents Type 1 or Type 2 exploitation.

A likely example of Type 1 terrorist exploitation of the charitable sector was the Tamil Rehabilitation Organization, which coordinated the activities of other Tamil organizations and effectively acted as an umbrella organization for other nongovernmental groups.[25] The Canadian chapter of this organization was reported to have sent more than $300,000 a year back to Sri Lanka and the Liberation Tigers of Tamil Eelam (LTTE). Writ large, the nonprofit or charitable organizations used by the LTTE are reported to have provided up to $2 million per month to their cause.[26] The donors were likely aware that some of their money would be provided to the LTTE. Of course, the LTTE also provided a variety of social services to the population in its area of control at various times in its existence and also diverted significant funds toward terrorist and insurgent activities.

Another example of a charitable organization that existed primarily to finance a terrorist group (in Type 1 charitable abuse) was Irish Northern Aid (NORAID), a charity established by Michael Flannery in New York that directed approximately $200,000 per year into Provisional Irish Republican Army (PIRA) coffers until the late 1970s.[27] The charity had approximately seventy chapters in the United States, although its supporters were concentrated in New York. The donations for the group were collected openly, meaning that donors were aware of the purpose and destination of the funds. NORAID is estimated to have raised between $3 million and $5 million for PIRA from fund-raising activities throughout the United States.[28]

Terrorist financing expert Matthew Levitt also cites the cases of Benevolence International Foundation, Holy Land Foundation for Relief and Development, and Islamic Committee for Palestine as examples of charitable organizations created specifically to fund terrorism.[29] According to UN sanctions information, the Benevolence International Foundation's predecessor organization was founded in 1987 in part to raise funds for fighters in Afghanistan, and the Benevolence International Foundation engaged in financial transactions on behalf of al-Qaeda, but the role of the Holy Land Foundation's involvement in terrorism remains contested.[30]

A likely example of Type 1 or 2 exploitation is the case of Adeel ul-Haq, who founded two charitable organizations in the United Kingdom. He used these organizations to buy a high-powered laser pointer, night-vision goggles, and a secret waterproof money pouch. The UK Charities Commission struck the two organizations from its official charity register in August 2016 after concluding that they had raised money and supplies for ISIL and al-Qaeda.[31] Ul-Haq's case is also noteworthy because it involves operational support for terrorist activity rather than the solicitation of funds for a terrorist organization. His donors were likely unaware of the purpose of the funds.

The Lashkar-e-Taiba (LeT) has also benefited extensively from charitable giving, using a combination of Type 1 and 2 exploitation of charitable organizations to raise funds for its activities. Two front organizations associated with the LeT are Jamaat-ud-Dawa (JuD) and the Falah-i-Insaniyat Foundation; both of these organizations were active in fund-raising and social activities for the group.[32] In both cases, these organizations have ostensibly charitable purposes but, in fact, provide significant funds to the militant wing of the organization. The LeT uses JuD's social welfare organization (which has more than 50,000 registered members) to raise funds. In Pakistan, donation boxes are placed in JuD offices and shops all over the country. At public gatherings, money is openly solicited for LeT, and the group also collects a land tax whereby farmers contribute 10 percent of their total produce to charity.[33] The Pakistani government has also seized assets and funds from charities associated with Hafiz Saeed, the founder of the LeT.[34]

In Type 3 and 4 charitable abuses, the organization is a partial terrorist front. This means the organization likely engages in some legitimate charitable activities and has at least a partially legitimate purpose, but some of the funds are diverted to terrorist activities. This diversion is done knowingly by the executive of the organization, and in Type 3 also with the knowledge of donors. For the most part, charitable organizations implicated in terrorist financing have dual purposes (charitable and terrorist) or also conduct charitable activities. An example of Type 3 or 4 charitable abuse is the International Islamic Relief Organization, believed to have given aid to terrorists in the Philippines in the 1990s. At the time, one of the branches of the charity was operated by bin Laden's brother-in-law. During his tenure, between 70 and 90 percent of funds that came into the charity were diverted for terrorist causes.[35]

Another example of Type 3 or 4 charitable abuse is from Hizballah; it runs a number of charities and receives support from sympathetic ones such as the Islamic Resistance Support Organization, Martyr's Organization, and Al-Mabarrat Charitable Organization.[36] In 2006, Lebanese women helped raise funds in support of Hizballah through the Islamic Resistance Support Organization. They sewed garments to be sold and arranged community dinners to raise funds. They also created a "sponsor a fighter" program that allowed women to provide money directly to specific Hizballah fighters.[37] However, when considering Hizballah as a terrorist organization, we must remember that it is also involved in governance and provision of social services, meaning that the charities are unlikely to be entirely terrorist fronts or diverting their funds solely to terrorist purposes. Some of LeT's charitable organizations might also fall into this category of charitable sector exploitation by terrorist actors.

In Type 5 exploitation, the charitable organization is not a terrorist front, but rather a person in a position of control is diverting funds toward terrorist purposes. In this case, the rest of the administration is uninvolved in this activity, and the donors are equally unaware of the diversion of funds for terrorist purposes. Type 5 abuse is one of the more common ways terrorists exploit the charitable sector, particularly in jurisdictions with more heavily regulated and monitored charities. In Type 5 abuse, the activity might resemble fraud more than other types of criminal activity. Funds are diverted from the charitable organization, but the ultimate destination might not be known. In cases of fraud, this would be for personal benefit, but in this case, it is for a terrorist cause. An example of Type 5 exploitation might be Chechen Islamist extremist groups such as Caucasus Emirate, a loose terrorist organization active in the southwestern region of Russia and in Syria that received donations from Islamic and international charities.[38] The Kurdistan Worker's Party (PKK) has also made use of charitable and nonprofit organizations to raise funds, including abroad. In Australia in 2010, approximately $200,000 of taxpayer money was granted to the Kurdish Association of Victoria. Shortly thereafter, the government had reason to believe the funds had been transferred to the PKK.[39] In this case, it is unlikely that the entire charitable organization's staff was aware of the links between the organization and the PKK; instead, one individual in a position of control or influence likely diverted the funds.

Khalistani extremists have also used this method to divert funds from charitable purposes toward operational activity. For instance, an alleged Khalistani extremist collected funds for ostensibly charitable purposes (the building of Gurdawas).[40] Funds were diverted from this purpose and distributed to terrorist families in Punjab.[41] That same extremist is also alleged to have provided financial support for an accused terrorist assassin.[42] In addition, the extremist facilitated a terrorist plot in 2017.[43] Although this type of charitable exploitation has much in common with Type 5, it can properly be conceived as a hybrid between Type 5 and Type 7 exploitation because of the lack of a person in a position of control or influence. In this case, the charity existed and was legitimate, but the funds were never given to the organization. Instead, the terrorists exploited access to cash.

In Type 6 charitable exploitation, the charitable organization is not diverting funds toward a terrorist entity or compromised from within by a person sympathetic to a terrorist entity. Instead, the organization is taxed by a terrorist organization (and in rare cases by cells or individuals) to operate within the area the terrorists control. This is a form of taxation or extortion but specifically applies to international aid or charitable organizations. Al-Shabaab provides a salient example of this type of predatory behavior. International aid groups are subject to the requirement to pay a percentage of their budget in protection fees to Al-Shabaab.[44] According to one leaked document, the UK government sent $723 million in aid to Somalia and admitted it was "certain" that portions of it would be used to fund Al-Shabaab.[45] The taxation of international aid organizations has been a lucrative source of funds for Al-Shabaab and something of a bête noir for the international community. Aid agencies have reportedly paid between $10,000 and $20,000 per month to operate in Somalia, along with further taxes demanded on top of this amount. Indeed, one UN agency allocated 10 percent of its budget to pay Al-Shabaab protection fees.[46] Of course, the most efficient way to stop terrorist fund-raising through this method would be to prohibit charitable and aid organizations from operating in the area, but this course of action would have devastating humanitarian consequences.

In Type 7 exploitation of the charitable sector, individuals, cells, or even organizations seek to raise funds for an ostensibly charitable purpose (e.g., humanitarian aid) but instead use the funds for terrorist purposes such as travel to join a terrorist organization or funding a terrorist attack. In Type 7 exploitation, no actual charities or organizations are exploited. Instead, the charitable sector is exploited through the use of a charitable cause for the fund-raising. In some examples, individuals go door to door asking for funds, but modern information technology has changed some of these practices, particularly through the use of crowdfunding websites. In one example of the exploitation of a charitable cause, a former al-Qaeda operative arrested in Germany raised funds for al-Qaeda and potential operational cells by soliciting contributions for religious or humanitarian purposes but diverted those funds to terrorist use.[47] In another example from 2011, eleven men were arrested in Birmingham on suspicion that they were planning an imminent terrorist attack (the Birmingham Rucksack bomb plot). The three leaders of the cell—Irfan Naseer, Irfan Khalid, and Ashik Ali—were handed significant sentences for their activities.[48] To raise money for their plan, they posed as charity workers. They used collection buckets and T-shirts from a charity to collect money on the streets of Birmingham during Ramadan. They collected more than £13,000 (approximately $18,000) in the name of the charity but told the charity that the amount was much smaller, keeping the undeclared funds for themselves. They sought to increase the amount of money at their disposal by speculating on currency but lost £9,000 (approximately $12,700) instead.[49] Ultimately, the group applied for loans to supplement its income after losing the money on the currency speculation scheme.[50]

The internet and social media have significantly enabled this type of terrorist fund-raising. For instance, crowdfunding can allow individuals to raise money in a short time online before the authorities or the companies themselves become aware of how these platforms are being used. Social media can also be used to fund terrorist organizations through charitable organizations. For instance, a charity in France raised money via a social media campaign primarily using Facebook. Some of the funds raised were given to foreign terrorist fighters.[51]

Above and beyond fund-raising, charities can be abused by terrorist entities in a variety of other ways. According to the Financial Action Task Force (FATF), charities and nonprofit organizations are abused by:

- diversion of donations through affiliated individuals to terrorist organizations;
- exploitation of some NPO authorities for the sake of a terrorist organization;
- abuse of programming/program delivery to support the terrorist organization;
- support for recruitment into terrorist organizations; and
- the creation of "false representation and sham NPOs" through misrepresentation/fraud.[52]

Many of these types of abuses are related to terrorist fund-raising, but some are used for recruitment and broader organizational support.

The charitable sector is considered high risk in terms of terrorist financing, not entirely without cause. Charitable organizations are sometimes established without the proper controls or authorities, and funds might not be provided to the appropriate people. For instance, Australia has experienced suspicious pop-up nonprofit organizations that seem to dissolve shortly after achieving their financial goal. These organizations were focused on raising humanitarian efforts in Iraq and Syria.[53] Although it is challenging to tie these organizations directly to terrorist organizations, at best, they likely lack the internal controls and due diligence to ensure that their funds were not being diverted to terrorist organizations. At worst, they might be fronts for terrorist groups, and funds might be sent directly to support terrorist activities elsewhere.

Terrorist groups that systematically abuse the charitable sector can do so with significant levels of sophistication. Al-Qaeda used a dual approach for its exploitation of the charitable sector. The group created its own network of charitable institutions as a cover for its fund-raising (Type 1 or Type 2), many of which originated during the jihad against Soviet occupation of Afghanistan. The group also employed a strategy of infiltrating the charities with employees to divert money toward the group and its illicit activities (Type 5).[54] The group likely used other methods in multiple charities and charitable organizations to raise funds as well.

The establishment of a charitable front for a terrorist organization is increasingly rare due to global efforts to stop the practice, but the diversion of funds or materials to terrorist groups by individuals involved in terrorist activity remains common. According to Shawn Teresa Flanigan, charities and extremism exist as two activities along a spectrum of possible actions used to address political or social concerns.[55] When activists' work is unable to advance their cause, they might advance toward the fringes of the political spectrum, in combination with other factors, which can include funding a terrorist organization, cell, or individual.

The ways terrorist groups, cells, and individuals use charitable organizations are plentiful, not least because of the vulnerabilities inherent in these organizations. The more informal the charitable organization, the greater the risks that it could divert funds to terrorist organizations or activities, either deliberately or not. Although the international community has made efforts to address this method of fund-raising for terrorist organizations, there is still a lack of understanding among financial intelligence units, charity regulators, staff at charities and nonprofit organizations, and law enforcement and security services about how terrorists use and abuse the charitable sector, in part because of the lack of well-articulated case studies. In some cases, overstatements about the involvement of terrorists in the charitable sector have increased skepticism about the abuse of the sector, hindering efforts by national and international bodies to tighten regulations and reporting on the sector. In other cases, fear of being portrayed as anti-Islamic has hindered regulation of the charitable sector, and the prospect of regulating and registering charities triggers considerations regarding constitutional and freedom of expression and freedom of religion in some countries.[56]

Approximately 20 percent of the terrorist organizations I studied have raised funds through charitable exploitation, but the actual number of terrorist groups exploiting the charitable sector is likely higher. Much of this activity might have gone undetected or might be limited in scope and scale. However, many of the terrorist organizations I studied do not have ready access to the charitable sector; it is a relatively restricted method terrorist groups can use to raise money. Operationally, only 2 percent of plots and attacks were funded in whole or in part through the charitable sector, which makes this one of the least-used methods of operational funding.

Businesses, Investments, and Cultural Activities
To ensure their longevity, terrorist organizations seek to solidify and diversify their sources of funding. One of the ways they do this is through investments, including in businesses, and to a lesser extent securities and currency speculation. They also seek to raise money through propaganda sales and cultural activities. Some of the groups involved in this type of activity include PIRA, Al-Shabaab, ISIL, al-Qaeda, and right-wing terrorist groups. Operationally, this type of activity is rare, although some cells and individuals do seek to raise money through businesses to support their terrorist objectives. Countering these types of fund-raising schemes requires a broad understanding of the structure of terrorist organizations and extremists (and to a lesser extent cells), the ability to track complex financial

paths, and the political willingness to investigate these types of activities for potential terrorist or extremist financing.

Above and beyond the taxation of legitimate businesses or their use as fronts, which I discuss in Chapters 4 and 8, respectively, terrorist organizations also invest money in them, control them, and in some cases finance their establishment. These businesses operate in a quasilegal space because the funds to start or expand them come from terrorist groups (and might have originated in criminal activity), and their profits are also diverted to terrorist organizations. However, the activities that occur between these terrorist bookends are often legal. It also helps to understand one of the incentives to invest in legitimate businesses: to solidify their financial position in such a way as to not raise suspicion and allow them to finance their activities (by raising, moving, and obscuring money) with ease over a longer time horizon.

Investing money in businesses is the hallmark of a successful terrorist organization and usually signals that the group has raised sufficient funds and requires a place to grow its money and protect it from inflation. Investing money in legitimate businesses signals that the terrorist organization intends to be in the "game" over the long haul, regardless of tactical (or strategic) military defeats. When terrorists invest funds, it is usually in businesses or in other relatively illiquid assets. Real estate in or near the territory in which they operate is a popular choice. Real estate offers several benefits; it is a tangible asset and can be sold to generate cash flow. Structures around the purchase can also be used to mask the identity of the owner and his or her links to a terrorist entity. Sometimes, terrorists set up entire businesses around investing in real estate or, in other cases, simply store their funds in real estate investments (I cover this in more detail in Chapter 7). Real estate can also serve as a safe house.

Adams argues that terrorist organizations need to become more sophisticated financially to survive, and he supports this argument with two case studies on the Palestinian Liberation Organization (PLO) and PIRA. Over time, they employed more stable (and legitimate) funding sources and invested those funds to supplement other sources of funds, eventually getting most of their money from investments and businesses.[57] These investments are usually initially funded by money raised through criminal activity or other terrorist fund-raising methods. For instance, PIRA raised funds by selling antiques.[58] Hamas has earned funds from the textile business and cattle raising.[59] The Popular Front for the Liberation of Palestine (PFLP) owned and operated metal works facilities.[60] Al-Shabaab is also alleged to run small businesses.[61] The types of businesses terrorists use to make money reflects the economic activity in the area they control or in the surrounding jurisdictions, meaning that an analysis of the economic terrain in and proximate to a terrorist group's area of operations can be used proactively to identify the types of businesses terrorist actors might use to raise funds.

More elaborate business structures are usually the purview of large, well established terrorist groups, as the LTTE amply demonstrated. That group created sophisticated structures and had a diversified portfolio of businesses in which it invested over the duration of its existence. In addition to running its own businesses (particularly within their area of control or influence), it provided start-up capital for Tamils all over the world who hoped to open a small business. In return, the group split the profits with the business owner.[62] These businesses allowed the group great diversity in funding sources and provided cover for the procurement and movement of funds, among other terrorist financing activities.

Indeed, there were multiple benefits for the LTTE in investing in some of these businesses, as illustrated by one of the LTTE's businesses, the Sea Pigeons. These constituted a fleet of deep-sea vessels registered in Panama, Honduras, and Liberia that carried both legitimate and illicit cargo. The shipping interests were managed by shell companies, distancing the activity from the terrorist organization. The ships carried rice, flour, sugar, cement, fertilizer, and timber, and they provided a mechanism for moving funds, weapons, people, narcotics, and a host of other commodities.[63] The vessels earned the LTTE significant profits and provided the group its own shipping line through which it could acquire more sensitive goods.

In the United Kingdom, the LTTE operated a range of businesses, including jewelry and video stores as well as gas stations and restaurants. In France, the group operated a supermarket, and in Canada it operated a travel agency and fruit canning company. In Europe, it operated several telecommunication retailers that provided prepaid phone cards. The group also operated a satellite channel with more than 22,000 subscribers in Europe alone.[64] Some of these businesses were likely created to achieve vertical integration in the LTTE's endeavors, such as newspaper production and printing presses, or to help in other pursuits such as the movement or use of funds (including procurement activities) and the dissemination of propaganda.

Over time, the LTTE diversified its asset base to include agriculture and finance companies. The finance companies might have served multiple purposes, including laundering criminal funds, generating profits in addition to the vital task of hiding the source of funds (the placement, layering, and integration of funds into the formal financial sector), and assisting the organization and its members to manage their resources effectively. Indeed, some of the funds generated from legal businesses (not the ones controlled or owned by the LTTE itself) were diverted to the group and laundered through Tamil-owned legal businesses and money exchange and transfer agencies.[65] Together, these businesses were estimated to have earned $2.75

million per month for the LTTE. Some cited as "LTTE businesses" might have been fronts for other activity as well. For instance, in Switzerland and Canada, the group set up its own hawala using Tamil jewelry shops. It balanced the books of the hawala using falsely declared gold jewelry from the gold market in Singapore, and human couriers and bank transfers were used to move the resulting cash.[66] These extensive business activities provided the LTTE with significant sources of funds, as well as the mechanisms to cover the movement of those funds and procurement activities, and a veneer of legitimacy in the communities in which they operated.

Although the LTTE might have had one of the most extensive business networks, other terrorist groups also use businesses to raise funds. For instance, the LeT has raised funds by operating fish farms, hospitals, markets, agricultural tracts, mobile clinics, and ambulance services. Often, legitimate business ventures combine an aspect of charitable giving with a cultural or religious context. During Eid, members of LeT collect the hides of slaughtered animals and sell them for a profit. In another instance, some of the money the LeT diverted from legitimate charitable aid for earthquake relief efforts was used to purchase real estate throughout Pakistan. At one point, the group had 1,500 offices operating in the country and invested money in legitimate businesses and enterprises such as Islamic institutions and schools.[67]

The Taliban has also raised funds from transportation businesses, import and export companies, and pistachio farming, all of which might contribute up to $15 million per year to the group's budget.[68] The initial funds for these businesses were likely obtained from other forms of terrorist or criminal fund-raising. Although the businesses might have been operating in the "legitimate" economy, they were likely also used to hide drug shipments and launder profits from the drug trade.[69] In this way, the Taliban benefited twice from the businesses: once through the profits they generated and again through the cover benefits they provided.

ISIL has blended the various ways of using businesses to dramatic effect. ISIL purchased businesses in Baghdad to move money from their extortion activities and oil sales into the legitimate economy in the region and abroad. ISIL invested in electronic companies, car dealerships, private hospitals, and the food and beverage industry. The companies were generally not owned by ISIL members; instead, they were owned by third parties who paid a "dividend" to the group.[70] Within its area of influence, ISIL also took control of a number of businesses, including mobile phone companies and tile, cement, and chemical factories, among others. The group ran the businesses and diverted portions of their profits to support its terrorist activities.[71]

ISIL is estimated to have moved $400 million out of Iraq and Syria to invest outside its territory as part of the group's strategy to ensure its long-term survival, even after the loss of the caliphate. ISIL likely has continued to benefit from these businesses, and the group also invested in businesses outside its direct area of control in Iraq and Syria. Much of this money was derived from its oil smuggling and extortion activities (among other fundraising mechanisms) and was invested in real estate companies, hotels, automobile dealerships, and carwashes. In some cases, the group invested in businesses relatively far removed from its terrorist membership, whereas in other cases ISIL operatives owned and controlled the companies. The group is believed to have invested those funds in businesses in the Middle East and Africa; funds were moved through the banking network in Turkey, and the United Arab Emirates (UAE), Iraq, and Syria.[72]

Examples of companies owned and controlled by an ISIL operative are Liiban Trading and Al-Mutafaq Commercial Company. These two companies were designated terrorist organizations by the United States because they were owned or controlled by Mohamed Mire Ali, an ISIL financial operative. Liiban Trading served as a front for ISIL-aligned groups in the Bari region of Somalia and likely generated profits for the group. Mire Ali also provided funds to Abdulqadir Mumin in support of ISIL-linked terrorist activities.[73] The funds have reportedly been earmarked to finance a future resurgence of the group.

Terrorists have, on occasion, also invested in cryptocurrencies in order to make money on a run-up in price. However, this is relatively rare, likely for several reasons. Currency speculation, regardless of whether it is on virtual or digital currencies, remains a relatively specialized activity. Cryptocurrency prices are volatile, meaning that terrorists expose themselves to significant potential losses if they invest in cryptocurrencies. Although experimentation is happening, and some terrorists undoubtedly earned significant funds during the Bitcoin price run-up of 2017, this does not appear to be a broad funding strategy adopted by terrorists to date.[74] Terrorist organizations such as Hamas have turned to Bitcoin as a way to solicit donations, but fundamentally this is about soliciting funds through a currency that provides some measure of anonymity and avoids the formal financial sector (in some cases it is about evading sanctions) rather than raising funds through cryptocurrency speculation.[75]

In addition to raising money through businesses and investments, cultural activities and propaganda production are also popular methods for terrorist groups to raise funds. This is particularly true with terrorist organizations that have a significant diaspora community. Two good examples of this are the PKK and the LTTE. In the 1990s, the PKK raised funds through festivals, concerts, plays, and magazine subscriptions.[76] Initially, the LTTE was involved in the film industry through trade and investment, but later it founded video and CD shops that generated sizable revenue.[77] In addition to being cultural, Tamil events were used to raise money for the LTTE.

Diaspora communities would hold cultural shows, spring events, and food festivals and would host guest speakers, with a portion of the proceeds going to the LTTE.[78]

Some terrorist groups also make money by selling propaganda. The right-wing terrorist group Atomwaffen Division might raise funds by selling books, specifically by James Nolan Mason, author of *Siege*, a critical piece of Atomwaffen ideological thought. The books are created and sold using Amazon's CreateSpace.[79] The creation of propaganda might be considered more of a "cultural" activity for the broader group of supporters. Atomwaffen Division is not the only right-wing extremist group in Europe that raises money in this way. Other groups are primarily funded by members through contributions and fund-raising or "cultural" events, such as concerts and parties.[80]

Organizational and Operational Financing Through Business and Investments

Terrorist groups, particularly those with successful fund-raising strategies, often find themselves in a position of having to invest their money, lest their cash lose value through inflation. This is particularly true if they hold significant amounts of local currency or are operating in a war zone where prices can fluctuate significantly and erode the value of their money.

In contrast, terrorist cells and individuals rarely need to invest their funds; they generally hold only operational funds, or funds specifically earmarked for operational activities or supporting the members of the cell in the lead-up to an attack or event. Some cells have, however, tried to expand their funding base by making investments. But generally speaking, these investments require a level of expertise and knowledge that escapes many cells and individuals. One notable example is the Birmingham Rucksack bomb plot, in which the plotters sought to increase the amount of money they had raised through their charity scheme by speculating on currency but lost £9,000 (roughly $12,700) instead.[81] This illustrates how difficult it can be for terrorist cells to manage their funds; they fall prey to the same investing pitfalls the rest of the world does, chasing quick profits with risks too high for their short-term plans.

Operationally, only one terrorist attack I studied involved the creation of businesses to fund it, whereas organizationally, approximately 30 percent of terrorist organizations used businesses and cultural activities (including the sale of propaganda) to raise funds. The vast majority of these organizations are well-established terrorist groups that have held or currently hold territory and have had or currently have a relatively sophisticated management and financial structure—two requirements for successful management of businesses within a terrorist organization's financial portfolio.

Conclusion

Fundamentally, investments in legitimate businesses are important for terrorist organizations that have acquired significant financial resources. They need places to store their funds, with the purposes of protecting that money from the costs of inflation and making more money to support their terrorist activities.

Terrorist organizations invest money in and start businesses related to the economic activity in the area of their operations. If farming is a significant source of funds in their area, they invest in and run farming businesses. If economic activity is more oriented toward the financial sector, real estate, or other businesses, then that is what the terrorist groups pursue. Businesses with several different benefits to the terrorist organization are likely to be more appealing than other types of businesses. Determining the main sources of economic activity within an area of operations for a terrorist group, along with focusing on businesses with multiple benefits for terrorist groups, might allow for the proactive identification of the types of businesses terrorist groups invest in and manage. The LTTE is illustrative. It had one of the most well-diversified fund-raising strategies in terms of the use of businesses. Part of the reason the group was able to diversify to this extent is that it had members is a wide variety of countries, which meant the group was able to take advantage of local economies around the world, finding fund-raising opportunities in a wide variety of sectors. This spread-out, diversified financial portfolio might well be something that other terrorist organizations seek to emulate.

Financially speaking, the most important types of organizations for terrorist groups are legitimate (or semilegitimate) businesses. This includes investments in cryptocurrencies as well as cultural organizations and activities. Terrorist patrons (other terrorist groups) are also important sources of funds, along with the charitable sector, as illustrated in Figure 3.1. Although the actual amount of funds each of these sources provides is unknown, their relative importance is likely reflected in the percentage of groups that employ them. However, there is also likely significant variation among terrorist groups regarding the amounts they raise from each of these sources.

Organizational funding for terrorist cells and individuals is far less prevalent than it is for terrorist groups, but it still plays a role in supporting terrorist plots and attacks, as illustrated in Figure 3.2. Terrorist patrons are the most important organizational source of funds, which makes sense because one of the main activities of terrorist groups is to perpetrate terrorist attacks. Investments are less prevalent in terrorist attacks but have played a role in some prominent attacks. The charitable sector is a much smaller direct source of funds, although this percentage likely underestimates the role the sector plays in funding terrorist attacks because much of

Figure 3.1 Terrorist Groups That Obtain Funding from Organizations, by Source

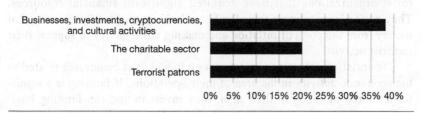

Figure 3.2 Terrorist Plots and Attacks That Obtain Funding from Organizations, by Source

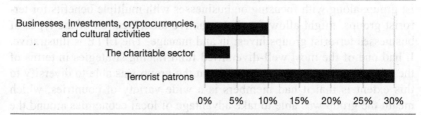

this money is likely funneled to terrorist organizations first before being provided for terrorist attacks.

The difference between group and operational funding from organizations, businesses, and terrorist patrons is significant. Operational terrorist activity is much less likely to be funded from these sources than terrorist groups. This finding has implications for counterterrorist financing policies aimed at addressing these sources of funds. Although these initiatives are important for tackling broader terrorist group funding, they might have limited utility in preventing operational terrorist activity in the jurisdictions in which they are implemented. Depending on the type of terrorist activity found in a particular country or area, jurisdictionally specific counterterrorist financing measures should be identified and prioritized for maximum effect.

Notes

1. Mironova, *From Freedom Fighters to Jihadists*, 236.
2. Bergman, *Rise and Kill First*, 548.
3. Croissant and Barlow, "Following the Money Trail," 136.
4. Humud, Rosen, and Pirog, "Islamic State Financing and U.S. Policy Approaches," 3.

5. Murdoch, "Marawi Uprising Funded by $1.9 Million"; UN Security Council, "Twentieth Report," 12, 17.

6. Egmont and Villamor, "ISIS' Core Helps Fund Militants in Philippines."

7. UN Security Council, "Monitoring Team Report," July 19, 2016, 13.

8. Monnier, "Islamic State, al-Qaeda Support."

9. UN Security Council, "Twenty-Second Report."

10. UN Security Council, "Monitoring Team Report," July 19, 2016, 12.

11. Olivier, "Nigeria."

12. Brisard and Poirot, "Le Financement des Attentats de Paris."

13. UN Security Council, "Monitoring Team Report," July 19, 2016, 12.

14. Oftedal, "Financing of Jihadi Terrorist Cells," 36.

15. Moghadam, *Nexus of Global Jihad*.

16. Levitt, *Hamas*, 62.

17. Looney, "Mirage of Terrorist Financing," 1–2.

18. Raphaeli, "Financing of Terrorism," 61.

19. Napoleoni, "Evolution of Terrorist Financing Since 9/11," 18–19.

20. Looney, "Mirage of Terrorist Financing," 2.

21. Raphaeli, "Financing of Terrorism," 62.

22. Ibid.

23. Basile, "Going to the Source," 173.

24. D. C. Alexander, *Business Confronts Terrorism*, 70.

25. Vittori, *Terrorist Financing and Resourcing*, 81.

26. Corley, "Liberation Tigers of Tamil Eelam," 121–122.

27. Vittori, *Terrorist Financing and Resourcing*, 70.

28. Clarke, *Terrorism, Inc.*, 29.

29. Levitt, *Hamas*, 62.

30. UN Security Council, "Benevolence International Foundation"; Peled, *Injustice*.

31. Bauer and Levitt, "Al Qaeda Financing," 98.

32. UN Security Council "Monitoring Team Report," June 16, 2015, 8.

33. Kamere et al., "Lashkar-e-Taiba," 81–82.

34. Associated Press, "Pakistan Begins Seizing Charities."

35. Germann et al., "Terrorist Financing in the Philippines," 152.

36. Vittori, *Terrorist Financing and Resourcing*, 105.

37. Cragin and Daly, *Women as Terrorists*, 26.

38. Wittig, "Financing Terrorism Along the Chechnya-Georgia Border," 251.

39. Ruehsen, "Partiya Karkeren Kurdistan," 69.

40. Bhagat Singh BRAR and Canada (Minister of Public Safety and Emergency Preparedness), No. T-669-16.

41. Ibid.

42. Ibid.

43. Chauhan, "Terror Module with Links."

44. Vilkko, "Al-Shabaab," 21.

45. Shabelle Media Network, "Somalia: UK Government Admits Funding Isil and Al Shabaab."

46. Keatinge, "Role of Finance in Defeating al-Shabaab," 23–24.

47. Raphaeli, "Financing of Terrorism," 61.

48. *BBC News*, "Terror Plot."

49. Oftedal, "Financing of Jihadi Terrorist Cells," 17.

50. *BBC News*, "Terror Plot."

51. Financial Action Task Force, *Emerging Terrorist Financing Risks*, 34.

52. Ibid., 13.

53. Bauer and Levitt, "Al Qaeda Financing," 98.

54. Miguel del Cid Gómez, "Financial Profile of the terrorism of Al-Qaeda," 8.

55. Flanigan, "Charity as Resistance," 642.

56. Levitt and Jacobson, "U.S. Campaign to Squeeze Terrorists' Financing."

57. Adams, "Financing of Terror," 393–405.

58. Horgan and Taylor, "Playing the 'Green Card'—Part 1," 8.

59. D. C. Alexander, *Business Confronts Terrorism*, 50.

60. Ibid., 51.

61. Schindler, "United Nations View," 89.

62. Vittori, *Terrorist Financing and Resourcing*, 42.

63. Corley, "Liberation Tigers of Tamil Eelam," 128.

64. Vittori, *Terrorist Financing and Resourcing*, 81.

65. Clarke, *Terrorism, Inc.*, 51.

66. Vittori, *Terrorist Financing and Resourcing*, 82.

67. Kamere et al., "Lashkar-e-Taiba," 85.

68. Brennan, "Nut Jihad."

69. Clarke, *Terrorism, Inc.*, 115.

70. Clarke and Williams, "Da'esh in Iraq and Syria," 37.

71. Ibid., 38.

72. Warrick, "Retreating ISIS Army."

73. Office of the Lead Inspector General "Operation Inherent Resolve," 113.

74. Tritten, "Dark Side of Bitcoin."

75. Arnold and Abu Ramadan, "Hamas Calls on Supporters."

76. Ruehsen, "Partiya Karkeren Kurdistan," 66.

77. Clarke, *Terrorism, Inc.*, 51.

78. Vittori, *Terrorist Financing and Resourcing*, 80.

79. Atomwaffen Division is responsible for several hate-based murders and celebrates all forms of violence, from the Columbine High School shooting to ISIL propaganda. The group advances the idea of preparing for a race war and cuts a broad swath of hate from National Socialism to the Islamic State. Epp and Hofner, "Hate Network."

80. European Union Agency for Law Enforcement Cooperation (Europol), *European Union Terrorism Situation*, 12.

81. Oftedal, "Financing of Jihadi Terrorist Cells," 17.

4

Designing
Business Models

Terrorists have developed or exploited a variety of criminal business models to raise funds for their activities. Many of these business models also have peripheral benefits that allow for the movement of goods and personnel. These business models include taxation, extortion, and protection rackets; kidnapping for ransom; drug trafficking; piracy; illegal gambling; and counterfeiting of goods and currency.[1] In some cases, terrorist organizations have also developed trafficking and smuggling networks of people and other goods and have been involved in maritime piracy, gambling, and prostitution rackets. These business models are more elaborate, sustained, and organized than the other criminal activities terrorist groups, cells, and individuals engage in, described in detail in Chapter 5. Criminal business models allow the terrorist actors to raise funds but, by and large, also require existing criminal networks or the development of parallel criminal networks, supplemental to their main terrorist activities. These business models are primarily the purview of terrorist organizations, but cells and individuals can occasionally be involved in these activities as well.

Terrorist organizations that design or exploit criminal business models to raise money can do so only if they are able to control territory or exert significant influence in an area. These business models require infrastructure as well as a monopoly on the use of force (ideally). The business models might also require that the terrorist group cooperate with nonterrorists, namely criminal entities, particularly in the realm of counterfeit and pirated goods and gambling and prostitution rackets. These organizations often have the characteristics of a criminal enterprise.[2] Even though terrorists and criminals leverage each other's respective capabilities, many of

these interactions exist simply through mutual convenience and are tempo-
rary in nature.[3] Despite these limitations, terrorist development of criminal
business models is well documented and has strategic implications for their
ability to support organizations and engage in terrorist attacks.

Taxation, Extortion, and Protection Rackets

Many of a terrorist organization's business models are essentially rent-seeking
activities that involve groups raising money from the population in the territory over which they have influence or control. Sometimes, this manifests as
taxation of local economic activities, and in other cases, it more closely
resembles extortion. In many cases, differentiating between these two activities is nearly impossible; the threats are implied or understood, so people give
money. Regardless, the end result is the same: taxes or fees on economic
activities of the population are used to fund terrorism.

In the same vein, protection rackets used by terrorist groups to raise
money overlap considerably with extortion and taxation. These activities also
prolong conflict because negotiating a settlement is difficult when actors can
extract resources from a region through taxation (or drug trafficking) and can
produce veto players.[4] Sometimes protection rackets are specific to a sector
of the economy, such as providing security to a particular shipment of goods
or movement of people. In other cases, the protection provided might be general and look more like the protection provided by police or security forces of
traditional states. The Liberation Tigers of Tamil Eelam (LTTE) forced remittances from Canada's Tamil diaspora are an excellent case in point. The
group identified diaspora communities worldwide as attractive sources of
revenue and subsequently exploited transnational social ties and threatened
the security of migrants' relatives or property still in Sri Lanka, creating victims on both sides of the migration system.[5]

Generally speaking, terrorist groups tax (or extort) money from the
population under their control or influence. It can be difficult to define
exactly what activities a terrorist organization engages in to raise funds versus activities the organization simply taxes. This lack of clarity can be compounded by media reports with often sensationalist and misleading headlines. This can be seen in the taxation of drug trafficking. Media and to
some extent analysts easily (and politically) conflate the taxation of drug
trafficking activity with the terrorist group's operational goals. In fact, evidence suggesting that terrorist organizations are directly trafficking in drugs
is rarely compelling and, in most cases, appears to conflate the taxation of
the activity with the actual activity. Of course, exceptions exist, and some
terrorist organizations (as well as cells and individuals) do traffic drugs,
particularly for operational financing. Terrorist groups derive funds from
the drug trade in various ways, such as taxing drug trafficking activity,

extorting money from the drug dealers, or protecting their activities in exchange for funds. For example, the Partiya Karkeren Kurdistan (PKK [Kurdistan Workers' Party]) imposed fees on drug traffickers, and in other instances, terrorist groups have been specifically recruited by criminals to provide security details in addition to the groups' more direct involvement in trafficking with Kurdish organized crime networks.[6] As this example of drug trafficking demonstrates, taxation, extortion, and protection rackets might be a Venn diagram, with significant overlap.

Taxation by terrorist actors occurs despite the presence of other resources and serves functions beyond just providing funds to the terrorist group. Revkin's work has contributed to our understanding of terrorist financing by challenging the commonly accepted theory that rebel groups (including terrorists) engage in taxation and other state-building activities only when they lack exploitable resources.[7] Revkin instead finds that taxation is codetermined by ideology and costs of warfare.[8] For instance, the Islamic State in Iraq and the Levant (ISIL) imposed several types of taxation. In her research, Revkin found seven types of revenue-extraction policies in the nineteen Syrian districts the group governed between 2013 and 2017, including income taxes, border taxes, excise taxes, fines, licensing fees, property taxes, and service fees.[9] This taxation system existed despite a number of exploitable resources such as oil, natural gas, hydroelectric dams, and phosphate mines.[10]

The line is blurry between terrorist taxation and extortion activities created by the threats and implications inherent in refusing to pay those taxes. Most of the time, taxation in a terrorist group's area of control is really extortion, and the difference between these two activities is likely in the eye of the beholder. For instance, if an individual lives in a territory controlled by a terrorist group he or she supports, the funds demanded by the terrorist group likely fall under the category of taxation. However, if the individuals in question are hostile to the terrorist group, they likely perceive these activities as extortion, particularly if or when there is a threat of violence related to nonpayment of the tax. Therefore, it is critical to remember this distinction: although the terrorist group might employ methods that look like traditional taxation, in reality, for people who do not actually support the group, this is a form of extortion.

Many groups engage in extortion and taxation of the population in their area of control or influence. The Provisional Irish Republican Army (PIRA) extorted funds from people and businesses and raised funds through coercion and protection rackets, targeting publicans, local businesspeople, and shopkeepers.[11] The group also generated funds by "riding shotgun," a euphemism for providing an armed escort in exchange for payment on international drug shipments and money laundering schemes in the United States, Northern Ireland, and the Republic of Ireland. The group also created "security companies" that provided a veneer of legitimacy to this activity.[12]

In some cases, protection rackets apply to particular economic activities, such as drug trafficking or cash movement, although they can also be more general in nature and apply to entire areas of the economy. The Revolutionary Armed Forces of Colombia (FARC) is known to have levied a 10 percent protection payment on coca growers in its region of control, providing protection from other groups and the state for the farmers who grew the coca.[13] Of note, however, is that in many cases the farmers were likely incentivized (sometimes through violence) by FARC to continue growing the coca on which they had to pay the protection tax. In Europe, the Armed Islamic Group of Algeria (GIA) used a combination of extortion and protection rackets to raise money, targeting illegal immigrants or people with relatives and property in Algeria.[14] The PKK has also relied on extortion, or forced donations, to raise funds. Information from 2007 indicates that the PKK extorted £2.5 million (approximately $6.1 million in 2020 dollars) per year; the group euphemistically called these donations "insurance fees." Many of these payments might have been made monthly, and those targeted for extortion payments were often businesspeople of Kurdish origin and other individuals of Kurdish background.[15]

Within Sri Lanka and Tamil territory, the LTTE taxed economic activity in its area of control as well as members of the Tamil diaspora abroad. The group charged sales tax on a variety of items including 10 percent on building materials, 7.5 percent on car parts, and 20 percent on cigarettes.[16] In the Tamil diaspora, the group also charged a variety of taxes or fees, generating significant sums of money. Although the diaspora was not under the group's direct control, family members and friends were, such that the diaspora was certainly under the group's influence. In Canada, the LTTE prescribed extortion fees for individuals and families of between CA$2,000 and $2,500 ($1,600 and $2,000). The group also charged more for business owners.[17] In France, the LTTE demanded that Tamil families pay €2,000 (roughly $2,400) per year and businesses contribute €6,000 ($7,300) per year in revolutionary taxes.[18] Fear drove the LTTE's taxation system: the LTTE would also occasionally outsource their collection efforts to street gangs, to whom they paid a 20 percent commission for services rendered.[19] Some individuals and families were required to borrow money to pay the taxes. They sometimes charged the fees to their credit cards or even remortgaged their homes. Business owners claimed to have been asked for hundreds of thousands of dollars in support of the cause.[20]

To augment their monthly or annual taxes, groups sometimes issue "special assessments" on the taxes to support the cause or a specific activity (e.g., an insurgent operation). During periods of heavy fighting, the LTTE collected urgent war funds, war taxes, or special contributions. In the early 2000s, the group petitioned families in the United Kingdom, Canada, and Australia for $1,000 per family to support their military efforts.[21]

A more contemporary example of an extensive taxation, extortion, and protection scheme occurred when ISIL held territory in Iraq and Syria in the 2010s.[22] In 2014 ISIL was believed to have raised $7 million ($7.5 million in 2020 dollars) per month through extortion.[23] As of February 2016, the group began to tax the most impoverished citizens living in its territory, people who had previously been exempt from taxation.[24] Reports indicate that the group might have earned as much as $30 million ($32 million in 2020 dollars) per month in 2016 from taxation of economic activities, as well as extortion, within its area of control. This estimate includes all rent-seeking activities such as business taxes, fees for electricity and water, rent (from seized real estate), and customs duties and passage fees. Over time, ISIL increased the rate and types of fees and taxes it collected but also provided fewer services as a result of its decreased cash flow. Of course, ISIL taxed all kinds of economic activity in its area of operations. Some of this taxation included the salaries of Iraqi government employees, money paid even after the government lost control of territory.[25]

As ISIL lost territory, the group also lost the bulk of its tax base but did not stop its practice of taxation and extortion. The group continues to extort funds wherever it operates (even if not in total control).[26] To do so, the group must maintain territorial control or significant influence to force the population to pay the taxes imposed; if the group loses its credible threat of being able to impose violence, then it will lose the ability to impose these fees. ISIL demonstrated its ability both to demand taxes and to take retaliatory actions when those taxes were not paid in May 2019. In Erbil, Iraq, ISIL cells torched several agricultural fields after farmers refused to pay the militants' taxes. ISIL remnants had demanded $4,000 for each combine harvester working in the fields and 15 percent (likely of the profits, or market value) of the crops.[27]

ISIL is not the only terrorist organization operating in Syria that raised funds through rent-seeking activities. In 2018, the Nusra Front was raising funds through extortion, including at checkpoints and through other forms of "taxation."[28] Many other groups engaged in this activity in areas over which they exert a significant amount of influence or control as well. The Lashkar-e-Taiba (LeT) has been known to engage in the extortion of money from the local population.[29] ISIL in Libya also funded itself through taxation and extortion, specifically through checkpoints it controlled in Sirte.[30] Other groups have also employed this taxation activity, such as Abu Sayyaf and the Taliban (which used the funds it collects from local populations to sustain local operations).[31] The PKK is known to extort funds from local businesses.[32]

When two terrorist groups operate in the same general territory, their rent-seeking activities can position them to compete, further exploiting the population in the region and splitting available income between the competing groups, although not always in a stable equilibrium. Examples of this are ISIL in Khorasan Province (ISIL-KP, the group's officially recognized affiliate in Afghanistan) and the Taliban. Both groups have derived a significant portion of their funding from the taxation of economic activity as well as other rent-seeking activities such as protection rackets and extortion.[33] For its part, ISIL-KP has controlled significant swaths of territory, but there have been mixed reports on its success at exploiting the area, likely a function of competition with the Taliban.[34] ISIL-KP's lack of ability on this front is also likely a function of the intense counterterrorism pressure it has been under, primarily by US forces.

The extractive sector and control, or taxation, of it are important sources of funds in Afghanistan. Correspondingly, ISIL-KP has demonstrated a specific interest in metal mining in Afghanistan. Areas under ISIL-KP control have included areas that produce talc and chromite as well as precious and semiprecious stones. These sites had been held by the Taliban before ISIL-KP took them over (although territorial control can be quite fluid in Afghanistan, such that whether ISIL-KP is able to maintain control of this asset is an open question). Even if ISIL-KP is not making significant money from the mines, it likely considers them a strategic asset.[35]

For terrorist groups, taxing a resource is not the only benefit derived from that control; it can also deprive their competition of important resources from a taxation base, eroding their ability to maintain their operations. For ISIL-KP, depriving the Taliban of a key resource is likely as important as acquiring it themselves.[36] Indeed, ISIL-KP has reportedly burned poppy fields rather than finance themselves through opium trafficking, an act that likely has less to do with ideological opposition to the drug trade and more to do with lacking the routes and methods to refine and smuggle the product themselves.[37] In this instance, ISIL-KP is likely seeking to deny its competition access to funding from the opium trade. Competition between the Taliban and ISIL-KP means that both of their funding bases are reduced, but overall they likely obtain enough money to survive, mount attacks, and in some cases build their wealth. Competition between these two groups might reduce the amount of money they have available but not to the extent of causing either of the groups to be nonfunctional.

For its part, the Taliban continues to raise money through opium (specifically the taxation, protection, and in a limited sense the production) and through roadside taxes.[38] The Taliban also collects approximately $100 million per year from usher (an Islamic tax) levied on local businesses and farms. The group also collects a land tax that funds their insurgency.[39] A variety of protection activities also generates significant funds for the Taliban and might make up a relatively significant portion of the group's income.

The Taliban also gains significant funds from other forms of protection payments. According to one journalist, 10 percent of US Department of

Defense logistics contracts consisted of payments to insurgents. As part of a quid pro quo, the payments were made to ensure that the Taliban refrained from attacking convoys delivering goods such as toilet paper, water, fuel, guns, and vehicles.[40] The supply chain itself was outsourced to questionable providers and fueled a vast protection racket.[41] This is not to suggest that the US Department of Defense provided funds directly to the Taliban; instead, the contractors who provided the services to the department were likely required to pay protection money to the Taliban to move freely in Afghanistan and avoid attacks, roadblocks, and kidnappings of employees. This type of rent-seeking activity occurs in many conflict zones where terrorist or rebel groups control or influence territory. In order to operate there, companies, states, and charitable organizations have to pay the taxes or meet the extortion demands.

ISIL-KP and ISIL in Syria are far from the only ISIL groups that use extortion and taxation and have competition for these resources among groups. Following Al-Shabaab's model, ISIL in Somalia is reported to have imposed heavy taxes on local businesses in Bosaso (Puntland) and to have extorted money from traders, raising as much as $72,000 per month from this activity.[42] Reports also indicate that ISIL in Somalia and Al-Shabaab are competing for resources in Somalia.

For taxation, extortion, and protection rackets, controlling territory is key, but so is the significance of the economic activity within that area of control. Al-Shabaab's control of the port of Kismaayo demonstrates this well. Although small, the port was a particularly lucrative piece of territory the group managed to control until September 2012; goods such as charcoal and imported sugar were taxed coming through the port facilities. Even after the group lost the port and the market, it continued to operate an extensive toll system and to benefit from trade in the area.[43] Estimates of the revenue generated by Al-Shabaab taxes vary significantly, ranging from $300,000–700,000 to $2–3 million per month.[44]

Sometimes, as part of the poorly named *diaspora financing*, diaspora communities are accused of supporting terrorist organizations because their remittance mechanisms are taxed or exploited by a terrorist organization. An example of this occurred in Somalia's much maligned remittance sector. Somalia's economy is reliant to a significant extent on diaspora remittances, believed to be surveilled and taxed by Al-Shabaab.[45] The group has monitored cash flows in the area and demanded information on incoming and outgoing transactions, presumably to augment its intelligence collection and related taxation activities.[46] Indeed, relying on taxation of diaspora remittances as a source of financing predates Al-Shabaab; the Islamic Courts Union relied on such taxation to fund its activities as well.[47] The tax rate applied to these transactions is unknown but is likely a relatively small percentage of the total transaction amount. But because of the high volume of transactions, the group generates a significant amount of money in this way. These taxes are not voluntary but instead are part of the cost of doing business for remittance companies in Somalia.

Along similar lines, terrorist groups are sometimes able to charge protection fees to international corporations operating in or near their area of control or influence, and this is a lucrative source of money. These corporations are likely charged well above the local tax rate. However, the higher fees charged to these companies need to be carefully calibrated so as not to disincentivize the company's ongoing operations in the terrorist's area of control or influence. Several examples of companies paying terrorist protection fees or taxes have been made public in recent years. The Moro Islamic Liberation Front (MILF) is believed to have charged $1.7 million over a three-year period to a Canadian mining company operating in Mindanao. Funds were provided by the company in exchange for protection and the continued ability to complete the project under safe conditions.[48] In Syria, ISIL and other extremist groups are believed to have charged companies protection money in their area of control as well. LafargeHolcim was investigated in 2018 for terrorist financing because the company's subsidiary in Syria was suspected of paying $5 million in protection money to keep its cement plant open.[49]

Roughly 38 percent of the terrorist groups I studied used rent-seeking activities to raise funds, and this is likely an underestimation of the prevalence of this method. Taxation and extortion by terrorist groups covers a broad range of economic activities, and both legal and illegal activities are taxed. Terrorist groups do not generally discriminate between these activities in terms of raising money, with the exception that they might charge a premium for illegal activities, such as drug trafficking, in their area of control. Taxation, extortion, and protection rackets are, for the most part, all rent-seeking activities. One of the underlying truths, however, is that these activities are based on the economic activity taking place in the area; if the terrorist organization takes over a poor area, it is likely to remain relatively poor. In contrast, if the terrorist group takes over an area with significant resources, its fund-raising base will be similarly lucrative. Taxes are imposed by terrorist groups when they are in a position of control or influence. However, behind those taxes is the implicit (or explicit) threat of violence if the taxes are not paid. In some cases, the terrorist organizations might provide services in exchange for these taxes (such as basic security, or "law enforcement"), but over time these services often deteriorate, and the rent-seeking activities become much more akin to extortion. The line between extortion and protection rackets is similarly blurry because the violence the terrorist group seeks to protect the business or individual from is often perpetrated by the group itself or its proxies. Terrorist groups like these create a sort of "self-cleaning oven" in the sense that they threaten the security of a population and then extract resources from it to prevent that threat from materializing. These rent-seeking activities are almost exclusively the purview of terrorist organizations; no terrorist cells or individuals were found to have engaged in taxation, extortion, and protection rackets.

For terrorist groups, extortion is about raising funds, but it is also about nonfinancial aspects such as consolidating political power and establishing themselves as the informal (or in some cases, formal) providers of public order.[50] All of these elements work together; the more terrorists can control the public space, the more room they have to raise funds and conduct operations, and the more political legitimacy they might be perceived to have.[51]

Conflating taxation, extortion, and support networks is common when terrorists govern territory. This is because terrorist groups able to govern to some extent have, as Zabyelina puts it, "re-shaped the victim-offender relations," transforming victims of extortion into involuntary terrorist funders and supporters.[52] In order to develop effective counterterrorist financing policies and practices, it is critical to separate these funding mechanisms and understand what is happening in specific contexts, ideally identifying the extent to which individuals support a terrorist group or movement or the extent to which they are being extorted.

Kidnapping for Ransom

Many terrorist organizations (but very few cells and almost no individuals) have raised funds through kidnapping people and ransoming them for money or political concessions such as prisoner exchanges. For terrorist organizations, kidnapping for ransom can be lucrative and relatively easy: it has a low barrier to entry in terms of required skill sets. However, doing it well, making it profitable, and indeed maximizing profit are more challenging. Kidnappers require infrastructure and expertise; otherwise, they will not extract maximum concessions, and the kidnapping victims have a higher chance of ending up dead. Victims might be relatively easy to find, and although the negotiations can be lengthy, governments, private companies, insurance companies, and family members can often be persuaded to pay the ransoms demanded.

Terrorists use two different types of kidnappings for ransom to raise funds, and groups might employ both methods: kidnapping and ransoming of local people or of foreign nationals. In the first instance, terrorists kidnap individuals in the area in which they are operating and ransom them to their family members or employers. These types of kidnappings rarely make international headlines and are relatively simple "snatch and grabs" with smaller ransoms.[53] Local kidnapping for ransom is essentially a predatory behavior (a form of extortion) that profits from territorial control. The ransom paid for a victim will depend on the resources of his or her company or family, information the terrorist organization might have acquired in advance of the kidnapping. Families pay these ransoms to get their loved ones back, and the terrorists can use the funds to execute further kidnappings or terrorist attacks or to sustain their organization.

In kidnappings of foreigners for ransom, the victims are often from relatively wealthy countries, so terrorist organizations seek to extract significant ransoms from their governments, their families, or their insurance companies. International kidnappings for ransom also involve longer, more drawn-out negotiation processes, and terrorists might also seek to extract propaganda value from their captives. Ultimately, the processes of local and international kidnappings for ransom are quite different, even if the end result is somewhat similar: funds for terrorist organizations.

Local Kidnappings
Small-scale kidnappings for ransom occur with much more frequency than the large-scale, multi-million-dollar acts, although it is challenging to estimate which has the larger impact on terrorist group finances given the information gaps, which are particularly acute in local kidnapping operations. As Shortland puts it, many kidnappings are only reported if there is a local police presence, police officers are not suspected of being complicit, and people expect a benefit from reporting the abduction.[54] As a result, a percentage of local kidnappings for ransom are never reported to the authorities at all or generate any media attention, making their proportional value in the total kidnapping for ransom ecosystem impossible to estimate.

Historically, terrorist groups have been able to conduct a version of local kidnappings for ransom without controlling territory by exploiting a relative state of lawlessness in the country in which they operated or by partnering with a criminal organization. The Italian Red Brigades used kidnappings for ransom to raise funds, splitting a $2 million ransom for an Italian political prisoner with the Camorra (a version of the Italian mafia). The Camorra acted as middlemen during the ransom negotiations, earning their share of the payment.[55] In this case, although members of the Red Brigades did not control significant territory, they were able to use their criminal network to secure the victim and evade police. PIRA also engaged in a series of raids and kidnappings to raise funds. Between the 1970s and 1980s, kidnapping for ransom brought in millions to the group.[56] Although the group's attacks were primarily aimed at bank managers, and the ransoms were generally paid swiftly, PIRA was also involved in the kidnapping but unsuccessful ransoming of a horse. The ransom was never paid, and the body of the horse was never found.[57]

A number of other groups also engaged in local kidnappings for ransom, including the LTTE.[58] The PKK used kidnapping for ransom to fund their activities, with a major source of funds being kidnapped businesspeople. [59] FARC had a dedicated unit for taking hostages. Local kidnappings were generally conducted in or near the territory the group controlled, and individuals were ransomed for relatively small sums.[60] In aggregate, however, the sums raised over the years through local kidnappings for ransom likely provided the groups important sources of funds in addition to their other fund-raising activities.

Groups that "specialize" in local kidnappings for ransom prefer to engage in quick negotiations to realize immediate gains, but sometimes they engage in lengthier negotiations. For instance, Boko Haram conducted lengthy negotiations and occasionally achieved high ransoms, such as the ransom paid for the Dapchi schoolgirls in 2018 of around €2 million ($2.3 million).[61] As of September 2018, the group generated significant sums from kidnapping for ransom.[62]

Not all local kidnappings for ransom are conducted by terrorist organizations. Sometimes, operational cells and individuals use this method to raise funds, although it exposes them to operational security considerations through potential detection by law enforcement. When used, this fund-raising method generally reflects a strong relationship with criminal elements. One example was the al-Qaeda-affiliated Pakistani jihadists living in Spain who engaged in "express kidnappings." These were quick "snatch and grabs" of locals that ended upon receipt of payment from their families in Pakistan.[63] The amounts of money demanded were lower than some other types of kidnappings, allowing the families to liberate their loved ones quickly without having to involve insurance companies or banks (for loans).

In aggregate, local kidnappings are far more frequently used by terrorists than foreign kidnappings to raise funds but might not raise as much money as the foreign ones do. Comparing local and foreign kidnappings and the money they generate is difficult; local kidnappings are less frequently reported and the ransoms paid even less so. Although local kidnappings might be far more prevalent than foreign kidnappings, they also garner significantly less money per incident, but over time this activity can still generate a significant amount of money for a group or cell.

Foreign Kidnappings

Foreign kidnappings for ransom occur in areas in which a terrorist group or cell is operating and involve kidnapping someone not from that area, such as an aid worker, journalist, or other person in the conflict zone. These kidnappings are often high profile and are used to generate funds but can also be used for propaganda purposes by the terrorist organization or cell.

Foreign kidnappings for ransom have been used by a number of groups over the course of recent history. Groups have kidnapped Westerners or individuals from wealthy countries to extract both publicity for their endeavors and a high ransom payment. In the 1960s and 1970s, the Argentinian Ejercito Revolucionario del Pueblo (ERP [People's Revolutionary Army], aka Montoneros) collected more than $1 million for an executive from the Ford Motor Company, $2 million for an executive from Arrow Steel, $3 million for an executive from Firestone, and $14 million for an executive from Exxon. These and other companies also paid ERP protection money to prevent the abduction of other employees.[64] Basque Homeland and Liberty (ETA) separatists also consistently relied on this method to raise funds.[65] Al-Qaeda, ISIL, and other like-minded groups have also generated at least $222 million in ransom payments between 2008 and 2014, according to US government estimates. Some of the groups that have used this fund-raising technique include al-Qaeda in the Islamic Maghreb (AQIM), al-Qaeda in the Arabian Peninsula (AQAP), ISIL, Harakat ul-Ansar (an Islamist militant group based in Pakistan, operating primarily in Kashmir), and several other groups in Pakistan.[66]

Al-Qaeda and affiliated groups engaged in significant kidnapping operations whenever and wherever they could and literally wrote the book on this fund-raising method. In 2004, al-Qaeda operative Abdelazziz al-Muqrin, the former head of al-Qaeda in Saudi Arabia, published a how-to guide to kidnapping.[67] The guide outlined the goals and objectives of kidnapping, which should serve one or more of the following purposes:

> Force the government or opponent to fulfill a specific set of demands, create a difficult situation for government in its relations with the countries where the kidnapped person comes from, obtain information about the hostages, obtain ransom money—as, for example, our brothers in the Philippines, Chechnya, and Algeria made happen and as our brothers in "Mohammed's Army" in Kashmir did when they obtained $2 million in ransom. This money can then serve as financial support for the organization. To draw attention to a specific concern—as occurred at the start of the Chechnya question or in Algeria, when our brothers hijacked a French plane.[68]

Regarding Iraq, having an accurate understanding of the scope and scale of kidnappings is particularly challenging because most victims have been locals (Iraqis) and reporting is "fragmentary at best."[69] Over time, al-Qaeda in Iraq (and other insurgents and jihadist groups) gradually embraced kidnapping as a funding source and for strategic purposes.[70] The group engaged in kidnapping for ransom and made millions from this activity with a combination of local and foreign kidnappings. Kidnappings of Iraqis are estimated to have peaked in 2006. Al-Qaeda's overall kidnapping of foreigners began in earnest in 2004. France, Germany, and Italy paid about $45 million for the release of eleven hostages, and other countries such as

Japan, Jordan, the Philippines, Sweden, and Turkey are also believed to have paid substantial ransoms. Private companies also paid ransoms to free their employees.[71]

Learning from its predecessor, al-Qaeda in Iraq, ISIL has also engaged in kidnapping for ransom, focusing on locals but combining the two approaches to significant effect.[72] The group used a combination of local and foreign kidnappings with payments averaging in the tens of millions of dollars between 2013 and 2016, including a ransom of between $9 and $30 million for 230 Assyrian Christians kidnapped in 2015.[73] ISIL has also advertised two hostages for sale in its magazine *Dabiq*, demonstrating that sometimes hostages are sold between criminal and terrorist organizations depending on whether they have been or are likely to be successful at obtaining a ransom.[74] When ISIL obtained an international kidnap victim, the group was likely to execute the hostage (particularly in the later years of the caliphate), possibly out of a desire to embarrass members of the anti-ISIL coalition and demonstrate that their lack of power could have real effects on their citizens. ISIL also might have been more likely to execute the hostage because of the ransom policies of some members of the anti-ISIL coalition against paying ransoms and the pressure others would be under not to pay ransoms either.

Some terrorist organizations combine the kidnapping of locals and foreign nationals not only to raise money but also for propaganda purposes. In March 2000, Abu Sayyaf kidnapped fifty-five schoolchildren, teachers, and a priest. The next month, the group conducted a raid on a resort in Malaysia, taking twenty-one tourists hostage. In July 2020, the group kidnapped three French journalists, ultimately receiving an estimated $15–$30 million ($22.5–$45.1 million in 2020 dollars) for the release of these hostages, funneled through the Libyan government.[75] This did not end their kidnapping activities. In May 2001, the group took another thirty tourists hostage.[76] Abu Sayyaf continues to rely on kidnappings to sustain itself.[77] The group has essentially developed into a professional kidnapping-for-ransom operation and uses the funds generated from this activity to support its terrorist activity and political objectives.[78] Government officials estimate that 90 percent of the group's funding (around $35 million between 1992 and 2000) came from kidnapping for ransom, with the majority of victims being local. Abu Sayyaf has also engaged in international kidnapping for ransom and in 2013 ransomed a group of hostages for around $85,000 each. The following year, the group exacted a ransom of $5.6 million ($6.4 million in 2020 dollars) for two German sailors.[79]

Other al-Qaeda-affiliated groups also continue to find kidnappings for ransom a lucrative source of funds. Al-Shabaab has raised money in this manner, netting a $5 million ransom for Spanish hostages kidnapped in Kenya in October 2011 ($5.8 million in 2020 dollars). As of 2014, AQAP, AQIM, and Al-Shabaab were still using kidnapping for ransom to generate a significant portion of their funds, estimated to be in the tens of millions of dollars.[80]

Jabhat al-Nusra/Jabhat Fatah al-Sham have also raised funds through kidnappings for ransom, including a high-profile kidnapping of Gulf royals.[81] The group also kidnapped a US journalist, UN peacekeepers, and a group of nuns. In what was probably the group's most lucrative endeavor, the organization likely facilitated the release of nine Qatari royals and sixteen Qatari nationals kidnapped by a Shiite militia group. Qatar provided millions of dollars to the group to facilitate the release of its citizens. Although the exact amount of money the Shiite militia group received is unknown because of the multiple groups involved in the incident, payments totaled at least $275 million to free the members of the royal family and other hostages, and the Shiite militia group received a cut of this.[82] Of course, the Qataris insisted that they gave the money to the Iraqi government for state-building purposes. However, the *Washington Post* reported that between $5 and $50 million went to Iranian and Iraqi officials and paramilitary leaders, $25 million was provided to Kata'ib Hezbollah, and another $50 million was earmarked for "Qassem," an apparent reference to the leader of Iran's Islamic Revolutionary Guard Corps (IRGC).[83]

AQIM might be the group that made the most use of kidnapping for ransom. Between 2008 and 2014, the group is estimated to have raised close to $100 million through ransoms paid for kidnap victims.[84] AQIM is not, however, a uniform group that engages in kidnappings for ransom and always succeeds in obtaining a high price. When two Canadian diplomats were kidnapped, Mokhtar Belmokhtar received only $1 million for the two and was reprimanded for negotiating the ransom on his own.[85]

Over the course of several years, some estimates suggest the Taliban has raised as much as $10 million per year from kidnappings for ransom.[86] The first reported ransom for kidnap victims was in 2006, when the group received $2.8 million ($4.5 million in 2020 dollars) for the freedom of Gabriele Torsello.[87] In 2007, the Taliban kidnapped twenty-three missionaries from South Korea. Ultimately, the government of South Korea paid $20 million ($25 million in 2020 dollars) for the release of nineteen surviving hostages. In 2008, the Taliban kidnapped Tariq Azizuddin, Pakistan's ambassador to Afghanistan. To free its ambassador, Pakistan released fifty-five detained Taliban operatives and paid several hundred thousand dollars in ransom.[88] The Taliban continues to kidnap victims and hold them, such as the American-Canadian couple it kidnapped in 2012 (freed in 2017).[89] They also kidnapped an American professor and an Australian professor in 2017.[90] The Taliban used the funds they received for their release to buy weapons and support all types of operational activities.[91]

Analysis of Kidnappings for Ransom

A basic requirement for either type of kidnapping for ransom is the control of some territory or a safe haven. Without this, a terrorist group has limited means of securing kidnap victims. Raising funds in this manner is therefore largely the purview of terrorist organizations, not cells or individuals. However, given that in the twenty-first century many terrorist organizations control some territory, the number of terrorist groups that use this fund-raising method corresponds in an expected manner. Broadly speaking, terrorist organizations charge ransoms in the millions of dollars for foreign victims but might charge as little as a few hundred or thousand dollars for local kidnap victims. In either case, the terrorist organizations charge what the market will bear.

There have frequently been international calls for a moratorium on payment of ransom for kidnap victims, but international consensus on the issue has proven elusive. Even if all governments refused to pay ransoms, private companies, insurance agents, and family members would likely continue to pay, particularly in local kidnapping events. In policy and practitioner circles, kidnapping for ransom (particularly of foreign victims) is seen as an international blight that provides terrorist organizations huge sums of money. At the same time, there is a lack of evidence to suggest that a moratorium would be effective or even possible. Kidnapping for ransom, particularly by terrorist groups, is a collective action problem.[92] Although it might be in everyone's best interest to cooperate and not pay ransoms (thus reducing or eliminating the incentive to take hostages), the benefit for politicians able to negotiate the release of their citizens is strong, whereas the costs of them failing to do so can be catastrophic for both their careers and the citizens involved.

One of the assumptions that underlies the push for a moratorium on ransoms is that terrorist groups make a lot of money from kidnappings for ransom (see Figure 4.1). Reporting frequently describes ransoms in the millions of dollars for foreign kidnapping victims. Although the ransoms paid have been large, the emphasis on the gross ransom ignores some of the real costs associated with kidnapping and holding hostages. In other cases, a lack of information on what ransoms have been paid prevents sound analysis of the profit for the terrorist organizations. Information is the basis for making sound and rational policy decisions, and unfortunately, in the domain of kidnappings for ransom, there is a dearth of reliable information.

The dataset in Figure 4.1 includes approximately 590 kidnapping incidents, some involving multiple victims, between 2000 and 2020.[93] In most cases the date of payment was not clear, so the date of the kidnapping incident was used as the date of ransom payment. In fact, many ransom payments occurred more than a year after the initial kidnapping event. Some of the individuals were ransomed together, whereas others were ransomed

Figure 4.1 Total International Ransom Payments, by Year (US$ million, 2020)

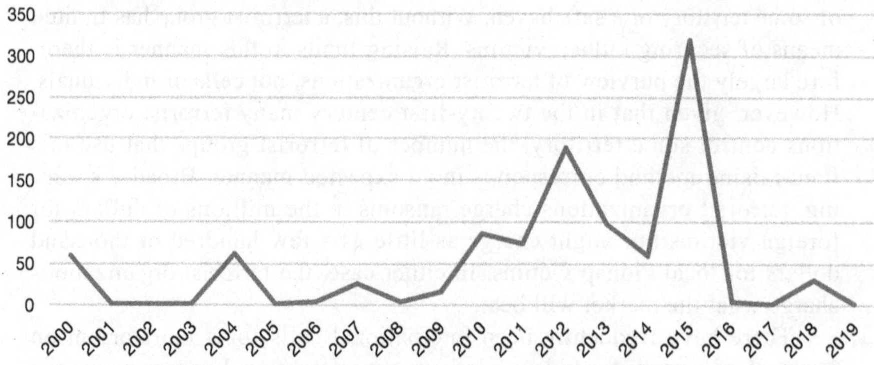

individually. Only 146 of these cases had sufficient information to determine if a ransom had been paid, and if so, how much. The amount of ransoms was adjusted to 2020 dollars for comparison purposes.[94]

On average, approximately $49 million is paid in ransoms to terrorist organizations every year. Because of the small dataset and one large ransom payment in 2015 (for the release of Qatari nationals), the average likely overstates the amount generated by terrorist groups each year. Discounting this large ransom payment, the average amount paid to terrorist groups each year is approximately $34 million—still a significant sum. Indeed, the median amount paid over this twenty-year period is $15 million.

There were insufficient data to draw a strong conclusion about trends in ransom payments. However, the number of incidents has decreased since 2013, and the average ransoms paid has also decreased since 2012 (excluding the 2015 payment). Two hypotheses could explain the decrease in ransom amounts. The first hypothesis is that the international community might be getting better at "negotiating down" ransom payments, and the second hypothesis is that terrorist expectations of ransoms have decreased. Other factors might have also featured in the observed decrease in number of ransom payments, such as counterterrorism pressures preventing groups from kidnapping more victims, a lag between the kidnappings and the ransoms being paid (i.e., some individuals are still being held), and a general lack of information on what ransoms have been paid.

At least 36 percent of the terrorist organizations I studied used kidnapping for ransom to raise funds. This estimate is likely to be on the low end of the spectrum because local kidnappings for ransom might have gone unreported. That being said, no terrorist plots or attacks were directly funded through kidnapping for ransom, making this fund-raising method one of the only methods that is exclusively the domain of terrorist organizations. Of course, as with other financing methods, terrorist organizations might have diverted funds from their ransom payments to support operations conducted directly by the terrorist group.

Two methods were used to estimate ransoms paid. There were significant data gaps in both methods, meaning that although this provides a starting point for understanding how much money terrorist organizations raise from kidnapping for ransom, greater data fidelity is required to understand the nature of kidnapping for ransom, trends, and ultimately best approaches to countering it. It is critical to remember that ransoms paid do not represent pure profit for these groups, because kidnappings for ransom generate significant costs and entire economies to support the endeavor. Those economies cannot be understated: everyone involved in supporting the kidnapping for ransom process gets paid. This includes the people who provide the logistical support (food, water, shelter, etc.), the guards, and the terrorists. Even the negotiators take a 10 percent cut of the ransom.[95] This means that the incentives for terrorists to conduct kidnappings for ransom are greater than the single payout. They are creating economies that in turn can mean support for the group itself.

When analyzing kidnappings for ransom from the perspective of terrorist financing, it is increasingly important to examine the economy of kidnapping, particularly in countries with well-developed kidnapping for ransom rackets. Kidnappings for ransom have developed their own subeconomies and local experts and facilitators in the regions where they are prevalent. They provide infusions of cash and take advantage of existing fund transfer mechanisms and skill sets in the area as well as other aspects of the existing economy, such as charitable or nonprofit organizations. The kidnappers have needs such as food, lodging, and security, and local economic actors where they are operating are likely co-opted into helping them and receive payment for those services. Part of this local economy involves partnerships between criminal and terrorist organizations, in part because of the prohibition on paying ransoms to terrorist groups. In some cases, payments are made to the "kidnappers" (criminal groups), when in reality they are simply the front for the terrorist organization.[96] This setup allows the payer of the ransom to have plausible deniability.

Partnerships develop with other economic actors as well, including nongovernmental organizations (NGOs) that facilitate the ransoming of individuals. For example, Gift of the Givers is the "largest disaster response non-governmental organization of African origin on the African continent."[97] The NGO has been involved in several hostage negotiations and payments over the years. In 2017, South Africa paid a ransom of €3.5 million ($4.3

million in 2020 dollars) for a tourist abducted in 2011 from Timbuktu, Mali, following negotiations through Gift of the Givers. Gift of the Givers had previously been involved in hostage negotiations in Yemen involving AQAP in 2013 that were ultimately unsuccessful.[98] In another example, a Swedish man was freed after six years in captivity, and €3.5 million ($4.2 million) was likely paid to AQIM for his release, again facilitated by Gift of the Givers.[99]

The host government fighting a terrorist group might also facilitate payments on occasion or have another government do so on its behalf. When European governments make ransom payments to terrorist organizations, they are sometimes written off as aid payments or delivered through intermediaries by companies such as Areva, a state-controlled company that paid €12.5 ($15 million) million in 2011 and €30 million ($36 million) in 2013 to free five French citizens.[100] The government of Mali has also ensured that a multimillion-dollar ransom from Germany for "humanitarian aid" reached an Islamist extremist group holding thirty-two hostages.[101] In 2009, two Swiss nationals were kidnapped in Mali and were later released with a German hostage for $8 million. Later that year, an additional $4.4 million of humanitarian aid to Mali was found in the Swiss national budget, meaning it was possible that a total of $12.4 million ($15 million in 2020) was paid to ransom the hostages, some of which was provided in cash and some of which was routed through the government of Mali.[102] According to an unnamed German official, in a 2003 hostage incident, it was understood by all sides that the "humanitarian aid for Mali" was bound for Islamist extremists in exchange for thirty-two European hostages. Suitcases of cash were delivered by cash couriers to fighters who would soon become an official arm of al-Qaeda.[103] By transferring the funds to Mali under the guise of humanitarian aid, European governments created deniability that they had provided funds to a terrorist organization.

Today, many terrorist groups use kidnapping for ransom to raise funds. In most cases, if they have not adopted this technique, it likely means that they lack sufficient territorial control or a safe haven to secure the kidnap victims, or they might lack potential victims, particularly in the case of groups seeking international kidnap victims. In cases of local kidnappings for ransom, it might mean that security forces in neighboring areas are sufficiently competent to prevent these kidnappings. The wealth of the region has little bearing on whether groups will adopt this technique—terrorist groups have engaged in local kidnappings for ransom in some of the poorest regions of the world, exploiting whatever available resources exist.

Although kidnapping for ransom is a lucrative business for most terrorist organizations, it is also logistically complicated and time-consuming. Negotiating ransoms can take months or years (particularly in the case of international kidnap victims), during which time provisions have to be acquired to keep the kidnap victim alive. This is one of the reasons kidnapping for ransom is largely the purview of terrorist organizations rather than cells and individuals. It also explains why the ransoms paid to the organizations likely overstates the amount of money the groups actually make from the operations—expenses must be deducted from that amount to get an accurate representation of the profit for the organization. For terrorist groups, kidnapping for ransom is not all profit. Instead, as Shortland puts it, kidnapping for ransom is big business, and there are many costs associated with this, including various professionals who work as messengers, mediators, and ransom couriers.[104] Other costs must also be factored into the profit margin of terrorist kidnapping for ransom. The costs of guarding and feeding hostages, for instance, can reduce those profits significantly, but these also depend on the country's price and wage level.[105]

Maritime Piracy, Gambling, and Prostitution Rackets

Maritime piracy, gambling, and prostitution rackets are used by terrorist organizations to raise funds, but these are geographically and contextually constrained activities. Only terrorist groups with sustained access to a coast and particular expertise are likely to engage in maritime piracy. Gambling and prostitution rackets usually require some connection to broader criminal networks and business models. These activities have many characteristics in common. They often involve significant overlap with criminal organizations and other types of criminal activity, involve criminal networks, and also involve the use of force to raise funds.

Understanding the specific mechanisms at play in the cases of maritime piracy, gambling, and prostitution rackets and the extent to which terrorist actors are implicated in the activity is critical to identifying potential areas for disruption. In some cases, terrorists profit from the pirate trade in the form of taxes and extortion. In other cases, terrorist organizations are fully engaged in the practice but hide this involvement behind a shield of criminality in an attempt to avoid having the pirate activities linked to them because this might make receipt of ransoms and release fees problematic from a counterterrorist financing perspective. Understanding the specific relationship between a terrorist organization and a piracy racket (or indeed, any criminal business model) is critical to identifying potential areas for disrupting this fund-raising activity.

Some terrorist organizations, such as the LTTE and Abu Sayyaf, have engaged directly in piracy. The LTTE, which controlled territory with a substantial coastline, developed advanced maritime capabilities. The group had submarines and an entire shipping line that they used to move people, goods, and sometimes conduct attacks against maritime targets. The group engaged in maritime piracy from time to time, although it appears that it transitioned away from this activity to instead providing protection to ships passing through the area, a form of "riding shotgun." Abu Sayyaf threatened to hijack vessels and used its maritime presence to kidnap two Malaysians and an Indonesian boating in the region in 2004. The group also collected money from drug smugglers by providing protection for syndicates moving goods on the water, reminiscent of the LTTE's maritime protection racket.[106]

Maritime piracy has limited application to terrorist financing writ large simply because of the requirement for relatively developed seagoing capabilities and access to the coast. The territorial and technical constraints on this fund-raising method mean it is relatively limited in application for terrorist groups but should not be discounted for future methods of fund-raising by groups that have access to the right terrain and personnel.

Al-Shabaab has notoriously been charged with using piracy to raise funds. However, there is little compelling evidence to suggest that the group itself engages in piracy. Instead, the group is much more likely to be involved in providing logistical support to the pirates (possibly including armed guards on the ships), taxing the activity, and providing other types of support. In 2010, the US Navy assessed that there was no evidence Al-Shabaab militants had financial or operational ties to pirates.[107] In contrast, more recent analysis suggests that Al-Shabaab might in fact have some relationship to the pirate trade and might receive between 15 percent and 20 percent of the ransoms paid (although probably not across the board on all ransoms ever paid to pirates).[108] Some of these funds might have been payment for training and weapons or user fees to operate out of Al-Shabaab-controlled territory.[109] There is consensus, however, that the group benefits at least passively from the economic activity generated by piracy in Somalia.

Some terrorist organizations also raise money through illegal gambling and prostitution rackets. For instance, the PKK might have raised money through these activities in Moscow.[110] Other terrorist groups might raise money from these activities as opportunities present themselves, but they are unlikely to publicize this source of funds, given that their supporters might find it particularly unsavory. When terrorist groups use illegal means to finance their operations, even activities to which they are ideologically opposed, this does not mean they have abandoned their ideology.[111] Instead, this activity should be seen simply as exploitation of local conditions or as a method to make money to advance their ideological goals.

Piracy and to a lesser extent gambling and prostitution rackets are mostly the purview of terrorist organizations rather than cells or individuals. An organizational-level resource base is generally required to engage in this type of activity. At the same time, individuals who have extensive criminal connections and have only recently turned to terrorism and politically motivated violence can use criminal activity to raise funds with greater ease. Approximately 29 percent of the terrorist organizations I studied engage in piracy, gambling, and prostitution rackets to raise funds. As noted, this is largely the purview of terrorist organizations that have access to a coast (for piracy), although gambling and prostitution rackets can be used by any group. Constraints on terrorist groups' fund-raising through these activities might exist as a function of other criminal enterprises already dominating these activities. Criminal organizations might not be willing to share space with terrorist actors in the gambling, prostitution, and piracy markets. Operationally, only one terrorist plot and one terrorist attack I studied were funded from this type of criminal activity, and in both cases, the individuals involved had preexisting inroads to this type of criminality.

As with any criminal activity that takes place within a terrorist group's area of control or influence, terrorist organizations likely benefit from piracy, protection, gambling, and prostitution rackets, and it remains possible that the group, or elements within the group, actively participate in it. Piracy, illegal gambling, and prostitution rackets are no exception given the sums of money involved and the requirement for weapons and funds for daily subsistence. Terrorists and criminals in this context make likely partners, particularly when a terrorist organization controls the territory in which this is occurring or can exert significant influence; however, they can also be competitors.

Smuggling and Trafficking: Drugs, Goods, and People

Many terrorist organizations make money from some version of smuggling and trafficking schemes, often involving drugs, goods, and people. The commodity smuggled or trafficked depends on the economy exploited by the terrorist group and what is available to smuggle. For instance, in Iraq, criminal and insurgent groups were involved in the theft and smuggling of crude oil, imported refined fuels, and locally produced gasoline. As Williams notes, "The insurgency was strengthened and sustained by criminal activities" and "sectarian conflict was funded by criminal activities and motivated by the desire to control criminal markets."[112] Most terrorist groups tax both smuggling and trafficking activities and might also participate in them directly. Terrorist cells and individuals are less likely to be involved in the smuggling or trafficking of goods and people, but there are notable exceptions: drug smuggling and trafficking.

Drug Smuggling and Trafficking

Many terrorist groups have engaged with the drug trade to some extent to generate funds. The exact nature of that engagement changes over time and can range from taxing the drug-related activities to full-scale involvement in the production of drugs. Our understanding of terrorist drug trafficking has been clouded by the politicization of both drug trafficking and terrorism.

Terrorist actors' involvement tends to be either over- or understated by individuals with vested interests in the involvement of terrorist groups in these illicit activities. In some cases, departments and agencies might be funded on the basis of their engagement in counterterrorism or with policing narcotics, meaning that they might have a motive to emphasize (if not outright exaggerate) the role of one or the other to secure their own funding.

Despite this caveat, we do know that some terrorist organizations have been involved in the drug trade. Terrorist organizations have used drug trafficking (the widescale movement of drugs to various locations, usually involving production, shipping, and protecting the drug trade) for decades to raise funds for their terrorist activities, but in recent years, significant doubt has been cast about the interplay between religiously motivated terrorist groups and the drug trade. The assumption appears to be that religiously motivated terrorist groups, particularly those aligned with or inspired by al-Qaeda or ISIL ideology, would not engage in drug trafficking to raise funds because it is not condoned religiously. Over time, it has become increasingly clear that terrorist groups do not adhere to their ideologies and belief statements when it comes to operational decisions such as targets, recruits, or financing.[113] Instead, terrorist organizations, even religiously motivated ones, operate opportunistically.

ETA was first reported to be involved in the drug trade in 1984, twenty-five years after its founding.[114] FARC has been involved to varying degrees in drug trafficking and raised a significant amount of money from this activity.[115] The Shining Path (in Peru) also protected the production of coca fields to raise funds. In some cases, growers in Peru were paid in advance by the traffickers to produce the coca leaf, and they did so under the (implicit or explicit) threat of death.[116]

Terrorist group involvement in the drug trade tends to evolve over time. FARC's involvement changed between the 1980s and 1990s; at first, it levied taxes on harvesters and buyers of coca paste and cocaine base cultivated and sold in FARC territory. Traffickers also paid FARC money to protect their laboratories and to gain access to airfields.[117] Eventually, FARC was directly implicated in the drug trade, including taking control of farms and participating in production. Eventually, the group was estimated to have obtained 50 percent of its funding from the drug economy.[118]

In the 1990s, the Islamic Movement of Uzbekistan launched an insurgency funded primarily through narcotics trafficking.[119] The group was reported to have controlled up to 70 percent of the opium and heroin that moved through Central Asia, with much of it originating in Taliban-controlled Afghanistan.[120] From the 1990s onward, Chechen Islamist extremist groups also raised funds through the production and trafficking of heroin.[121]

Other terrorist groups, such as the LTTE and Hizballah, have also been involved in drug trafficking to varying degrees. The LTTE's involvement constituted (for the most part) taxation of Tamil organized crime. The group diverted profits from this activity as either a "donation" or taxation.[122] Few sources cite the LTTE's involvement in the drug trade as significant. In fact, the group likely earned some money from drug trafficking simply through this diversion of funds from supporters who earned their money through the drug trade.[123] It is important to note a subtle distinction here. Although these criminal groups were described as Tamil, they were not necessarily part of the LTTE. As such, the terrorist organization might not have been directly implicated in the drug trade but likely benefited from it in the form of donations, extortion, and protection fees.

Hizballah is yet another terrorist organization believed to raise funds through drug trafficking, specifically cocaine trafficking in the tri-border area of South America, and the group's involvement in the illegal drug trade dates from at least the 1980s.[124] In 2003 Ciudad del Este, the largest city in the tri-border area, generated between $12 and $13 million ($16.7–$18 million in 2020) from drug proceeds and other criminal profits. Some portion of these funds made their way back to Hizballah.[125] In Lebanon, Hizballah finances its activities through the Bekaa Valley's agriculture as well as heroin and hashish production, activities that would be impossible without some form of territorial control.[126] In 2005, it was estimated that 13,000 acres were under control of the group in Lebanon's Bekaa Valley and that the group produced 300 tons of hashish each year that it exported to Europe, grossing $180 million ($236 million in 2020 dollars). As of 2008, the US Drug Enforcement Administration (DEA) believed that Hizballah was raising $1 billion per year from drugs and weapons trafficking.[127] This estimate might include the proceeds of all Lebanese organized crime, not just the funds raised by Hizballah-linked or -directed elements, and almost certainly overstates the amount of money Hizballah received directly from this activity. More recently, the group is thought to be involved in the production, trafficking, and sale of the stimulant Captagon throughout the Middle East.[128] Hizballah's drug trafficking activities might be conflated with the same activities of Lebanese organized crime, although there is certainly overlap between the two.

A good example of the evolution and complexity of a terrorist group's involvement in drug trafficking is the Taliban. At any given time, its actual involvement in various aspects of the trade is subject to debate; what is not debatable is that it earns a significant portion of its revenue from the opium trade. The Taliban has charged poppy farmers a 10 percent tax on the profits of their labor, and the group has been known to encourage and force farmers to plant poppies. The Taliban receives money, vehicles, and weapons from drug lords as payment for protecting them within its territory. Opium traffickers pay the group to let them transport narcotics to neighboring nations. The Taliban also provides security for the processing labs and for the shipments of chemicals required to make heroin and has been known to help drug lords fight poppy eradication efforts. Increasingly, the group is implicated in every aspect of the drug trade, although core Taliban fighters are not believed to cultivate poppies directly and process or distribute opium.[129] Instead, the Taliban leaves that to its criminal allies.[130]

Over the course of their existence, many groups have dabbled in the drug trade or been implicated in it in a more sustained way; this also changes over the course of many groups' existence. The PKK is estimated to have controlled about 70 percent to 80 percent of the heroin trade in Europe in the early 1990s; as of 2012, the group is still estimated to make significant money from the trade.[131] MILF and Abu Sayyaf both obtained large amounts of money from the illegal drug market. Abu Sayyaf has specifically been linked to the marijuana trade, with police destroying more than $10 million worth of marijuana belonging to the group in 1999.[132]

ISIL in Libya might have benefited from the drug trade as well. According to news reporting, the Greek government accused entities associated with ISIL of importing Tramadol, involving a shipment originating in India and destined for Libya.[133] Some reports suggest that a transactional relationship has evolved between ISIL in Libya and the Calabrian 'Ndrangheta organized crime group, likely around the trafficking of drugs through their territory.[134]

Of course, there are exceptions to the widespread taxation and use of the drug trade to raise funds for terrorist organizations. Some terrorist groups do not appear to have engaged in or benefited from drug trafficking. Few sources identify much of a connection between PIRA and the drug trade.[135] There are also limited reports of the LeT's involvement in drug trafficking,[136] with most reports suggesting guilt by association. Because there are huge potential profits and the group enjoys geographical proximity to drug trafficking areas, it is possible that it has raised money by providing security to drug traffickers or by taxing their routes. For instance, in 2002, there was a large opium harvest—an estimated 5,000 tons—on the border between Afghanistan and Pakistan. The drugs were smuggled by Inter-Services Intelligence (ISI) narcotics smugglers and had an estimated net worth of $2.5 billion. The profits were alleged to have been transferred to the Taliban and to Jammu and Kashmir, presumably at least in part to the LeT.[137]

As with terrorist groups, significant differences of opinion and fact exist on the extent of terrorist involvement in the drug trade at the operational level. Some analysts have argued that terrorist cells and individuals do not engage in drug dealing because they do not want to expose themselves to potential law enforcement scrutiny, but some notable terrorist attacks have been funded in this way. Terrorist organizations tend to engage in drug trafficking, whereas terrorist cells and individuals usually engage in smaller-scale drug dealing to raise funds for their terrorist plots and attacks.

Organizationally, groups might become involved primarily on the periphery of the activity, taxing or facilitating it if they control territory. For the cells, this can be a main means of financing their activities. Indeed, investigations into several al-Qaeda plots in Europe suggest that the cells were often flush with cash obtained from drug dealing and credit card fraud and often raised far more than was necessary for the operation.[138] For example, Mohamed Merah, the perpetrator of a series of shootings in France in March 2012, had a main income source from criminal activities. He engaged in theft and robbery as well as drug trafficking.[139]

A widely cited example of a terrorist cell's involvement in drug trafficking was the 2004 terrorist attack in Madrid, Spain. On March 11, 2004, ten bombs detonated on four commuter trains in Madrid, killing at least 192 people and wounding more than 1,400.[140] A significant aspect of the attack was funded through the sale of illicit drugs and through trade: the drugs were traded for the explosives, stolen from a mine in Spain, required for the attack.[141] It is also critical to note that the drug trafficking skill set was already well developed among the cell members; one of the plot's ringleaders and several accomplices were drug dealers and traffickers.[142] Indeed, some of the funding is alleged to have come from robberies and muggings of individuals involved in the drug trade.[143]

The differences between organizational and operational involvement in the drug trade are significant. Terrorist organizations are much more likely to be involved, with at least 20 percent of the groups I studied engaging with the trade. Operationally, the scope of this activity is far more limited, with only 6 percent of terrorist plots or attacks I studied raising funds from drugs. However, a broader look at more plots and attacks would likely reveal a higher percentage, particularly in Europe, where the crime-terror nexus is well documented and where individual terrorists might exploit their access to criminal activity for funding.[144] Other estimates of terrorist organizations' involvement in drug trafficking are higher. In 2008, the chief of operations at the DEA said that of forty-three designated terrorist groups, nineteen profited from drug trade (44 percent).[145] In 2010, the US Department of Justice reported that 46 percent of the top international drug syndicates were associated with terrorist groups.[146] Of course, precise information on how terrorist groups interact with the drug trade can be difficult to obtain, and the relationship between these groups and organized crime is likely fluid, changing over the course of the terrorist groups' existence and based on organizational needs.

Trafficking and Smuggling Goods and People
In addition to drug trafficking, terrorist organizations, cells, and individuals all make use of smuggling and trafficking. For instance, the sale and trafficking of weapons is a lucrative source of funding for terrorist organizations

and sometimes cells. Mokhtar Belmokthar, who leads one of the Khatibs (brigades) for AQIM, focuses on criminal activities such as theft (weapons smuggling and stolen vehicles) and the sale of contraband to raise funds.[147] Terrorists often go well beyond goods, smuggling and trafficking people to raise funds.

The specific goods smuggled are often less illustrative of the financing mechanisms involved than the actual efforts involved in smuggling and trafficking, because these can point to the extent of the relationship between the terrorists and criminal elements. When terrorist groups control territory, they make use of existing smuggling and trafficking networks, either taking them over or demanding a cut of their proceeds. Some terrorist organizations frame this as a "tax," whereas others consider it a form of protection money. In some cases, terrorist groups engage in the smuggling activity directly, whereas in others, they impose a tax on the activity within their area of control or influence. For example, Hizballah is reported to have received taxes on the profits of diamond smuggling operations in West Africa.[148] Hamas is believed to raise funds through smuggling tobacco products (both genuine and counterfeit) as well as counterfeit T-shirts and other apparel.[149]

The goods smuggled or trafficked depend on both the economy and geography where the terrorist groups are operating. For instance, PIRA engaged in smuggling and trafficking goods, both legal and illicit, such as pigs, cattle, livestock grain, and animal antibiotics.[150] The use of the agricultural sector as a basis from which to derive revenue is not unique to PIRA, but this type of fund-raising activity is specific to the economic, cultural, and geographical area in which a group operates. Boko Haram has also exploited agricultural resources within its area of operations to raise funds, stealing and selling the resources and in some cases taxing their transportation and sale. Other goods and commodities have also been used to raise funds for terrorist organizations. Al-Shabaab has smuggled illicit goods out of Somalia, raising as much as $7 million per year smuggling charcoal.[151] (Somali charcoal exports were banned in 1969 because of the environmental degradation caused by harvesting acacia trees, from which the charcoal was derived.)

Trafficking small weapons has also been a source of funds for terrorist groups. This source has dual benefits: not only do the groups raise funds from the trafficking of these weapons, but they are also able to exploit sources of weapons for their own purposes. As Colin Clarke notes, this phenomenon was especially prominent following the end of the Cold War, when the end of superpower subsidies led terrorist and insurgent groups to traffic small weapons such as AK-47s. Groups that have engaged in this source of funds include PIRA, LTTE, al-Qaeda, the Taliban, FARC, and ISIL.[152]

Much has been made of terrorist organizations' involvement in the commodities trade, specifically diamonds. Passas and Jones examine this issue in some detail and note that although commodities have long formed part of the economy of conflict, studies of this phenomenon in terrorist groups are supported with conflicting and weak evidence and plagued by vague language.[153] Passas and Jones's study, however, used two cases—al-Qaeda and Hizballah—as well as primary and secondary data to explore the links between the diamond trade and these groups. They concluded that al-Qaeda in particular is not seriously engaged in the diamond trade, but some people associated with the group appear to have engaged in diamond transactions.[154] Whether this benefited the terrorist groups was not clearly identified.

Human smuggling and trafficking have also been used by terrorist groups to raise funds. Human smuggling (the provision of a service to individuals who voluntarily want to gain illegal access to a foreign country) is used by terrorist groups to make money as well as to preposition terrorist operatives. The LTTE acquired substantial funds through human smuggling, although those funds had to be split with their criminal partners in the endeavor. The LTTE shared between $18,000 and $32,000 per person smuggled from Sri Lanka to India or to the West (specifically the United States and Canada).[155] The profits on this activity ranged from $180,000 to $226,000 per year. Some of these individuals were facilitated into other countries as refugees. The group would extract payment from them later by forcing them to carry money for drugs or arms purchases. In addition to acquiring weapons for its own needs, the group also engaged in arms smuggling for profit.[156]

Other terrorist organizations such as the PKK, Chechen groups, and Al-Shabaab have also raised funds through human trafficking.[157] Human trafficking involves the exploitation of men, women, and children for the purposes of forced labor or commercial sexual exploitation.[158] Al-Shabaab's human trafficking has included children to serve as soldiers.[159] Human smuggling and trafficking is a lucrative source of funds for terrorist organizations, and in other cases, it is both a source of funds for and a means of intimidating and retaliating against their enemies, such as the case of ISIL's enslavement of Yazidi women and girls. In this case, Yazidis were sold as slaves for approximately $13 each, but ISIL also ransomed them to their families, generating far greater profits (closer to $13,000 each).[160] Similar patterns of activity have also been seen with Boko Haram's trafficking of women and girls.[161]

Almost any product or resource can be smuggled, as terrorist groups have demonstrated over the years. The Taliban has derived significant funds from the trade in (unspecified) goods smuggled from Dubai to Pakistan.[162] AQAP has raised funds by appropriating oil and selling it.[163] ISIL in Libya is alleged to have close links with criminal groups and smugglers.[164] All of these groups and smuggling activities have access to resources terrorists can exploit and markets for them in common.

Smuggling and trafficking are not solely the purview of terrorist organizations; cells and individuals can also use them to raise funds. A former al-Qaeda operative, Shadi Abdullah, was arrested and interrogated in Germany, where he admitted to raising hundreds of thousands of dollars by forging passports and smuggling militant Muslims and asylum seekers into that country.[165] However, for the most part, cells and individuals do not engage in this activity because of the general requirement for a network of preestablished criminal associations. There are major barriers to entry for individuals seeking to raise funds in this manner without those criminal networks.

A more complex variant of smuggling involves sales tax arbitrage. Some terrorists have purchased goods in one jurisdiction with a lower sales tax and then resold the goods for a profit in a jurisdiction with a higher sales tax. This is considered smuggling or trafficking, even if the goods themselves are legal in both jurisdictions, because taking advantage of the difference in sales tax is illicit. A well-known example of this involved a Hizballah cell in the United States that raised a significant amount of money through taxation arbitrage on cigarettes, taking advantage of differences in tax rates between Michigan, New York, and North Carolina.[166] A less well-known example is PIRA. The group took advantage of differences in sales taxes on luxury goods and alcohol, buying them in a lower sales tax jurisdiction and then reselling them in higher-priced jurisdictions. The group also took advantage of different rates of excise duties on either side of the border for fuel oil (gasoline and diesel).[167]

Smuggling and trafficking in goods and people are not widespread terrorist fund-raising methods, but they have been used by some groups, cells, and individuals and continue to allow terrorists not only to raise funds but also to move people and goods illicitly. At least 29 percent of the terrorist organizations I studied have funded themselves through smuggling and trafficking of goods, people, and commodities, although actual numbers are likely higher. There are significant added benefits for terrorist groups that can control trafficking and smuggling routes, in that they can overcome logistical hurdles such as the movement of explosives, weapons, and people. Terrorist cells and individuals might exploit links to criminal elements in advance of their terrorist ambitions to raise funds or acquire goods or services for their plots and attacks.

Counterfeit and Pirated Goods

Counterfeiting, which involves the creation of fake goods, and piracy, which involves the illegal reproduction of real goods, can be used as long-term strategies to raise funds by terrorist groups as well as cells (but almost never individuals). In most cases, terrorist groups traffic in or sell counterfeit goods to raise funds, but in other instances, they can be involved in counterfeiting themselves, particularly when it comes to currency. For instance, Indian terrorists fighting British colonialism in 1906–1907 attempted to counterfeit coins. The Croatian Ustashe also forged Yugoslav 1,000 dinar notes in the 1920s, and the Jewish Lohamei Herut Israel (Lehi) group printed fraudulent government bonds.[168]

Other groups in more recent history have also used the forgery of currency to raise funds. Al Aqsa Martyr's Brigade is reported to have funded its activities with counterfeit money, although it is unclear if the group created the money themselves.[169] Louise Shelley alleges that al-Qaeda financed its activities through counterfeit notes and believes that the 9/11 hijackers visited casinos in Las Vegas prior to the attacks in an effort to dispose of the notes.[170] In Europe and Australia, LTTE members were involved in the counterfeited currency racket as part of the group's diversified efforts to raise funds.[171] The ISI is reported to give both real and counterfeit money directly to the LeT, comingling genuine cash with counterfeit money, obscuring both the source (through the use of cash couriers) and the counterfeit money, making all of it appear legitimate.[172]

Pirated goods are also used by terrorist groups, cells, and individuals to raise money for terrorist activity.[173] PIRA dealt in both pirated and counterfeit goods, including compact discs, computer games, contraband cigarette lighters, and brand-name jeans.[174] Hizballah is widely understood to have profited from music piracy operations in the tri-border area of South America.[175] Other pirated goods or counterfeit goods created, bought, or sold by a variety of terrorist groups include movies, video games, clothing, electronics, pharmaceutical products, tickets to sports and music events, and so forth. In more recent years, some of these goods and services have been bought and paid for on the dark web using Bitcoin and other cryptocurrencies.[176]

Trafficking in counterfeit goods might appear to be primarily the purview of terrorist organizations, but terrorist cells and individuals also use this method to raise funds. The Charlie Hebdo attack was financed at least in part through the sale of counterfeit goods. At the time of the attack, the perpetrators did not have regular jobs.[177] Some of the funds used to purchase the weapons might have been provided by Cherif Kouachi, who bought and resold €8,000 ($9,500) worth of counterfeit items, mostly Nike shoes from China.[178]

These examples represent the bare minimum of terrorist fund-raising through counterfeit and pirated goods and demonstrate that at least 13 percent of terrorist organizations benefit from counterfeiting. The ubiquity of these goods and the growing interplay between terrorists and criminal activity make this an increasingly likely source of funds, particularly for cells or individuals looking to raise funds quickly but without a significant investment of resources. Provided the terrorists have the right connections, the barriers to entry for selling counterfeit goods are few, and significant profits can be made. For terrorist organizations, cells, and individuals to create or take advantage of a market for pirated or counterfeit goods, they must have existing means to obtain or create the goods and networks in which to sell them. These types of terrorist activities often require existing contact with criminal organizations, in some cases partnerships, and they require a market for resale.

Organizational and Operational Fund-Raising Through Criminal Business Models

There is a significant difference between how terrorists use criminal business models for funding their organizational and operational needs. Terrorist groups use criminal business models to fund their organizational needs (see Figure 4.2), whereas operational terrorist actors (cells and individuals) rarely use these methods (see Figure 4.3). The only real criminal business model terrorist cells and individuals employ is drug trafficking (and some counterfeit sales), and they do this by exploiting preexisting criminal networks and capabilities.

Other types of criminal activity, such as kidnapping for ransom, are almost exclusively the purview of terrorist organizations and are likely to stay that way for the foreseeable future. Both local and foreign kidnapping require some territorial control or a safe haven in which to secure the hostage. Logistical requirements for this fund-raising activity are also largely outside the capabilities of cells and individuals. In recent years, incidents of kidnapping for ransom have decreased, as have the ransoms paid. Whether this trend continues depends on a number of factors, such as the types of terrorist actors likely to emerge or become more prominent in the future, the willingness of families and governments to pay ransoms, and the other costs to terrorists who engage in this activity (such as retri-

Figure 4.2 Organizational Financing Through Criminal Business Models

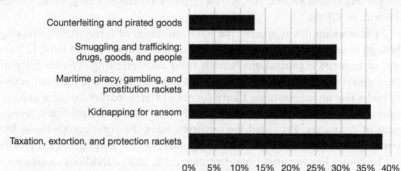

Figure 4.3 Operational Financing Through Criminal Business Models

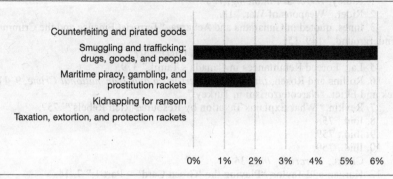

bution in the form of drone strikes or terrorist decapitation). Regardless of these factors, terrorist organizations are likely to be tempted to engage in kidnapping for ransom.

Conclusion

Terrorist criminal business models involve a variety of activities, and terrorists engage in whatever criminal activity is prevalent in the area in which they are operating or have access to. For it to rise to the level of a business model, however, the activity generally requires some control or significant influence over territory and access to criminal networks. These networks can either be preexisting or can be developed specifically by the terrorist entity. Many of these business models, such as taxation, extortion, and protection rackets, overlap; drawing clear lines between them is difficult, if not impossible. The majority of the time, criminal business models are used by organizations, although in some instances, these models have been used for operational financing, and they have generated funds well in excess of those needed for the attack, as was the case in the Madrid bombing.[179] However, specificity of language and understanding the mechanisms involved in these activities are critical for this source of funds to be effectively countered. Terrorists obtain far more from these business models than funds: they also gain freedom of action and legitimacy and support from the population (what Felbab-Brown calls political capital).[180] Without understanding the exact role of criminal business models in a terrorist organization's funding strategy, an effective counterterrorist financing policy is impossible to implement. At the same time, these criminal business models have significant footprints that can make tracking, and potentially countering, this aspect of terrorist financing within the realm of possibility.

Notes

1. Ridley, *Terrorist Financing*, 123.
2. Rider, "Weapons of War," 18.
3. Innes, quoted in Gunaratna and Acharya, "Terrorist Finance and the Criminal Underground," 149–151.
4. Fearon, "Why Do Some Civil Wars Last?" 297.
5. La, "Forced Remittances in Canada's Tamil," 379.
6. Rollins and Rosen, *International Terrorism and Transnational Crime*, 9–11; Pek and Ekici, "Narcoterrorism in Turkey."
7. Revkin, "What Explains Taxation by Resource-Rich Rebels?" 757.
8. Ibid., 758.
9. Ibid., 759.
10. Ibid., 759.
11. Clarke, *Terrorism, Inc.*, 34.
12. Horgan and Taylor, "Playing the 'Green Card' —Part 1," 7, 14.
13. Vittori, *Terrorist Financing and Resourcing*, 36.
14. Lia and Kjøk, *Islamist Insurgencies, Diasporic Support Networks*, 26.
15. Ruehsen, "Partiya Karkeren Kurdistan," 68–69.
16. Vittori, *Terrorist Financing and Resourcing*, 77.
17. Financial Action Task Force, *Emerging Terrorist Financing Risks*, 17.
18. Corley, "Liberation Tigers of Tamil Eelam," 120.
19. Ibid.
20. Vittori, *Terrorist Financing and Resourcing*, 80.
21. Corley, "Liberation Tigers of Tamil Eelam," 118.
22. UN Security Council, "Twenty-Second Report."
23. UN Security Council, "Monitoring Team Report," November 14, 2014, 22.
24. UN Security Council, "Monitoring Team Report," July 19, 2016, 8.
25. Financial Action Task Force, *Emerging Terrorist Financing Risks*, 17.
26. UN Security Council, "Monitoring Team Report," January 13, 2017, 9–10.
27. Rudaw, "ISIS Burns Crop Fields."
28. UN Security Council, "Twenty-Second Report."
29. Kamere et al., "Lashkar-e-Taiba," 83.
30. UN Security Council, "Monitoring Team Report," July 19, 2016, 12.
31. UN Security Council, "Twenty-Second Report."
32. Financial Action Task Force, *Emerging Terrorist Financing Risks*, 17.
33. *Global Witness*, "At Any Price We Will Take the Mines," 14.
34. Ibid., 16.
35. Ibid.
36. Ibid., 14, 16, 29.
37. Ibid., 14.
38. Phillips, "U.S. Attacks Taliban's Source."
39. Mahendrarajah, "Conceptual Failure," 109.
40. Roston, "How the US Funds the Taliban."
41. US House of Representatives and Tierney, *Warlord, Inc.*
42. *Garowe Online*, "Somalia."
43. Keatinge, "Role of Finance in Defeating al-Shabaab," 17, 19.
44. Vilkko, "Al-Shabaab," 19.
45. Keatinge, "Role of Finance in Defeating al-Shabaab," 5.
46. Vilkko, "Al-Shabaab," 17.
47. Ibid., 7.
48. Germann et al., "Terrorist Financing in the Philippines," 151.

49. Agence France-Presse, "Lafarge Charged with Complicity."

50. Bantekas, "International Law of Terrorist Financing," 317.

51. Mironova, *From Freedom Fighters to Jihadists*, 243.

52. Zabyelina, "'Capone Discovery,'" 1.

53. Williams, *Criminals, Militias, and Insurgents*.

54. Shortland, *Kidnap*, 3.

55. Vittori, *Terrorist Financing and Resourcing*, 56.

56. Ibid., 68.

57. Horgan and Taylor, "Playing the 'Green Card'—Part 1," 9–10.

58. Roethke, "American Law," 173.

59. Koseli et al., "Use of Kidnapping and Extortion."

60. Rollins and Rosen, *International Terrorism and Transnational Crime*, 18.

61. Shortland, *Kidnap*, 112; Sahara Reporters, "Lai Mohammed Lied."

62. RFI Afrique, "Une nouvelle forme de banditisme." Whether Boko Haram or the Islamic State in West Africa was responsible for this kidnapping is the subject of debate. See UN Security Council, "Twenty-Second Report."

63. Clarke, *Terrorism, Inc.*, 139.

64. Vittori, *Terrorist Financing and Resourcing*, 56.

65. Horgan and Taylor, "Playing the 'Green Card'—Part 1," 9.

66. Financial Action Task Force, *Emerging Terrorist Financing Risks*, 18.

67. Callimachi, "Paying Ransoms."

68. Musharbash, "Al-Qaida Guide to Kidnapping."

69. Williams, *Criminals, Militias, and Insurgents*, 105.

70. Ibid., 115.

71. Clarke and Williams, "Da'esh in Iraq and Syria," 32–33.

72. UN Security Council, "Monitoring Team Report," July 19, 2016, 18.

73. Clarke and Williams, "Da'esh in Iraq and Syria," 34.

74. Thachuk, "Gangsterization of Terrorism," 21.

75. Croissant and Barlow, "Following the Money Trail," 135.

76. Germann et al., "Terrorist Financing in the Philippines," 150.

77. UN Security Council, "Twenty-Second Report."

78. Schindler, "United Nations View on al-Qaeda's Financing," 89.

79. Shortland, *Kidnap*, 200.

80. UN Security Council, "Twenty-Second Report"; US Department of the Treasury, "Remarks of Under Secretary for Terrorism."

81. UN Security Council, "Monitoring Team Report," November 14, 2014, 19.

82. Moore and Browne, "Qatari Hostage Payments Funded Al Qaeda."

83. Warrick, "Hacked Messages Show Qatar."

84. Bauer and Levitt, "Al Qaeda Financing," 93. One of those kidnappings involved ransom payment in 2017 of 3.5 million euros. See Anderson, "Former Hostage Held by Al Qaeda."

85. Callimachi, "Paying Ransoms."

86. Clarke, *Terrorism, Inc.*, 117.

87. Ibid., 116–117.

88. Reese, "Financing the Taliban," 103.

89. Ahmad, "Taliban Video Shows Sons."

90. Rasmussen, "Kidnapped Professors Beg Trump."

91. Vittori, *Terrorist Financing and Resourcing*, 36.

92. Sandler, "Collective Action and Transnational Terrorism."

93. These data were compiled from the Global Terrorism Database (GTD) and augmented with additional open-source research. National Consortium for the Study

of Terrorism and Responses to Terrorism (START), Global Terrorism Database. Data are current to January 2021.

94. Many thanks to Jillian Hunchak, who worked as a research analyst on the kidnapping for ransom dataset.
95. Callimachi, "Paying Ransoms."
96. Shortland, *Kidnap*, 102.
97. Gift of the Givers Foundation, "About Us."
98. Callimachi and Chan, "Hostage Held by Al Qaeda."
99. Anderson, "Former Hostage Held by Al Qaeda."
100. Callimachi, "Paying Ransoms."
101. Shortland, *Kidnap*, 153.
102. Ibid., 192–193.
103. Callimachi, "Paying Ransoms."
104. Shortland, *Kidnap*, 76.
105. Ibid., 112.
106. Croissant and Barlow, "Following the Money Trail," 136.
107. Rollins and Rosen, *International Terrorism and Transnational Crime*, 30.
108. Vilkko, "Al-Shabaab," 24.
109. Keatinge, "Role of Finance in Defeating al-Shabaab," 23.
110. Ruehsen, "Partiya Karkeren Kurdistan," 67.
111. Bantekas, "International Law of Terrorist Financing," 318.
112. Williams, *Criminals, Militias, and Insurgents*.
113. Davis, *Women in Modern Terrorism*, 4.
114. Shelley, *Dirty Entanglements*, 109.
115. Rollins and Rosen, *International Terrorism and Transnational Crime*, 9.
116. Vittori, *Terrorist Financing and Resourcing*, 36.
117. Ibid., 17.
118. Ibid., 18.
119. Thachuk and Lal, "Introduction to Terrorist Criminal Enterprises," 4.
120. Vittori, *Terrorist Financing and Resourcing*, 36.
121. Wittig, "Financing Terrorism Along the Chechnya-Georgia Border," 254.
122. Clarke, *Terrorism, Inc.*, 53.
123. Ibid., 52.
124. Vittori, *Terrorist Financing and Resourcing*, 106; Ruda, "Hezbollah."
125. Philippone, "Hezbollah," 57.
126. Vittori, *Terrorist Financing and Resourcing*, 61.
127. Ruda, "Hezbollah."
128. Clarke, "ISIS Is So Desperate."
129. Mashal, "Afghan Taliban Awash in Heroin Cash."
130. Rollins and Rosen, *International Terrorism and Transnational Crime*, 21.
131. Ruehsen, "Partiya Karkeren Kurdistan," 70.
132. Germann et al., "Terrorist Financing in the Philippines," 150.
133. Clarke, "ISIS Is So Desperate."
134. Clarke and Williams, "Da'esh in Iraq and Syria," 36.
135. Horgan and Taylor, "Playing the 'Green Card'—Part 1," 16.
136. Kamere et al., "Lashkar-e-Taiba," 83.
137. Ibid.
138. K. McGrath, *Confronting Al Qaeda*, 75.
139. Oftedal, "Financing of Jihadi Terrorist Cells," 36.
140. Sciolino, "Bombings in Madrid."
141. Oftedal, "Financing of Jihadi Terrorist Cells," 15.

142. Rollins and Rosen, *International Terrorism and Transnational Crime*, 19.
143. Reinares, *Al-Qaeda's Revenge*, 43.
144. Basra and Neumann, "Criminal Pasts, Terrorist Futures."
145. Braun, "Drug Trafficking and Middle Eastern Terrorist Groups?"
146. Rollins and Wyler, "Terrorism and Transnational Crime," 3.
147. Chelin, "From the Islamic Maghreb of Algeria," 9.
148. Rabasa et al., "Convergence of Terrorism, Insurgency, and Crime," 103.
149. Clarke, *Terrorism, Inc.*; 101.
150. Ibid., 34.
151. *Maritime Executive*, "Charcoal Smuggling Finances Somali Terrorist Groups."
152. Clarke, "Small Arms and Light Weapons."
153. Passas and Jones, "Commodities and Terrorist Financing," 1.
154. Ibid., 29.
155. Vittori, *Terrorist Financing and Resourcing*, 31.
156. Corley, "Liberation Tigers of Tamil Eelam," 124–125.
157. Wittig, "Financing Terrorism Along the Chechnya-Georgia Border," 252.
158. Immigration and Customs Enforcement, "Human Trafficking vs. Human Smuggling."
159. Shelley, *Dirty Entanglements*, 178–179.
160. Financial Action Task Force, *Financing of the Terrorist Organization*, 13.
161. Shelley, *Dark Commerce*, 161.
162. Clarke, *Terrorism, Inc.*, 114.
163. UN Security Council, "Twenty-Second Report."
164. UN Security Council, "Monitoring Team Report," July 19, 2016, 12.
165. Raphaeli, "Financing of Terrorism," 61.
166. Arena, "Hizballah's Global Criminal Operations."
167. Clarke, *Terrorism, Inc.*, 31–34.
168. Vittori, *Terrorist Financing and Resourcing*, 53.
169. Darshan-Leitner and Katz, *Harpoon*, 73.
170. Shelley, *Dirty Entanglements*, 32.
171. Clarke, *Terrorism, Inc.*, 53.
172. Kamere et al., "Lashkar-e-Taiba," 81–83.
173. Treverton et al., "Film Piracy."
174. Clarke, *Terrorism, Inc.*, 34.
175. Rabasa et al., "Convergence of Terrorism, Insurgency, and Crime," 103.
176. Zehorai, "Richest Terror Organizations in the World."
177. Financial Action Task Force, *Emerging Terrorist Financing Risks*, 11.
178. Treicher, "When Transaction Laundering Finances Terror."
179. Reinares, *Al-Qaeda's Revenge*, 74.
180. Felbab-Brown, *Shooting Up*, 5.

5

Making
Crime Pay

One of the most significant ways terrorist organizations, cells, and individuals raise money is through criminal activity. Some of that criminal activity follows criminal business models (explored in depth in Chapter 4), whereas other forms are smaller in scale and opportunistic but can still yield a significant windfall for terrorists. Criminal activity (outside of that conducted in criminal business models) encompasses a range of financial crimes from theft to resource exploitation. Of course, some of these other forms of criminal activity can also be part of criminal business models. However, terrorists can also function relatively independently of larger criminal models and networks to raise funds for their activities. These criminal activities allow all levels of terrorist actors to raise money, ranging from a significant amount to just enough to conduct a low-level operation. These smaller-scale criminal activities are usually the purview of terrorist cells, but some individuals seeking to fund-raise for groups try to make crime pay as well.

Financial Crimes
Financial crimes are, generally speaking, types of theft of property and can include fraud, robbery, blackmail, and corruption, to name a few methods. Financial crimes also increasingly have an online component: victims might be identified online, or the entire criminal activity might be carried out online. The amount of financial crime that happens online generally reflects the extent to which a country or region is connected; for those with little internet connectivity, financial crimes are often still perpetrated offline.

Terrorist groups, cells, and individuals use financial crimes to generate profits used in turn to fund both organizational and operational needs. Some of the types of financial crimes by terrorist actors have included credit card fraud, tax fraud, and student loan and welfare benefit fraud. Terrorists who raise funds in these ways are generally able to do so because they exploit a preexisting criminal skill set they have diverted to terrorism. Groups that have used crime to finance organizational and operational activity include the Provisional Irish Republican Army (PIRA), the Liberation Tigers of Tamil Eelam (LTTE), Hizballah, al-Qaeda, and the Islamic State in Iraq and the Levant (ISIL), to name a few.

When analyzing the financial crimes committed by terrorist actors, it is important to separate fact from hypothesis. For instance, securities fraud has been posited as a way terrorists might make money, but there is little evidence to support this hypothesis.[1] Of course, with nearly every terrorist financing method, it is conceivable and possible they will use it to their advantage; the question becomes to what extent has it been used, and what evidence is there to support policy changes to address the method?

One of the first terrorist organizations to raise funds through financial crime might have been PIRA.[2] The group used tax scams, specifically income tax fraud and false tax exemption certificates, to raise funds. Income tax fraud involves purposely not reporting income to evade taxes or to receive a refund for prepaid taxes and can constitute a variety of schemes. For instance, groups obtain false taxation exemption certificates and purchase goods without paying taxes, then resell them for a profit. This scam is estimated to have yielded PIRA £28.5 million ($36 million).[3] The group also committed welfare fraud to raise funds.[4]

The LTTE also used financial crime, specifically credit card fraud, to generate funds. The group tended to outsource this activity to the more technologically proficient individuals within its ranks or associates. In 2007, sixteen LTTE operatives were caught in Norway skimming $890,000 (more than $1.02 million in 2020 dollars) from bank accounts using legitimate credit card data.[5] That same year, a group of LTTE members was busted for automated teller machine and credit card fraud. The scheme yielded $250,000 (more than $306,000 in 2020 dollars) in New York and millions worldwide.[6] These one-year totals demonstrate that the extent to which the LTTE profited from financial crime was significant.

Financial crime does not have geographical bounds limiting organizations to raising funds in areas they control. In fact, there might be a preference by groups to employ these techniques outside their territory because many terrorist organizations exist in developing economies that might not be the best targets for financial crime (particularly online). Instead, terrorist organizations (as well as cells and individuals) tend to conduct their financial crime schemes in countries with well-developed and largely internet-based financial sectors. They exploit the speed of transactions to make money quickly. Operational cells and individuals can also use their target countries (for operations) as a base from which to raise funds. One example of this was the 1993 World Trade Center attack, funded by credit card theft and other low-level financial crimes. A similar pattern of activity funded the December 1999 plot to attack the Los Angeles International Airport, known as the millennium plot. To raise money for this plot, the cell members believed to be associated with al-Qaeda committed check fraud, credit card fraud, and identity fraud.[7]

The internet is increasingly an efficient place for terrorists to conduct illicit transactions, in particular financial crimes. Criminals and terrorists use the internet to identify victims of their planned activity, illicitly obtain credit card information, and deploy malware and ransomware to gain direct access to people's accounts. In 2006, Younis Tsouli, using the moniker Irhabi 007, helped to generate $2.5 million ($3.2 million in 2020 dollars) for jihadi operations through cybercrime.[8] Following his arrest, police found stolen credit card information in his house; the cards had been used to pay US internet providers to host extremist propaganda.[9] Tsouli used a combination of online presence and financial crime to raise money, a trend likely to grow as more financial activity is conducted online.

The internet also facilitates the procurement of goods for terrorist activity.[10] For instance, the terrorists involved in the attacks in France and Belgium in 2015 and 2016 are thought to have purchased their weapons online from sources in the Balkans.[11] More recently, an ISIL facilitator created a scheme to sell fake personal protective equipment during the Covid-19 pandemic in a likely bid to raise money for his own terrorist activities or for ISIL writ large.[12]

Not all financial crime is committed online, and Hizballah has been committing offline financial crimes for decades to raise funds. One of the most well-known schemes was the cigarette scam in North Carolina and Michigan, known as Operation Smokescreen. Michigan had a 75 cent tax per pack on cigarettes, whereas North Carolina charged only 5 cents per pack. Between 1996 and 2000, Mohammed and Chawki Hammoud transported cigarettes from North Carolina for resale in Michigan to take advantage of the tax difference, profiting by approximately $8 to $10 per carton, or $13,000 per van load. Over the course of eighteen months, the brothers generated approximately $7.9 million (approximately $12.2 million in 2020 dollars).[13] This activity was essentially a form of tax arbitrage.

Hizballah is also reported to have used credit card fraud to raise funds. Members of the fraud ring obtained credit cards and made "purchases" from companies that were in fact fronts controlled by Hizballah. The cardholders then declared bankruptcy. The credit card companies and banks paid the front companies for the purchases made, and thus the profits of this scheme were transferred to Hizballah.[14]

Other terrorist organizations have also employed credit card theft to raise funds and to acquire material. In some schemes, terrorists extract cash from the cards and purchase goods, making their use of the funds more difficult to identify. Al-Qaeda and other terrorist groups might have also used the credit cards of their kidnap victims to purchase equipment and material. Former al-Qaeda and Nusra Front hostage Matthew Schrier has stated that during his imprisonment, he was asked to provide his passwords and social security number. He later learned that his credit card was used to purchase two tablet computers subsequently delivered to an address in Westmount, Quebec, to an individual suspected of having traveled overseas to join a terrorist group.[15]

Al-Qaeda has specifically taught operational cells how to raise funds through financial crime instead of relying on the core organization to provide money. Manuals developed by al-Qaeda have been found that provide detailed instructions on how to engage in this type of criminal activity, and the group is reported to have established a special training camp in Afghanistan to teach people how to fraudulently use credit cards.[16] Those efforts paid off: al-Qaeda's Algerian-dominated European network once raised nearly $1 million per month through credit card fraud.[17]

Operational cells and individuals have also used other financial crimes such as student loan fraud and welfare benefit fraud to finance their activities. Sometimes, these benefits were obtained legitimately and then diverted to terrorist activities, whereas in other cases, the loan applications themselves were fraudulent in nature, with the individual never having intended to attend school. In particular, suspected foreign fighters have applied for and fraudulently used student loans to finance their travel overseas.[18]

Other, lower-tech financial crimes have also been used to fund terrorist attacks. In advance of the 7/7 bombing in London, one of the perpetrators, Jermaine Lindsay, made a series of small purchases with checks that bounced in the weeks before July 7, some of which might have been used for preparations or for Lindsay's living expenses while plotting the attack (rather than his earning a legitimate income). Bank investigators looking into the anomalous check activity visited his house the day after the bombing, prior to his name being released in the media as one of the attackers. Lindsay had bought perfume, which he then traded on the internet for material useful in the bomb-making process and for goods and funds to provide for his family.[19]

Another example of financial crime related to organizational terrorist activity was the failed 2005 plot in Australia. The Melbourne cell plotting the attacks paid taxi drivers to provide them with the credit card numbers of unsuspecting passengers.[20] However, this activity might have been unrelated to their planned attacks because some of them also engaged in profit-motivated criminality. Third parties had provided funds to the cell from a car rebirthing racket, meaning that the group essentially had a support network that generated its funds through crime.[21]

Terrorists involved in plots and attacks have used fraudulent student loans to generate money. For instance, the Charlie Hebdo attack in Paris in 2015 was financed in part through fraudulent loans. One of the attackers obtained a €6,000 ($7,200) consumer loan with forged documents. The Manchester bomber also used student loans and benefits to finance his terrorist plot.[22] He was given at least £7,000 ($9,800) from a taxpayer-funded student loan company for a business administration program he started in 2015, funds he might have used to travel to Libya and buy materials for his bomb.[23] In some of these examples, the financial crime might have been used to fund the attack, or it might have been part of preexisting criminal activity. For terrorists who raise funds through criminal activity, preexisting criminal behavior is common, and there is rarely a clear delineation between their criminal and terrorist activity.

Another form of financial crime often undertaken by operational cells involves welfare benefit abuse, misuse, or fraud. In 2015 and 2016, the Paris and Brussels terrorists used welfare fraud in the United Kingdom to finance their attacks. Mohamed Abrini, believed to have been involved in the planning and execution of the attacks, was given £3,000 ($4,200) by two men in Birmingham, having been sent by Abdelhamid Abaaoud (the presumed leader of the Paris attack) to collect the money just months prior. The funds were withdrawn from the account of Anouar Haddouchi, who had left the United Kingdom to join ISIL but was still receiving benefits.[24] These financial crimes were but one element of their operational financing. The perpetrators also financed their activity through drug trafficking and theft as well as from their income and other benefits. Financial support from ISIL might have also played a role.

Supporters of ISIL have also used financial crime to generate funds (in the form of donations), and some have combined multiple methods to significant effect. In December 2017, Zoobia Shahnaz, a twenty-seven-year-old New Yorker, was arrested for raising more than $85,000 ($89,000 in 2020 dollars) to send to ISIL.[25] She used false information to acquire loans and multiple credit cards to raise the funds. She then purchased Bitcoin and other digital currencies and sent the funds through shell companies in Pakistan, China, and Turkey to ISIL.[26] The case of Shahnaz is exceptional, particularly in the ISIL-support scene in the United States, for its complexity.[27] Ironically, that complexity might have led to its detection.

Sometimes, scholars and analysts assert that terrorists launder money to raise funds. Certainly, terrorist groups, cells, and individuals periodically use this technique (primarily to obscure the source or destination of funds), but it is rare. In some cases, they might raise money this way if an individual terrorist has the skills to launder money for other groups and can charge a fee for services rendered, usually a cut of the laundered funds. In other cases, money laundering might generate funds as a by-product of the act itself, such as funds raised through a legitimate venture serving as a front for an organization, a place in which to deposit significant sums of cash, or other investments.[28] Some of the techniques involved in money laundering, such as over- or underinvoicing for goods or services, might generate funds in and of themselves. For instance, purchasing, shipping, and invoicing for goods might have at their root the purpose of moving money with a plausible excuse through overinvoicing goods, but those goods can then be resold in other jurisdictions, often generating a profit for the money launderers. Other techniques that can generate revenue include "coloring up," or lending low-denomination cash to individuals to use for gambling. The individuals then pay a portion of their profits (or interest on the loan), and the money launderers benefit from receiving either higher-denomination bills or a wire transfer or check for the money loaned. These are just examples of money laundering techniques used to generate proceeds, although this remains a rare fund-raising technique for terrorist actors.

Other financial crimes are common ways terrorist cells and individuals fund their operational activities. At least 16 percent of the terrorist plots and attacks I studied have been funded using financial crime. In coming years, plots and attacks and plots are increasingly likely to be financed through criminal activity and, in particular, through online financial crime. At the organizational level, financial crimes are a less popular way to fund terrorist activities. Only 13 percent of terrorist groups I studied used this type of criminal activity to raise funds. However, the terrorist organizations that do use financial crimes to generate money span the ideological spectrum. Generally speaking, terrorists look for crime with low barriers to entry, such as schemes that can easily be implemented by cells or individual members.[29] Financial crimes fit that description, particularly low-level scams (including student loan or welfare benefit fraud). The types of financial crime terrorist groups use to raise money evolve over time and have no limit of creativity. Terrorist groups, cells, and individuals take advantage of existing access to criminal markets or knowledge of criminal activities and adopt these techniques for their own purposes to raise money. However, financial crimes are not without their costs in terms of operational security: they alert law enforcement to terrorist activity because banks and other financial institutions have fraud-detection tools that far outstrip terrorists' abilities.

Theft and Resource Exploitation

Terrorist groups, cells, and individuals all engage in various types of opportunistic theft to raise money. Bank robberies (and other violent tactics), theft of high-value goods, petty theft, and resource exploitation are all ways terrorists steal resources to fund their plots and attacks. How terrorists accomplish this depends entirely on the places in which they operate as well as the operational activities they intend to undertake. Over time, terrorists who control territory tend to move away from theft (particularly robbery) as a fund-raising tactic. For some terrorists, stealing is prohibited by their ideology or their interpretation of religious or political texts, so they limit this activity to when it is absolutely necessary, such as in setting up their terrorist organization. For others, stealing from the population in their area of control would mean a decrease in popular support, often another important source of funds. Terrorist organizations might move away from theft at different points in their existence, but for cells and individuals intent on undertaking terrorist activity, this tactic remains a viable means of generating funds.

Bank Robberies

Bank robberies are critical for terrorist organizations and operational cells because they provide a onetime influx that can augment their funds. Bank robberies generate significant windfalls for terrorist groups and in some cases provide important seed or startup money.

The terrorist practice of robbing banks dates back at least to Russia in 1879.[30] This fund-raising tactic was also popular in the 1960s, 1970s, and 1980s, when a variety of terrorist groups across the ideological spectrum used it. Between 1966 and 1977, Euskadi Ta Askatasuna (ETA [Basque Homeland and Liberty]) raised more than $1 million ($6.6 million in 2020 dollars) from bank robberies; in 1978, the group conducted more than fifty robberies, netting $4 million ($15.7 million in 2020 dollars).[31] In the 1970s, the German Red Army Faction committed a number of bank robberies, netting more than a million deutsche marks ($275,000), and the Palestinian Liberation Organization (PLO) targeted British banks in Beirut.[32] In a similar vein, the Weather Underground obtained funds by attacking a Brinks armored vehicle in 1981.[33] In 1985, a right-wing group stole $3.6 million ($8.6 million in 2020 dollars) from another Brinks armored vehicle in California.[34] Bank robbery was the sole financing means of the November 17 organization.[35]

PIRA also raised funds through bank robberies.[36] Over time, the group moved away from armed robberies because of negative publicity and a decrease in public support for the robberies, particularly following a few poorly executed ones that resulted in civilian casualties and police murders. Other groups operating in Northern Ireland also used armed robbery as a method of fund-raising but over time moved away from banks and post offices toward cash-in-transit and goods-in-transit robberies.[37]

In more recent years, ISIL's bank robberies in Iraq and the millions of dollars it obtained in the process have garnered significant media attention. However, characterizing ISIL's actions as bank robberies might not be entirely accurate. As Clarke and Williams note, ISIL asserted control over the banks and everything in them rather than merely robbing them.[38] Certainly, the group used force to take over the territory in which the banks existed, but after it accomplished this feat, the threat of force might not have been necessary in the context of taking over the banks' resources (but was likely implied). These acquisitions of banks provided the group significant funds, but they were onetime influxes of cash and paled in comparison with the group's other ongoing sources of funds.

At various points in the startup phase, ISIL and its affiliates have used bank robberies to finance their operational activities. ISIL in Libya robbed banks or took control of them, essentially controlling the resources and certainly robbing the citizens of their funds. Press reports indicate that ISIL closed all the banks in Sirte and demanded they convert to Islamic banking before reopening.[39] ISIL supporters in the Philippines overran a number of banks during the siege of Marawi, including the city's three main banks, and is estimated to have stolen about $38.3 million pesos (roughly $800,000 in 2020 dollars).[40] In October 2017, ISIL affiliates in the Sinai robbed a bank in al Arish and are believed to have obtained approximately $1 million ($1.05 million in 2020 dollars).[41] ISIL in Somalia has also resorted to bank robberies (among other criminal activities) to fund its operations.[42]

In recent years, al-Qaeda and affiliated groups have also robbed banks to finance their activities. In December 2017, al-Qaeda in the Arabian Peninsula attempted (but failed) to rob a private bank in Mukalla.[43] Indeed, in the early 2000s, Jemaah Islamiyah used Poso, Indonesia, as a valuable staging ground for its economic activity. Between 2003 and 2006, Jemaah Islamiyah's wing Tanah Runtuh carried out religiously sanctioned robberies when the group was short on funds.[44]

Operational activity might also be supported through bank robberies; in Europe, a Dutch returnee from Syria was arrested while in possession of firearms. He was planning to rob a bank to fund an act of terrorism.[45] In Spain and Switzerland, terrorists inspired by al-Qaeda committed robberies to finance armed attacks and terrorist training abroad. They also used the theft and sale of designer watches, gold bracelets, and emerald necklaces to generate funds, which in turn were used to fund assassinations in Algeria and Mauritania.[46] In Jordan, al-Qaeda operatives sustained themselves for the millennium attacks through bank robberies, burglaries, and forged checks.[47] In Indonesia, one of the terrorists involved in the 2002 Jemaah Islamiyah attack in Bali was financed by a bank robbery.[48] That attack was believed to have been funded largely through petty crime, trade in natural resources, and robbery of a gold store. Samudra, one of the key figures in the attack, robbed Elite Gold, stealing about $2,000.[49] This provides an example of theft of high-value goods, looting, and petty theft to fund operational activities. These criminal activities are largely opportunistic, provide onetime influxes of funds, and risk the possibility of the terrorists being caught by law enforcement prior to engaging in their plots.

Petty theft can be used to finance terrorist plots or to serve as a means for terrorist cells or individuals to obtain the material for their attacks. Members of an Australian plot were caught shoplifting batteries, maps, and electronic timers. Through the execution of search warrants, investigators also found stolen railway detonators.[50] Members of the Toronto 18 plot also stole some of the equipment for their training camps.[51] This type of shoplifting is rare, likely because many of these items are inexpensive, so the cost-benefit analysis of whether to steal them and risk getting caught versus raising the funds to purchase the goods generally ends in favor of using the money. These examples illustrate that terrorist actors might look for onetime windfalls to fund their plots, generate the seed money for the plot, and increase their capabilities by removing the financial constraints on their planning.

At least 33 percent of the terrorist organizations I studied use theft to raise money for their activities, and many of them seek high-value targets to infuse their organizations with a significant amount of cash from a single criminal act. However, to maximize benefit from these crimes, terrorist organizations generally need to be in a position of significant territorial control or influence and retreat to a safe haven to avoid arrest. A few plots and attacks have been funded (in part) from bank robberies and other types of theft, but these numbers remain low at less than 9 percent of those I studied.

Most terrorist organizations that have used bank robberies to finance their activities have done so early in their existence and have used these funds as seed money. Terrorist groups have demonstrated a decided preference for rent-seeking crimes such as extortion and taxation, possibly because, like all large organizations, they seek fiscal stability to effectively manage their organization and operations. Bank robberies, although lucrative, are difficult to execute, particularly in areas where a terrorist organization is not able to operate freely. Certainly, the success of bank robberies, along with their scope and scale, has to do with whether the perpetrators can expect a swift response from law enforcement.

Terrorist cells and individuals face inherent limitations on their ability to rob banks to raise funds. To successfully execute a bank robbery, they likely require prior criminal experience, preferably in a similar operating environment. Bank robberies might not appeal to terrorist cells and individuals because they could attract law enforcement scrutiny, are high risk (though high reward), and might not be worth the trouble given the relatively low cost of financing attacks that can garner significant media attention in the twenty-first century. For cells and individuals, the cost-benefit analysis might lead them to undertake other forms of fund-raising that are less risky and less likely to expose them to law enforcement scrutiny. Despite these barriers, bank robberies are likely to remain one source of funds for terrorist groups, particularly when they are able to control territory.

Exploitation of Antiquities, Natural Resources, and High-Value Goods

Theoretically, terrorist organizations, cells, and individuals steal and exploit any goods and resources they can access to raise funds. However, in practice, whether they enjoy territorial control affects if this occurs. If they control territory, terrorist groups (or, in rare cases, cells) impose taxes on local people; extort goods, services, and funds from them (covered in Chapter 4); and develop or co-opt resource extraction services. When they do not have complete control of territory, terrorist groups, cells, and individuals can still steal and resell a variety of goods, including natural resources or antiquities.

One of the most notable examples of profiting from stolen goods is the theft and sale of antiquities, an activity for which ISIL is well known. However, it was not the first terrorist group to engage in this activity. In 1999, Mohammed Atta, one of the key organizers behind the 9/11 attacks, attempted to raise money by selling stolen antiquities from Afghanistan.[52] Antiquities have also been exploited to raise money for extremist groups in Iraq, Libya, Syria, and Yemen. The local populations can play a role in this trade by removing the antiquities and bringing them to collectors. Collectors regroup them and pay fees to terrorist groups to sell the products outside of the region.[53]

Although ISIL has been reported as a facilitator and profiteer from this activity, the group was more involved in antiquities exploitation than many observers initially believed. The group, over time, became involved in the excavation of the antiquities as well as the smuggling and sale of the items. The group might have also been involved in the direct movement of the goods into Dubai, Jordan, Lebanon, and Turkey.[54] Even as ISIL was fighting to maintain control of territory, it expended resources excavating antiquities and continued to market them in a professional manner.[55] Some analysts have gone as far as to claim that antiquities were ISIL's second largest source of funds.[56] However, as with many assertions about terrorist group funding sources, supporting data are scarce. Some estimates appear to be based on the final price paid for antiquities in European and North American markets; however, this is far higher than the price ISIL would have obtained, given the many layers of sellers between the terrorist group and the ultimate purchaser.[57]

The theft of antiquities (and the terrorist taxation of this activity) demonstrates the importance of geography in raising funds. Only a group operating in specific parts of the world can do it, and it is not available to every terrorist group, cell, or individual. Geography and connections with existing smuggling networks and criminal entities play significant roles in terrorists' ability to raise funds in this manner.

As with antiquities, theft of high-value goods and other resources is entirely dependent on the area in which a group, cell, or individual operates. Sometimes, those high-value goods are in extractive sectors such as mining and logging but can also be in hunting or poaching. The Moro Islamic Liberation Front (MILF) is estimated to have earned $74,000 per month from illegal logging.[58] In Afghanistan, the forests of Kunar Province have provided a source of funds for both the Taliban and ISIL Khorasan Province. Although the exportation of wood from the provinces was banned in 2016 because of deforestation and desertification, both groups have illegally logged the forests. Each tree is estimated to generate about $1,125, with between 20,000 and 30,000 trees logged each year. This could generate as much as $33.8 million for the terrorist organizations each year, although costs (such as bribery and transport) reduce the profits of this endeavor.[59]

Wildlife poaching has also been used, albeit to a lesser extent, by terrorist organizations. This method of raising funds is highly geographically specific. A terrorist group has to control or influence a significant territory or cooperate with existing criminal networks to exploit this resource. Insurgent groups such as the Lord's Resistance Army raised funds by poaching elephants in the Democratic Republic of Congo, South Sudan, and Uganda, and the Janjaweed militia in South Sudan has been accused of poaching elephants in Cameroon, Chad, and the Central African Republic.[60] The Taliban might have also poached wildlife to raise funds. The group is reported to have facilitated the hunting of houbara buzzards, snow leopards, and falcons for wealthy Saudis and Emiratis.[61] Some analysts also suggest that Al-Shabaab has benefited from the illicit ivory trade and to a lesser extent the trafficking in exotic wildlife.[62] One example suggests that an Al-Shabaab broker exported ivory at $200 per kilo; however, whether the broker actually conducted this activity on behalf of Al-Shabaab is an open question.[63] Some researchers believe the group simply taxes the activity and is not directly involved in it.[64]

Although much has been made of the potential link between gold, precious metals and stones, and terrorist financing, these assessments might be overblown. The Financial Action Task Force (FATF) and the Financial Transactions and Reports Analysis Centre of Canada (FINTRAC) have both identified a number of vulnerabilities in the trade of these goods for money laundering, but evidence of their use to finance terrorism is more limited.[65] For the most part, terrorist actors use high-value goods such as gold and precious metals to move value across borders (see Chapter 8 for more details) or within their territory, rather than using them as a means to generate funds. Certainly, when they come across these goods, they sell them for profit, but their exploitation of this sector is more limited.

The terrain in which a terrorist group operates has a significant impact on what they steal or exploit. Theft by terrorist groups, individuals, and cells depends on what there is of value in the area. If electronics are plentiful and valued, then they will steal and sell electronics. If cattle are valued in the area, then they will steal cattle, as Boko Haram has done in Nigeria. The group is reported to have stolen more than $6 million worth of livestock in Nigeria since 2013, which amounts to 17,000 herds of cattle as well as thousands of sheep and goats.[66] Other types of criminal economic activity within the terrain will also be exploited by the terrorist organization, and they will steal and sell anything of significant value that has the potential for fund-raising activities. This can include oil, other natural resources, high-value goods from the individuals in the area, and so forth. Widescale theft is often the purview of terrorists, but cells that have significant links to criminal organizations can also make use of it to raise money.

There is significant overlap between these natural resource thefts and the criminal business models explored in Chapter 4. In many cases, exploitation of natural resources requires something of a criminal business model, along with smuggling networks, to gain maximum benefit. Although terrorist groups can partner with criminal entities to smuggle goods, or sell their resources to criminal groups, there is far more profit in them engaging in this activity themselves and reducing the number of individuals in the chain taking a cut of the profits.

As with many other types of fund-raising, terrorist groups', cells', and individuals' ability to raise funds through theft is constrained by their geographical operating environment, their criminal skills, and their ability to control or influence territory. For organizations, theft requires resources to be present in their area of influence, but terrorist groups are adept at figuring out ways to steal whatever is of value in those areas. Cells and individuals tend to focus on higher-value, smaller goods that can be sold relatively easily to generate swift profits for their activities.

Conclusion

In terms of criminal activity that does not rise to the level of criminal business models, there are key differences between organizational and operational funding. Although both terrorist organizations and operational actors (cells and individuals) use financial crimes to fund their activities, kidnapping for ransom is exclusively the purview of terrorist organizations. Theft is also primarily done by terrorist groups, although some operational actors have engaged in this activity as well. Resource exploitation can also be part of a criminal business model, although it is more often an organizational source of funds than an operational one. These main differences are illustrated in Figures 5.1 and 5.2.

The scope and scale of criminal activities undertaken by terrorist actors depends largely on whether they are able to control territory. If they are,

Figure 5.1 Organizational Funding Through Crime

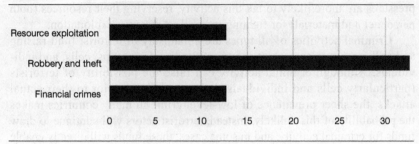

Figure 5.2 Operational Funding Through Crime

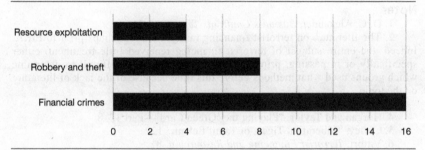

then their activities are much more brazen, large scale, and lucrative. If they do not control territory, then their activities are generally smaller in scale, less lucrative, and more likely to expose them to law enforcement and security service scrutiny.

For criminal activities such as financial crimes that increasingly take place online, territorial control is largely irrelevant. Certainly, providing safe haven to individuals undertaking this activity can be useful if it is done on a broad scale, but it has primarily been undertaken by individual terrorist supporters. Over time, more financial crime is likely to migrate online and might become a more prominent method of fund-raising for terrorist organizations, cells, and individuals alike.

Terrain is the most prominent determinant of whether terrorists engage in theft and resource exploitation, particularly at the group level. Organizationally, when terrorists have access to these types of high-value resources, they are likely to at least tax them and might also become involved in their direct exploitation. Over time, groups can become more directly involved in direct exploitation, particularly if they gain more territory and better access to smuggling and international markets. Groups facing strong counterterrorism pressures are more likely to tax this activity, reserving their resources (both personnel and material) for fighting rather than resource exploitation.

Criminal activities of all types are a mainstay of terrorist fund-raising and will remain an important source of funding for groups, cells, and individuals. Although criminal activity can raise the possibility of terrorists (particularly cells and individuals) being interdicted prior to their actual attacks, the sheer prevalence of low-level crime in many countries makes the probability of this unlikely. Instead, terrorist actors will continue to draw funds for criminal activity, and in some cases, these funds will directly enable their attacks. For terrorist groups, criminal activity will be used wherever possible and practicable.

Notes

1. D. C. Alexander, *Business Confronts Terrorism*, 70.
2. The literature on terrorist financing rarely includes groups prior to PIRA. Indeed, the entire subject of terrorist financing received little treatment, either specifically or in passing, prior to the 1980s–1990s. It is difficult to determine which groups used what methods before this time because of the lack of literature on the topic.
3. Clarke, *Terrorism, Inc.*, 34.
4. Horgan and Taylor, "Playing the 'Green Card'—Part 1," 8.
5. Corley, "Liberation Tigers of Tamil Eelam," 127.
6. Vittori, *Terrorist Financing and Resourcing*, 81.
7. Clarke, *Terrorism, Inc.*, 136.
8. Thachuk, "Gangsterization of Terrorism," 21.
9. Katz and Kern, "Terrorist 007, Exposed."
10. Davis, "How Terrorists Use the Internet."
11. Prothero, "Inside the World of ISIS."
12. US Department of Justice, "Global Disruption of Three."
13. Vittori, *Terrorist Financing and Resourcing*, 33.
14. Clarke, *Terrorism, Inc.*, 73.
15. Desmarais, Lavigne, and Bastien, "Identities of 2 Quebec Men."
16. K. McGrath, *Confronting Al Qaeda*, 75.
17. Ibid.
18. Willgress, "Teenager Who Spent Student Loan."
19. House of Commons, "Report of the Official Account of the Bombings," 14–15, 18, 23, 25.
20. Australian Financial Intelligence Unit (AUSTRAC), "Terrorism Financing in Australia 2014."
21. In a car rebirthing racket, a stolen car has some or all of its parts replaced with parts from other (often stolen) vehicles and is resold for a profit. The VIN from the car is often replaced as well, masking the origins of the car.
22. Willgress, "Teenager Who Spent Student Loan."
23. Financial Action Task Force, *Emerging Terrorist Financing Risks*, 11.
24. Evans and Finnigan, "British Benefits Payments Used."
25. Cuen, "New York Woman Charged with Laundering Bitcoin."

26. H. Alexander, "New York Woman Charged with Sending $85,000."

27. Vidino, Lewis, and Mines, "Dollars for Daesh."

28. Clarke, *Terrorism, Inc.*, 28.

29. Ibid., 135.

30. Shelley, *Dirty Entanglements*, 112.

31. Horgan and Taylor, "Playing the 'Green Card'—Part 1," 10.

32. Vittori, *Terrorist Financing and Resourcing*, 35, 55.

33. Shelley, *Dirty Entanglements*, 109.

34. Vittori, *Terrorist Financing and Resourcing*, 55.

35. Bantekas, "International Law of Terrorist Financing," 319.

36. Horgan and Taylor, "Playing the 'Green Card'—Part 1," 11.

37. Evans, "Organised Crime and Terrorism Financing," 4.

38. Clarke and Williams, "Da'esh in Iraq and Syria," 31.

39. UN Security Council, "Monitoring Team Report," November 19, 2015, 18.

40. UN Security Council, "Twentieth Report," 17; Office of the Lead Inspector General "Operation Inherent Resolve," 101.

41. Magdy and Sweilam, "Militants Rob Bank."

42. UN Security Council, "Twenty-Second Report."

43. Ibid. See also Allard, "Exclusive: Looted Cash, Gold."

44. Hwang, "Dakwah Before Jihad," 26–28.

45. Financial Action Task Force, *Emerging Terrorist Financing Risks*, 15.

46. Clarke, *Terrorism, Inc.*, 139.

47. K. McGrath, *Confronting Al Qaeda*, 75.

48. Financial Action Task Force, *Emerging Terrorist Financing Risks*, 15.

49. Shelley, *Dirty Entanglements*, 35.

50. Australian Financial Intelligence Unit, "Terrorism Financing in Australia 2014."

51. Davis, "Financing the Toronto 18."

52. Shelley, *Dirty Entanglements*, 31.

53. UN Security Council, "Twenty-Second Report."

54. Clarke and Williams, "Da'esh in Iraq and Syria," 34–35.

55. UN Security Council, "Monitoring Team Report," January 13, 2017, 10.

56. Humud, Rosen, and Pirog, "Islamic State Financing and U.S. Policy Approaches," 6–7.

57. *France24*. "Syria: On the Trail of Looted Antiquities."

58. Germann et al., "Terrorist Financing in the Philippines," 151.

59. Glinski, "Afghanistan Forests Are Turning a Profit."

60. Felbab-Brown, "Making a Killing."

61. Ibid.

62. Foundation for Defense of Democracies, *Al-Shabaab*.

63. Keatinge, "Role of Finance in Defeating al-Shabaab," 22.

64. Liang, "Criminal-Jihadist," 6.

65. Financial Action Task Force, *Money Laundering/Terrorist Financing Risks*; Financial Transactions and Reports Analysis Centre of Canada (FINTRAC), "Operational Brief."

66. Mbodiam, "Cameroon."

PART 2

Using Money

6

Deploying Funds

How terrorist groups, cells, and individuals use funds is often given short shrift in the literature on terrorist financing, in part because it is relatively obvious: they use money to conduct terrorist attacks. However, more nuance around the specifics of how terrorists use funds can help illuminate the full scope of their procurement of goods and materials for their activities as well as the relatively more quotidian needs of a terrorist group, all of which are important for understanding the true cost and techniques of terrorism. This accounting can help balance the conversation around the wealth of terrorist organizations by illustrating that although many terrorists (particularly organizations) generate significant revenue, they also have substantial costs, and even low-cost terrorist attacks might require more financial resources than is evident at first glance.

Terrorist organizations, cells, and individuals all need food and shelter; money to pay for travel (either locally or internationally), communications, and internet access; and a host of other basic human necessities. Where they differ from the norm, however, is in their desire for weapons, operational security measures, and funds to engage in a host of terrorist activities. Identifying all of these uses of terrorist funds can help shed light on differences between organizational and operational financial needs; although there are many aspects that overlap, differences can help identify various types of terrorist activity as well as opportunities for detection and disruption.

Organizational Use of Funds

Terrorist uses of funds have been fairly well articulated in prior analysis of their financing, even if this is a less discussed and analyzed component compared to fund-raising and the movement of money. For instance, Ehrenfeld notes that terrorist networks need money to spread their ideology, recruit members, and hold training camps. They also pay for housing and food, equipment, explosives, conventional and unconventional weapons, forged identity and travel documents, intelligence gathering, communications with organizational components, bribery, and day-to-day maintenance.[1] Terrorists' organizational use of funds can be broken down into a handful of categories that encompass a variety of activities:

- terrorist attacks, including weapons, components, and training
- terrorist group patronage
- propaganda and recruitment
- social services, sustenance, salaries, and support
- intelligence gathering and operational security
- corruption and political lobbying

Terrorists' operational activity also falls into many of these categories and of course differs in scope and scale from their organizational use of funds.

Terrorist Attacks, Weapons, Components, and Training

Terrorist organizations use a significant amount of money to equip and train their fighting forces, particularly if they are maintaining insurgent forces and territory, because they require continual access to weapons, ammunition, and other war-fighting equipment. Gaining and maintaining territory are some of their largest organizational uses of funds. Although most terrorist organizations use their funds operationally for attacks, some also use their resources to expand their territory and gain further control, an issue widely demonstrated by ISIL and Al-Shabaab. Al-Qaeda in the Arabian Peninsula, which received funds for the European hostages it kidnapped, used those funds to finance its $20 million campaign to seize territory in Yemen between 2011 and 2012.[2] The costs of obtaining, maintaining, and securing territory are significant. They include weapons and ammunition, expert trainers for the fighting force, and logistics for fighting, and these costs are also often compounded by inflationary pressures in war zones.[3]

Weapons might be one of the largest expenses terrorist organizations incur. Although weapons, including assault rifles, are thought to be relatively plentiful, terrorists still need to acquire them and keep them in working order as well as obtain ammunition for them. Some terrorists, particularly ones that hold territory, also manufacture their own weapons and components.[4] Ensuring that all their weapons remain operational and that every fighter has access to one can be a significant expense. The Provisional Irish Republican Army (PIRA) illustrated this through how it spent money on weapons and materials for homemade munitions and maintained significant caches of arms and bomb-making factories.[5] To grow the organization, PIRA relied on the gray and dark economy and used the money it raised to purchase sophisticated weaponry as well as on operations and logistics.[6] The Taliban also uses the money it raises to buy weapons, such as AK-47 assault rifles, BM-1 field rockets, RPG-7 rocket launchers, and machine guns, as well as to pay for suicide bombers and to build improvised explosive devices.[7] In some cases, terrorist groups get a break on their equipment costs thanks to state sponsors of terrorism and might receive in-kind donations from their sponsors. For instance, Libyan leader Muammar Qaddafi provided a significant number of weapons to PIRA, which meant that the group could devote less of its budget to acquiring weapons.[8] The cost of weapons (such as AK-47s) depends on where the terrorist group operates, whether it has access to state sponsors (who might provide a deal on the weapons), and the number of weapons it needs to buy. For the most part, weapons are a terrorist organization's most significant line item.

Terrorist groups often expect their cells and operatives to finance their own attacks, but in other instances, the terrorist group provides at least some of the money to get the plot off the ground or increase the scale and expected impact of the attack. Hizballah generally provides funds for its cells' and individuals' terrorist operations, and in recent years, the organization has allocated as much as $100,000 for an operation.[9] Al-Qaeda has also provided funds to cells and individuals to perpetrate attacks, and in 2002, the main perpetrator of the Djerba, Tunisia, synagogue bombing was given $20,000 ($28,504 in 2020 dollars) to fund a truck bomb attack that killed twenty-one people.[10] In the attack, the perpetrator welded a gas tank onto the back of the vehicle and filled it with either propane or butane. He also traveled to Pakistan to attend a terrorist training camp.[11]

ISIL has also used some of its considerable operational wealth to finance attacks by cells and individuals. On January 14, 2016, in Jakarta, Indonesia, terrorists were responsible for multiple explosions and shootings near the Sarinah shopping mall. Eight people (including the four attackers) were killed, and twenty-three other people were injured. According to the Jakarta police, Bahrun Naim, an ISIL-linked Indonesian extremist, was behind the attack.[12] It was later determined that funds for this attack were transferred from Syria through an international money remitter.[13] This was not an isolated case of ISIL funding terrorist operations. Abdelhamid Abbaoud, an organizer of the ISIL attacks in France and Belgium in November 2015 and March 2016, had contact with ISIL members in Libya relating to financing and travel, potentially indicating that he received some financial support for these attacks.[14] ISIL in Libya also provided financial and logistical support to other cells, such as those who carried out the attacks in Tunisia in 2015 and 2016.[15]

Other terrorist groups also fund operational activity directly. The October 2009 Jyllands-Posten plot, in which two individuals planned to retaliate for the printing of cartoons of the Prophet Mohammed in 2005, was financed in part by the Lashkar-e-Taiba (LeT).[16] The main perpetrator (Headley) met with a mid-level LeT commander in Pakistan and received €3,000 (roughly $3,600) to travel to Denmark and conduct surveillance on his target.[17] Following the Mumbai attacks of November 2008, the LeT put Headley's attack on hold, likely because of increased counterterrorism pressures. Headley subsequently reached out to another group, Harkat ul-Jihad al-Islami (HUJI), to sponsor the plot. The group gave him $1,500 and told him to travel to Europe, produce more surveillance videos, and meet with contacts about weapons. These contacts did not want to participate in Headley's plot or supply the weapons, but they did offer him $15,000.[18] The plot was ultimately disrupted, and Headley was imprisoned in the United States. The majority of funds were used by Headley for his surveillance and planning trips but also demonstrate that he would have had access to ample funds to perpetrate the attack had the planning progressed. The LeT plot was not the only one to incur travel expenses—Chechen groups spent a considerable amount of money on weapons as well as the cross-border smuggling of fighters in addition to training and general sustenance.[19]

Sometimes, terrorist organizations use their funds to support other terrorist organizations (as terrorist patrons) or to support would-be terrorists not aligned with their group whose activities support their broader objectives. For instance, individuals associated with ISIL supported al-Qaeda operatives in planning a potential attack in Kenya in 2015.[20] The LeT supported Jaish-e-Mohammed (JeM) in its attack on India's parliament in December 2001, and the LeT has also supported Indian and Western jihadist organizations by providing logistical and financial support, for example to Richard Reid, who attempted to detonate explosives hidden in a shoe.[21]

Most terrorist organizations and cells train their members in basic weapons handling, combat, operational security, and bomb-making as well as other skills. Training provides terrorists with a sense of camaraderie and morale along with real skills that make their attacks more deadly. Training can be a significant expense for terrorist organizations, as the Liberation Tigers of Tamil Eelam (LTTE) demonstrated. By the mid-1980s, more than 20,000 fighters had been trained, with the average training lasting about four months.[22] During their training, the LTTE likely provided its recruits room and board and might have even provided them a stipend. This means that for each individual the group trained, even modest expenses amounted to a significant amount of funds spent in this early phase of the conflict.[23]

Professionally run training camps can be costly; terrorist organizations use them to train their own fighters but might also use them to train the fighters of other terrorist organizations, regardless of whether they have a strategic alliance. One group that has spent a significant amount of money on training is Hizballah, which held training camps in the Bekaa Valley.[24] However, training camps can also be a source of funds if the group charges fees to attend, either to their own recruits or to operatives from other organizations.

Many operational cells and individuals also undertake training activities at specified camps, although this varies significantly in levels of sophistication. Mohammed Merah, the perpetrator of the 2012 shootings in France, is an example of an individual who undertook terrorist training before engaging in activity elsewhere. In 2011, he traveled from France to Pakistan to attend a training camp held by the Tehrik-i-Taliban Pakistan (TTP) and al-Qaeda. To pay for his trip, he sold his car for €4,400 (about $5,300) and also raised money by acting as a drug courier between France and Spain and engaging in other petty criminal activity.[25] Jemaah Islamiyah has also sent individuals to Syria to train, likely in an effort to reconstitute its terrorist organization.[26] The Toronto 18 terrorist plot in Canada also involved several training camps, although these were relatively simple affairs that might not have contributed significantly to the group's operational capability.[27]

All terrorist organizations have expenses relating to weapons, components, and training, and the same can be said for many cells and individuals, although documented evidence of this use of funds occurs far less than 100 percent of the time. The actual costs associated with each terrorist group depend on the group's particular circumstances, including whether it has access to low-cost weaponry, the cost of improvised explosive device material in its region, and a variety of other factors. Determining what these costs are can affect assessments of how much money a terrorist group has at its disposal for operational activities, including for gaining and maintaining territory.

Terrorist Group Patronage

As I discussed in Chapter 2, some terrorist organizations provide funds to other groups to help them get established, spread their brand, and conduct operations. These funds are often significant for the receiving organization and for the donating group. For the patrons, donating money to other terrorist groups is often a choice to expand their political and geographical influence. Many groups have engaged in this activity, such as al-Qaeda, ISIL, al-Qaeda in Iraq, al-Qaeda in the Islamic Maghreb (AQIM), Hizballah, and some of ISIL's affiliates. These donations are not always about establishing organizational relationships between terrorist groups and funding specific activities; they are also about expanding the brand and can serve as an insurance policy for the umbrella movement to create alternative safe havens in response to counterterrorism pressures.

Al-Qaeda is known to have used some of its funds to sponsor other terrorist organizations and cells. According to Vittori, al-Qaeda was the first group to provide seed money to terrorist cells to establish an organizational structure and conduct attacks that would enhance its profile internationally.[28] ISIL has also provided startup capital to some of its affiliates, likely learning from al-Qaeda's success in funding offshoot groups. ISIL has moved funds to these affiliates using cash couriers, alternative remittance systems, and banking channels.[29] ISIL has likely spent significant sums in helping its provinces establish themselves. During one period, up to $100,000 per month is estimated to have been transferred from the group in Iraq and Syria to its affiliate in Afghanistan despite a substantial decline in ISIL's income.[30] Indeed, financing the establishment of ISIL in Afghanistan was likely an insurance policy for the main organization; knowing that the international military intervention against ISIL was closing in on its territory, the group sought to establish a safe haven and provide its fighters and leaders a place to escape.

Terrorist patronage is often seen as a matter of the original umbrella organization providing funds to smaller startup organizations. But in some cases, this relationship can shift as the fortunes of those groups change relative to each other. In 2006 and 2007, al-Qaeda in Iraq was financially self-sufficient, so it sent funds to the al-Qaeda leadership in Pakistan.[31] In these cases, the changing funding patterns can also illustrate a shift in the financial center of gravity for a terrorist movement; this is often in response to counterterrorism and sometimes counterterrorist financing pressures.

At least 13 percent of terrorist organizations I studied have provided funds to others, allowing the patron to spread its own particular ideology, support related groups and operations, and generally increase its brand recognition. Providing funds to other groups is an insurance policy for terrorist organizations, in that the brand and objectives can live on if the patron group is defeated and provide safe haven for the leadership if positive relations are established and maintained. The actual cost of this activity for terrorist groups might be as low as several thousand dollars or as high as into the millions. How much the group dedicates to patronizing other organizations depends on its budget as well as its future prospects and its relationship with the client group.

Propaganda and Recruitment

Costs of propaganda and recruitment add up. Although initial outlays of funds in this area tend to be modest, they increase over time and can become significant as the need for operational security increases. Historically, propaganda and recruitment costs have involved printed materials or physical copies of lectures, texts, and so forth, but today these costs are primarily for website hosting and production value for videos. For example, PIRA used some of its funds to pay for its newspaper, which it used to disseminate its propaganda. The newspaper also provided an outlet for Sinn

Fein and to explain the group's overall strategy.[32] But over time, a substantial amount of money raised in the United States for PIRA never made it to Northern Ireland. Instead, the funds were used to pay the salaries of people in the United States involved in the fund-raising and propaganda effort.[33] The LTTE also used funds it raised for media and public relations. In Toronto, the group operated four twenty-four-hour radio stations and ten weekly newspapers as well as Tamil-language television programs.[34] Hizballah has also spent significant sums in support of the al-Manar TV network.[35] The Taliban uses money to pay for propaganda that it disseminates via the radio, internet, DVDs, and magazines.[36] Radio and television stations have significant costs that terrorist organizations have to devote funds to, and relatively few groups do this.

Today, many of the costs associated with propaganda and recruitment of terrorist members have gone down considerably thanks to the internet. At the same time, many terrorist groups must now pay for propaganda with higher production value or recruit or train members within their ranks to produce it. Terrorist organizations have also had to devote funds to their social media presence and their online footprint. Although many individuals assume that terrorist propaganda in the age of social media is free, that is not necessarily the case. ISIL had to pay for website-hosting services, something the group was reported to have done through Bitcoin.[37] Terrorist groups also turn to crime to generate funds for these services: in 2006, Younis Tsouli used stolen credit cards to pay US internet providers to host extremist propaganda.[38] Contemporary terrorist groups pay dedicated content producers to produce high-quality material. They also need to ensure their operational security, which in turn requires resources for salaries, software, and equipment.

Beyond propaganda, terrorist organizations also spend money to recruit new members. Recruitment incurs costs such as the maintenance of recruitment cells and the travel of the recruiters.[39] Indeed, in many cases, a recruiter and a financier can be the same person, as demonstrated in several cases in Europe.[40] Funds are used for the personal needs of the recruiter and to create propaganda as well as to facilitate recruitment channels.[41] These recruiters might also pay costs for recruits, such as food, travel, and salary.[42] For example, al-Qaeda and the group Ansar al-Islam funded the travel of recruits from Europe to fight in Iraq and Chechnya.[43] Al-Shabaab has also used its funds to recruit members. In Somali diaspora communities such as the Stockholm suburb of Rinkeby, the group has provided funds for airfare for recruits to get to Somalia, if required.[44]

Terrorist groups might also offer financial incentives to get people to join; these are effectively signing bonuses, and groups might also offer initial salaries, particularly to recruits with much-needed skill sets.[45] Although economic incentives are rarely the sole motivating factor for someone to join a terrorist organization, depending on the region, signing bonuses and salaries help. ISIL in the Philippines used some of the funds it stole to offer parents a onetime payment of $1,340 plus a monthly salary of $574 to send their sons to train as militants. Recruits were also promised a bonus of $191 for killing a soldier.[46] The group also used the funds to win over boys and young men in the province of Lanao del Sur, essentially buying their support.[47]

Approximately 18 percent of the groups I studied are known to have used funds to pay for propaganda or recruitment of members, but many others are believed to use funds for this purpose as well. However, in many cases the amount of money they spend for these purposes might be limited given the relatively small size of most terrorist organizations. Over time, and as terrorist groups extend their reach, their propaganda expenses can actually increase because they need to reach new audiences. They also face greater counterterrorism pressures that require them to adopt new technologies, recruit for specialized skill sets, mask their locations, and maintain their content.

Intelligence Gathering and Operational Security

One of the less studied terrorist uses of funds involves intelligence and counterintelligence activities. Many terrorist groups have an intelligence function, although they likely go to some lengths to keep information on it to a minimum. Despite little concrete information on this activity, it is probably more common than not within terrorist organizations. For instance, Al-Shabaab has a relatively well-developed intelligence and counterintelligence function. The group used prostitutes to solicit information from their clients and report relevant information to its operatives.[48] In another example, Hamas used some of its funds to bribe officials in an attempt to penetrate various intelligence agencies of the Palestinian Authority (such as the General and Preventive Intelligence Services), and it also used its intelligence apparatus to target suspected collaborators.[49] The LTTE is also believed to have had a well-developed intelligence function that likely also supported the group's extortion and taxation work.[50] The Taliban is believed to have an extensive intelligence apparatus, with an intelligence capability on both sides of the Afghanistan-Pakistan border and spies in the Ministry of the Interior as well as the Ministry of Defense.[51]

Some of the costs associated with intelligence and counterintelligence functions are salaries and bribes as well as communication security devices (starting with basic telephones and increasing in complexity and cost to encryption, etc.). The costs of maintaining these functions are likely proportional to the size of the terrorist network as well as how much support it has in the area in which it operates. When terrorist groups enjoy high levels of popular support, they are more able to find people who might provide information for ideological reasons rather than financial incentives, reducing the cost of intelligence gathering.

Above and beyond the intelligence and counterintelligence function, terrorist organizations also need to provide for other operational security measures. Much of this need constitutes electronics and communications security, but some of it is in the form of physical security measures. For instance, PIRA maintained safehouses.[52] The LTTE also purchased safehouses and communication centers in Tamil Nadu as well as factories to create uniforms.[53]

Other operational security costs terrorist groups, cells, and individuals incur are cell phones, prepaid credit cards, email, and secure communications channels.[54] Although these might seem like minimal expenses for terrorist organizations, if they are serious about their operational security, their burn rate for this equipment might be substantial, increasing costs. They might also need to pay for virtual private network (VPN) services and secure email, again generating monthly costs that can eat into their bottom line, particularly if they need to provide these services to a significant number of their members.

Approximately 13 percent of the terrorist organizations I studied had a defined intelligence and counterintelligence function or spent money on other communications and operational security measures. But this number likely underestimates the prevalence of intelligence and counterintelligence functions in terrorist groups along with the costs of operational security measures.

Social Services, Salaries, and Support Activities

One of the most common uses of funds by terrorist organizations is to pay the salaries of members. Territory-controlling groups also use funds to establish social services and support activities. These activities can range in scope and scale significantly, but for groups that aspire to govern an area, they are critical components in establishing legitimacy and popular support. The maintenance of social services and support activities also serves another function: to support the economy, which in turn enables taxation of the local population. Research also demonstrates that nonstate groups provide social services as part of their attempt to undermine the state, and their provision of these services "represents an extension of the broader political goals" of the groups.[55]

Most terrorist organizations use some form of tiered system to pay their members, with leadership and key figures receiving a more robust salary than those at the lower tiers, such as the average fighter. Economic incentives might not be the primary motivation for most individuals to join a terrorist organization, but the practical realities of life are such that most need ongoing support while in the organization. Rare is the person without any outside responsibilities who will forgo remuneration, no matter how committed to the cause. The Taliban illustrates this point well; at first, it did not offer salaries to officials or soldiers and provided only food, clothes, shoes, and weapons. Recruits were supposed to be motivated by the ideology to volunteer. Over time, the group started to have to pay recruits. Members received a signing bonus of $300 and a monthly salary of $150, as of estimates from 2006.[56] In the 1990s, the Islamic Movement of Uzbekistan paid salaries to its fighters of between $100 and $500 per month, money the group gained through the control and trafficking of opium and heroin in central Asia.[57] Most terrorist groups likely provide some form of financial compensation to their core membership group and fighters, although insurgents and terrorists are not compensated for the risks they take. Instead, terrorist groups (and specifically al-Qaeda in Iraq, although the findings can likely be applied to other groups as well) use wages as a screening mechanism to identify uncommitted individuals.[58] Although terrorist groups acknowledge that they must pay wages, they are hesitant to do so at market rates for fear of recruiting materially motivated members. These types of recruits can pose significant challenges for groups and can be incentivized to join other competing groups relatively easily, depleting the fighting force of the original group.[59]

Some terrorist groups offer what is better understood as a total compensation package, and these are often more complex and sophisticated than simple monthly or weekly payments. In the LeT, recruits receive monthly remuneration and receive financial incentives for big terrorist acts. After two years with the group, they also receive tenure payments.[60] PIRA also had a more flexible benefits structure that evolved over time. The group had between 400 and 500 members who received weekly salaries of between £30 and 40 ($40 to $55). However, sometimes additional funds had to be spent on members. In one case, an operative in Dublin received £6,000 (approximately $8,400) to "keep him happy."[61] Terrorist groups might offer these types of payments to help members cover onetime expenses (such as medical expenses for a family member or to repay debt). This might serve to demonstrate that the organization cares for its membership and that the loyalty and commitment within the terrorist organization is rewarded.

Although large terrorist organizations are often seen as a substantial threat, size can be a financial burden for the group itself. For instance, the Moro Islamic Liberation Front (MILF) and the Moro National Liberation Front (MNLF) have had a significant number of members, with MILF maintaining a payroll for between 10,000 and 15,000 fighters at one point in time. The leaders and fighters earned between $50 and $100 per month, adding up to a significant cost for the terrorist organization.[62] Even the lowest estimated monthly salary for all its members cost the organization more than $500,000 per month. For the Abu Sayyaf group, which kept a smaller roster of members in the 2010s, costs were comparable. The group had a membership of 100–280 and paid fighters and hostage guards between $1,000 and $2,200 per month.[63] Again, even this smaller total of fighters would have cost the organization at least $100,000 per month in salary alone.

Even modest salaries for a relatively small group of people can become costly. In 2019, reporting indicated that Jemaah Islamiyah was resurgent in Indonesia, that the group had between 70 and 140 people, and that the group was paying its officers $707–$1,061 per month.[64] A separate report suggested that all members were being paid at least $707 per month.[65] Officers are almost always paid more than foot soldiers, but the report gave no indication of how many officers were present within the group. Even with only one officer per province, the group would have ongoing expenses of about $5,000 in salary per month and possibly much more.

Terrorist organizations also have a requirement to sustain imprisoned members and the families of deceased members. For instance, PIRA used its funds for the sustenance of prisoners and families of the deceased members. Like many other terrorist organizations, the group paid allowances to members in jail and to members who had little or no chance of finding legitimate employment.[66] Some of the wealthiest terrorist groups in history have likely struggled with the cost of maintaining a salaried membership group. The costs of maintaining a cadre of fighters must be kept in mind when estimating how wealthy a terrorist organization is.

Any terrorist group that controls territory and aspires to governance has significant expenditures related to state-building and maintenance and encompassing expenses for security, social services for citizens within the area of control, and other state-related expenses. In some cases, the terrorist organization will develop entirely parallel systems of governance, as the LTTE did, which creates expenses for the group in salaries for officials and social services for the residents of its territory.[67] Hizballah runs a system of governance that includes schools, hospitals, and dispensaries; provides microfinancing loans; and runs construction companies to rebuild after attacks on its infrastructure.[68] ISIL provided a variety of governance services including hospitals, police, taxation, and other bureaucratic functions as well as an attempt at monetary policy. During the pandemic, Al-Shabaab used some of its funds to set up a Covid-19 assessment center in Jilib that functioned as an isolation and care facility[69]

When a terrorist group controls territory, it is likely providing at least some basic form of social assistance that can cost a lot of money. For instance, Hamas provides a significant range of public services including schools, scholarship funds, hospitals, garbage collection, and rebuilding roads and businesses when they are destroyed. In the early 2000s, it was estimated that the group spent 95 percent of its resources on social welfare programs.[70] Many other groups, including those that do not control significant territory, might provide social services. The Idarah Khidmat-e-Khalq (IKK) provides social services on behalf of the LeT, and the LeT was the first to come to the aid of people in the northwest frontier province during the October 2005 earthquake.[71] The political wing of the LeT in Pakistan uses significant funds to run Dawa schools, madrassas, science colleges, mobile clinics, blood banks, and ambulance services. The group's humanitarian wing, Jamaat-ud-Dawa (JuD), also provided assistance in 2010 to those affected by severe flooding.[72] MILF and MNLF are also reported to have spent a significant amount of money on social works programs.[73]

Most terrorist groups do not need to spend such a significant proportion of their money on social welfare; however, the more entrenched a group becomes and the larger its territory, the more significant a program the group likely has to provide to the population under its control. They need to expend funds on these programs to maintain public support, gain control, and generate revenue. As with almost all aspects of terrorist financing, charities and nonprofit organizations are also involved in the provision of social services. Terrorist groups, particularly those that control (or aspire to control) territory, use funds to provide humanitarian aid and social services to individuals. Those activities are often delivered through humanitarian or charitable organizations.

Not all terrorist groups that control territory provide social services; in fact, empirical cases of groups providing these types of services exist for 49 percent of the groups I studied, although the actual number is likely higher. The groups more likely to provide these services include those with foreign allies and religious orientations, and groups are more likely to provide services when they have governing aspirations and seek to counter the authority of the state.[74] Social service provision has little to do with recruiting fighters.[75]

Of course, provision of social services and salaries is not something terrorist cells or individuals generally need to do. However, in considering the operational implications of terrorist use of funds, it remains critical to remember that terrorist cells and individuals need to have ongoing sources of funds to pay for their daily needs; without these funds, they can become distracted from their terrorist activity (as they seek basic employment), turn to criminal activity to raise funds for themselves and their plot, and reduce the complexity of their planned terrorist attack to better fit within their means.

Corruption, Lobbying, and Political Activities

As with any organization, terrorist groups are vulnerable to internal corruption and diversion of funds from its members; this happens with or without the leadership's knowledge and acceptance. For instance, German terrorists in the 1970s and 1980s were notorious for their lavish lifestyles, including BMWs and expensive stereos.[76] Some of these expenses included paying residence fees to their host countries, along with bribing police or other public or security employees, lobbying politicians and governments, and undertaking other political activities.[77] Depending on the area where the terrorist groups (and in some cases, cells or individuals) operate, these expenses can be significant.

Some terrorist groups incur costs related to corruption or payments to government officials in order to conduct their activities and operations. According to Shelley, "Terrorists could not recruit collaborators, develop their organizations, or maintain a broad support network if it were not for the pervasive corruption that undermines quality of life and is repellent to many innocent civilians."[78] Corruption is a key facilitator of terrorism: for instance, Chechen groups have used their funds to pay off corrupt officials and to buy weapons on the black arms market in the region.[79] Terrorists use money to pay border guards, police officers, and other state officials to turn a blind eye or facilitate their activities. This is particularly true of groups that rely on cross-border illicit trade to raise funds.

Additional costs can be incurred as a result of internal corruption of members of terrorist organizations. Individuals in positions of authority or financial control might siphon funds from the organization's coffers to advance their own personal comfort or status. This internal theft might be a function of the nature of terrorist organizations. As Shapiro notes, terrorist organizations are (or try to be) decentralized and compartmentalized and for that reason must operate with fewer checks and balances than most other organizations. Not all members of the organization are uniformly committed to the cause.[80] For instance, some of the funds the Palestinian Liberation Organization (PLO) obtained through its 1976 bank robbery were used by senior PLO members at casino tables in Monte Carlo.[81] The Taliban did not always use its funds raised through the drug trade to invest in terrorism. Instead, some of the leaders built flashy mansions and bought luxury cars such as Toyota Land Cruisers.[82] Hassan Nasrallah, the secretary general of Hizballah, is believed to have a personal net worth of $250 million thanks to the group's drug trade.[83] The Ulster Defence Association (UDA) and Ulster Volunteer Force (UVF) are both believed to have allowed senior members to draw "expenses" from the organization, which motivated the group to fund-raise well in excess of its actual needs.[84] Many terrorist groups suffer from internal theft, corruption, and lifestyle inflation of their members and leadership, all of which depletes the organizations' bottom line.

Terrorist organizations that aspire to political legitimacy might also use funds to support political parties. PIRA used some of its money to support the growth of the political wing Sinn Fein.[85] Sinn Fein had regional offices in thirty-two Irish counties and took up considerable financial resources. PIRA paid the election costs, traveling expenses, and payroll for this political arm. In 1988 PIRA revenues were split 80 percent to 20 percent in favor of the political activities carried out by Sinn Fein.[86] Other groups that have had political costs include the LTTE, the Kurdistan Workers' Party (PKK), and the Taliban, to name a few. Overt lobbying activities are relatively rare among terrorist groups. Generally, if groups are more structured and international in scope and have a legitimate front organization, then they will engage in this type of activity and use money they obtain in a variety of legal or illegal ways to fund it. Terrorist organizations might also engage in lobbying to have a government remove them from the terrorist designation list, as the LTTE tried to do (unsuccessfully). The group spent money to lobby for its removal from the US Department of State foreign terrorist organization list, tried to bribe US officials, and hired a law firm to pursue legal mechanisms.[87]

To date, political influence and corruption costs have largely been accumulated by a few terrorist organizations, with evidence suggesting that approximately 16 percent of those I studied made payments to public officials, politicians, or state employees. As with other elements of the data for this book, these are likely low estimates because it is entirely likely that many other terrorist organizations have also incurred expenses related to corruption and potentially other legal or political activities.

Operational Use of Funds

Terrorist attacks are often said to be low cost, but this assessment does not take into consideration the variety of costs actually incurred through the planning and preparation for those attacks. Even for terrorist groups conducting attacks within their area of operation, costs can be substantial. For instance, for al-Qaeda in Iraq, individual attacks were relatively expensive, but not because of the material the group used to conduct them. The group had to pay salaries to fighters as well as to the families of imprisoned and deceased members. The organization also had to secure and maintain safehouses and transportation for its operatives. The attacks themselves are estimated to have cost around $2,700, but this underestimates the overall cost that the group incurred for each attack.[88] Taken as a whole, terrorist attacks (and terrorist organizational support) cost far more than is often assumed, meaning that the amount of money terrorists have to dedicate to these activities is far more than the numbers suggest.

In terms of operational financing, the use of funds is generally relatively straightforward. The cells or individual members usually use the funds for direct operational requirements. Terrorist cells and individuals have many of the same expenses terrorist organizations have, such as transportation, housing, and security measures. They might also share some expenses such as salaries, although in the case of individuals, this might simply be a matter of ensuring that funds are in place to sustain them during the course of any intensive planning and preparatory periods during which they might not be able to work at regular jobs. Their principal cost is, of course, procuring weapons, components, and explosive devices and carrying out the attack.

Examples of the types of expenses incurred for a terrorist attack abound. For instance, in the Madrid attack of 2003, the terrorist group used the money raised to pay for safehouses, phones, logistical support, and the weapons used in the attack.[89] The cars used before and after the attack were likely stolen.[90] The Manchester bomber also incurred operational security expenses. In the weeks before the attack, he rented a second flat several miles from his home, paying £700 for it (about $1,000).[91] Indeed, terrorists often make use of staging areas outside their actual residences to construct their bombs or materials to avoid having any neighbors, friends, or family members become aware of changes in their behavior because of attack preparations. Some of the planning and preparation costs for PIRA operations were transportation for people and materiel to and from the scenes of attacks, maintenance of weapons, storage sites, safehouses, and communications equipment. Costs have also included train, bus, or airplane tickets to and from international operation sites and payments to individuals who allowed their homes or property to be used during the planning, preparation, and attack.[92] The 9/11 attack cost somewhere between $400,000 and $500,000 (close to $724,000 in 2020 dollars). The group spent the majority of the money on flying lessons, rent, travel, and daily subsistence; the remaining money was returned to al-Qaeda and the original financiers. In the 2002 Bali attack, Jemaah Islamiyah robbed a gold store to fund travel, buy or rent vehicles, and purchase chemicals and explosives used in the attack.[93]

Terrorist cells and individuals spend the bulk of their money on weapons and attack components. Depending on the type of attack, its level of sophistication, and the individuals involved, costs can vary from tens of dollars to hundreds of thousands of dollars. As part of my research for this book, I analyzed the costs of individual terrorist attacks and plots. Based on a sample of almost fifty terrorist attacks and plots, those involving firearms were, on average, thousands of dollars more expensive than those involving just improvised explosive devices or other simple tactics. This is likely a function of the relatively high cost of weapons desired for terrorist attacks, such as AK-47s. In many jurisdictions, AK-47s cost more than $1,000 each. Of course, the territory in which the attack is planned affects the availability of such weapons, the costs involved, and how the terrorists use the funds. Also, terrorist actors (including cells and individuals) might dedicate a significant portion of their budget and time to training in the lead-up to their mobilization to violence; it might be one of the first acts in which prospective terrorists engage.[94]

The way terrorist groups use funds for operational activities has shifted dramatically over the past ten years. Whereas terrorist organizations once provided the bulk of the funding for operational cells, today those cells are much more likely to be self-financed. In many cases, terrorist organizations provide at least some seed money. Analysis by the Norwegian Forsvarets

Forskningsinstitutt (FFI [Norwegian Defence Research Establishment]) found that cells with foreign fighters in their ranks received funds from international terrorist organizations more often than cells without such members.[95] This points to at least one role terrorists with foreign or field experience can bring to a cell—that of liaison or financial facilitator. The FFI report indicates that nine out of ten attacks funded by terrorist groups from abroad involved a member who had fought or trained overseas.[96] In many other cases, particularly those without a foreign fighter connection, cells and individual terrorists finance their own operational activity, including some or all of the uses of funds detailed in Figure 6.1.

Compared with terrorist organizations, terrorist cells and individuals do not incur a number of categories of expenses. They rarely provide funding for other terrorist groups, although individuals or cells involved in planning an attack might divert surplus funds to a terrorist organization after their own operational needs have been met. They also spend significantly less on propaganda and recruitment, although they might use some of their funds to recruit specialists with particular skills required for a terrorist plot, such as bomb-making. Cells and individuals do not spend significant funds on intelligence and counterintelligence, instead dedicating their money to operational security measures and reconnaissance of targets. Prospective terrorists also do not generally provide support for members in prison or families of deceased members because their concerns are more immediate, focused on conducting the terrorist attack rather than providing long-term support for members. Given their small size and covert nature, terrorist cells and individuals do not provide social services or residence fees to a host country, particularly because they tend to operate within the countries they target. Terrorists acting as part of a cell or as individuals also do not dedicate significant funds to political parties, lobbying activities, or legal expenses.

Figure 6.1 Organizational Use of Funds (in percent)

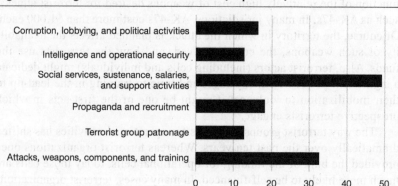

Conclusion

Across the board, and regardless of whether the actor is a terrorist group, cell, or individual, all terrorists want weapons and device components for their attacks, and many undertake training and travel prior to these events. Regarding terrorist attacks, often little information was available about the specifics of their funding, although it can always be assumed that terrorists acquired weapons or device components, even if it was as simple as renting a van or buying a knife. Similarly, although details of terrorist group attacks, weapons and components are not available in 100 percent of cases, every terrorist group has conducted attacks and therefore has had expenses in this category at least once. Details of these expenses are available about 33 percent of the time for organizations and 52 percent of the time for terrorist plots and attacks, illustrated in Figures 6.1 and 6.2, respectively.

The data suggest that the majority of operational uses of funds for terrorist cells and individuals include explosive device components, transportation, weapons, safehouses, and operational security measures.

Other interesting findings indicate that terrorist use of intelligence and operational security measures are present only in 10 percent of the terrorist groups, plots, and attacks I studied. However, it is likely that far more resources are allocated to this than my evidence suggests. Although not necessarily a large proportion of a terrorist group's or cell's budget, these measures are important nonetheless and can add up, particularly when a group or cell is under intense counterterrorism scrutiny, requiring more sophisticated and dynamic operational security efforts (and a higher burn rate for operational security measures), which increases costs.

Terrorists deploy their funds across a broad spectrum of activities and use them to acquire training, weapons, and components; establish and maintain relationships with other groups and individuals; recruit and spread

Figure 6.2 Operational Use of Funds (in percent)

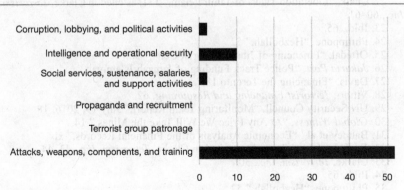

propaganda; sustain populations in their area of control; obtain intelligence and operational security; and engage in corruption and political activities. These broad categories represent an effort to itemize terrorists' uses of funds. This somewhat neglected analysis in terrorist financing is critical: by understanding how terrorists use their funds, a better appreciation of their capabilities and costs can be developed. This categorization also sheds further light on the actual financial health of terrorist organizations by expanding our understanding beyond their revenue-generating activities, accounting for expenditures as well.

Notes

1. Ehrenfeld, "Funding Evil," 27–28.
2. US Department of the Treasury, "Remarks of Under Secretary for Terrorism."
3. Komar, Borys, and Woods, "Blackwater of Jihad."
4. Castner, "Exclusive: Tracing ISIS' Weapons."
5. Horgan and Taylor, "Playing the 'Green Card'—Part 1," 5–7; Vittori, *Terrorist Financing and Resourcing*, 71.
6. Clarke, *Terrorism, Inc.*, 27.
7. Giustozzi, *Koran, Kalashnikov, and Laptop*, 147.
8. Horgan and Taylor, "Playing the 'Green Card'—Part 1," 4
9. Philippone, "Hezbollah," 53.
10. Zelin and Bauer, "Development of Tunisia's Domestic Counter-Terrorism," 29.
11. *Guardian*, "Deadly Attack Keeps World on Alert."
12. *BBC News*, "Profile of Jakarta Suspect."
13. UN Security Council, "Monitoring Team Report," January 13, 2017, 19.
14. Brisard and Jackson, "Islamic State's External Operations," 11.
15. UN Security Council, "Monitoring Team Report," July 19, 2016, 12.
16. Oftedal, "Financing of Jihadi Terrorist Cells," 31.
17. Ibid., 32.
18. Ibid., 33.
19. Wittig, "Financing Terrorism Along the Chechnya-Georgia Border," 251.
20. Schindler, "United Nations View," 89.
21. Kamere et al.,"Lashkar-e-Taiba," 86.
22. Chalk, "Liberation Tigers of Tamil Eelam," 131, as cited in Clarke, *Terrorism, Inc.*, 60–61.
23. Ibid., 65.
24. Philippone, "Hezbollah," 52.
25. Oftedal, "Financing of Jihadi Terrorist Cells," 36.
26. *Jakarta Post*, "Police Track Funding of Jamaah Islamiyah."
27. Davis, "Financing the Toronto 18."
28. Vittori, *Terrorist Financing and Resourcing*, 62.
29. UN Security Council, "Monitoring Team Report," July 19, 2016, 18.
30. *Global Witness*, "At Any Price We Will Take the Mines," 14.
31. Bahney et al., "Economic Analysis of the Financial Records," xiv.
32. English, *Armed Struggle*, as cited in Clarke, *Terrorism, Inc.*, 43–44.
33. Clarke, *Terrorism, Inc.*, 30.
34. Ibid., 65.
35. Philippone, "Hezbollah," 52.

36. Clarke, *Terrorism, Inc.*, 128.
37. Financial Action Task Force, *Financing of Recruitment for Terrorist Purposes*.
38. Katz and Kern, "Terrorist 007, Exposed."
39. Rudner, "Using Financial Intelligence," 37.
40. Nesser, *Islamist Terrorism in Europe*, 124.
41. Financial Action Task Force, *Financing of Recruitment for Terrorist Purposes*.
42. Ibid.
43. Levitt, "USA Ties Terrorist Attacks."
44. Keatinge, "Role of Finance in Defeating Al-Shabaab," 6.
45. Financial Action Task Force, *Financing of Recruitment for Terrorist Purposes*.
46. Office of the Lead Inspector General, "Operation Inherent Resolve," 101.
47. Allard, "Exclusive: Looted Cash, Gold."
48. Through its main line of work, the group compensates them for this information. Petrich, "Al-Shabaab's Mata Hari Network."
49. Clarke, *Terrorism, Inc.*, 104.
50. Vittori, *Terrorist Financing and Resourcing*, 78.
51. Clarke, *Terrorism, Inc.*, 121.
52. Horgan and Taylor, "Playing the 'Green Card'—Part 1," 5–7.
53. Clarke, *Terrorism, Inc.*, 60.
54. Miguel del Cid Gómez, "Financial Profile of the Terrorism," 5.
55. Asal, Flanigan, and Szekely, "Doing Good While Killing," 1.
56. Reese, "Financing the Taliban," 96.
57. Vittori, *Terrorist Financing and Resourcing*, 36.
58. Bahney et al., "Insurgent Compensation," 521.
59. Mironova, *From Freedom Fighters to Jihadists*.
60. Kamere et al., "Lashkar-e-Taiba," 85.
61. Vittori, *Terrorist Financing and Resourcing*, 71.
62. Germann et al., "Terrorist Financing in the Philippines," 155.
63. Ibid.
64. Chew, "Why a Resurgent Jemaah Islamiah."
65. *Jakarta Post*, "Police Track Funding of Jamaah Islamiyah."
66. Vittori, *Terrorist Financing and Resourcing*, 71.
67. Clarke, *Terrorism, Inc.*, 61.
68. Vittori, *Terrorist Financing and Resourcing*, 102.
69. Guled, "Extremist Group Al-Shabab."
70. Shelley, *Dirty Entanglements*, 82.
71. Kamere et al., "Lashkar-e-Taiba," 85.
72. Shelley, *Dirty Entanglements*, 81.
73. Germann et al., "Terrorist Financing in the Philippines," 156.
74. Asal, Flanigan, and Szekely, "Doing Good While Killing," 15.
75. Ibid., 16.
76. Hewitt, "Costs of Terrorism," 171.
77. Miguel del Cid Gómez, "Financial Profile of the Terrorism," 3–4.
78. Shelley, *Dirty Entanglements*, 66.
79. Ibid., 42, 52.
80. Shapiro, "Terrorist Organizations' Vulnerabilities," 58.
81. Vittori, *Terrorist Financing and Resourcing*, 35.
82. Thachuk and Lal, "Introduction to Terrorist Criminal Enterprises," 5.
83. Ruda, "Hezbollah."
84. Silke, "In Defense of the Realm," 336.
85. Clarke, *Terrorism, Inc.*, 28.

86. Vittori, *Terrorist Financing and Resourcing*, 71.

87. Corley, "Liberation Tigers of Tamil Eelam," 111, 130.

88. Bahney et al., "Economic Analysis of the Financial Records," xv.

89. Rollins and Rosen, *International Terrorism and Transnational Crime*, 19.

90. Reinares, *Al-Qaeda's Revenge*, 72.

91. Mendick, Evans, and Ward, "Exclusive: Manchester Suicide Bomber."

92. Clarke, *Terrorism, Inc.*, 39.

93. Shelley, *Dirty Entanglements*, 35.

94. Canadian Security Intelligence Service, "Mobilization to Violence (Terrorism) Research."

95. Oftedal, "Financing of Jihadi Terrorist Cells," 21.

96. Ibid.

7

Managing, Storing, and Investing Funds

Terrorists, particularly groups with substantial assets, need a secure place to store and protect their funds from inflation, require strategies to generate and deploy funds, and have to invest the money for the future. Although these are fundamental needs for terrorist organizations (and to a lesser extent cells and individuals), this subject has not received significant attention from scholars or policymakers. The lack of analysis relating to terrorist management, storage, and investment of funds, and the lack of theorizing about terrorist financing in all its possible and likely forms, might be because of a dearth of information about these techniques. Managing and storing funds, however, is important for terrorist groups, particularly those that control territory. For cells and individuals, the management occurs at a microlevel and is primarily intended to ensure that attacks or other terrorist activities can be carried out and that cell members are not stealing funds, a perennial concern of all levels of terrorist actors. How terrorist actors manage, store, and invest their funds can illuminate significant aspects of their internal structures, shed light on long-term plans and strategies, demonstrate key vulnerabilities and strengths, and provide opportunities for intelligence collection and disruption.

Money Management
Terrorist groups need to manage their finances well if they want to move beyond subsistence levels of funding, aspire to state-building projects, and control territory. Without a sophisticated management strategy, terrorist groups quickly lose money to unscrupulous middlemen, corrupt members,

and other thieves. The level of complexity involved in money management is tied (although not linearly) to the funds the group has. In some cases, even groups with a large amount of money might have simple management strategies, particularly if their funds are derived from one or two sources, they are not involved in extensive international transactions, and most of their activities take place within their area of control.

Cells and individuals must also manage their money for their operations, which can present significant challenges and thus result in diminished capabilities on the part of the terrorists. For those who do manage to correctly identify their short- and long-term funding needs and manage their finances accordingly, their attacks can be more impactful and their cells and organizational structure more resilient against counterterrorist efforts.

The main tools and methods terrorist organizations, cells, and individuals use to manage their money include dedicated financial managers, companies, investors, financial committees, bankers, accountants, auditors, intelligence services, and tax collectors. The financial managers for terrorist organizations can be singular, multiple, or members of a committee. The size of the organization might dictate its management needs: a small group (and certainly cells and individuals) might require only one individual to handle the funds, but when organizations control territory and generate significant funds, they might be more inclined toward adopting multiple managers and financial committees, which has the advantage of avoiding concentrating all the financial power and information in the hands of one individual.

Most terrorist groups that exist for more than a few years adopt a hierarchical and bureaucratic funds management system. They use these systems to make decisions and account for how money is being raised, especially useful if the group is relying on rent-seeking activities. Although certainly not the first group to do so, al-Qaeda had a sophisticated financial network that employed professional bankers, accountants, and financiers.[1] One of the most notable, well-articulated examples of a terrorist group managing funds was the Provisional Irish Republican Army (PIRA). The group learned hard lessons about funds management early: PIRA's financing was initially disjointed, which led to the 1962 ceasefire because of the group's inability to acquire the necessary funding to continue fighting.[2] This was likely a turning point for the group, and its financing quickly became more sophisticated. The southern command of the group acted as the quartermaster and was responsible for volunteer training. It also bought, stored, and moved armaments. PIRA established a series of holding companies that concealed the true ownership of the businesses it used to raise funds and thus obscured their involvement.[3] These basic management practices allowed the group to raise and deploy its money on weapons and training, simultaneously obscuring it from law enforcement and security services through the front companies, which likely also served as places to comingle legal and illegal funds.

The circle of financial trust in most terrorist organizations is relatively small, and in some cases, terrorists might also employ individuals who do not know the ultimate beneficiary of their professional services. PIRA entrusted few individuals within the organization with these roles, although over time it had to expand its circle of trust to accommodate its growing financial activities. PIRA employed at least four accountants; three had republican sympathies and one was unwittingly employed.[4]

Over time, PIRA developed a formal finance department, entrusting its funds to a small group of people. A financing director had overall responsibility for the money, and a ring of advisers handled finances for both PIRA and Sinn Fein. The financing director supplied cash to PIRA units for operations, meaning that in large part, the group had a centrally controlled financial structure.[5] As terrorist organizations grow, it is common for them to adopt specialized skills within the group and to trust only a handful of people with their finances.

PIRA's financing committee was not run by amateurs. The group had an accountant who advised them and a front man who purchased businesses for money-laundering purposes. He owned a hotel and two pubs in his own name, but the PIRA benefited from them. In addition to these professional moneymen, the group also hired freelance accountants who would occasionally do work for PIRA and its political arm, Sinn Fein. They were employed mainly to provide advice to firms and to falsify tax returns and other documents for the pubs in PIRA's employ. The group also had an additional ring of sympathizers that included at least one bank manager and an auctioneer, both of whom were willing to provide services such as creating false documents for the group.[6] The Ulster Defence Association (UDA) and Ulster Volunteer Force (UVF) had specialized units with responsibility for fund-raising, and those responsible for this activity were senior members of the group.[7]

Recruiting skilled individuals into the ranks of terrorist groups, or as peripheral sympathizers, has many benefits regarding money management. Terrorists can exploit the expertise of these individuals to avoid law enforcement and security service scrutiny and can ensure their funds are managed professionally, preserving capital and making investments as required. It might even be more beneficial for a terrorist group to have individuals with few links to it performing this function. These "clean" individuals are often outside the initial scope of investigation for law enforcement and security services, given their lack of terrorist group connections, but the groups can rely upon them to ensure their funds are managed professionally.

Above and beyond organizational and operational financing, terrorist funds are also managed toward their longer-term costs, such as financial support for incarcerated and deceased members' families. For instance, Hamas and the Palestinian Islamic Jihad were reported to use financial institutions to disburse funds to families of martyrs. The Arab Bank based in Jordan allegedly administered accounts of Saudi donors who allowed families of the martyrs to withdraw up to $5,300.[8] These long-term requirements often fall outside the organizational financing of terrorist groups, and separate accounts might be set up to ensure funds are always available and are not subject to internal corruption or other financial pressures that might decrease their availability and ultimately force the terrorist organizations to withdraw their promised support payments, which could have consequences for future support from the population in their area of control.

Terrorist organizations often have the challenge of managing a significant amount of cash. Many terrorist organizations receive cash from state sponsors, other terrorist groups, donor networks, and their own taxation or extortion activities. Managing an organization or, in some cases, an entire economy based largely on cash can be a complex affair that requires significant countertheft measures to prevent the cash from being stolen by members, deserters, corrupt leaders, or anyone else who might come into contact with it. For example, PIRA tried to maintain accountability for its funds, meticulously tracked its assets, and made public examples of those who mishandled its money through punishment and beatings.[9] Terrorist groups recognize the temptation for their members when they handle a significant amount of cash. Even smaller groups that maintain a more operational focus seek to adopt these techniques, as evidenced by ISIL in Libya as it prepared to launch a state-like financing system inspired by ISIL in Syria in 2015.[10]

As with many aspects of financing, the Liberation Tigers of Tamil Eelam (LTTE) provide a useful case study in how a terrorist organization might structure its financial management. The group maintained systematic records of community members containing their addresses, telephone numbers, email addresses, and bank account numbers.[11] It used these records as the basis from which to conduct fund-raising efforts. The LTTE established a fixed contribution system based on family income, ranging from $50 to $500 per month per family.[12] The various means the LTTE had for raising money necessitated a relatively sophisticated mechanism of funds control, particularly given how internationally dispersed its fundraising activities were. The group employed a main financial controller and a subgroup for finances. These subgroups were known as the Aiyanna Group, the KP Directorate (named for its leader, Kumaran Pathmanathan), and the Sana Group.[13]

The Aiyanna Group was responsible for securing and monitoring fundraising streams and served as the clandestine intelligence and operations body of the LTTE. The KP Directorate was in charge of the entire international financing network and was also responsible for some procurement activities, including weapons.[14]

The Sana Group included a principal controller and eight trust managers in Europe, North America, and Southeast Asia. These managers ensured that transfers took place through banking institutions, human couriers, and the misinvoicing of goods. The trust managers were also responsible for meeting collection targets within their communities set by LTTE headquarters in Sri Lanka. The financiers did not fight for the group, were not on any watchlists, and deliberately kept a low profile, particularly during highly profitable financial operations.[15] This separation likely necessitated the use of proxies and third parties to keep their names out of transactions. The principal controller did not deal with funds but managed the books detailing where the funds were located. The trust managers were responsible for transferring the funds, often through formal financial institutions and into the bank accounts where the money was required.[16]

Al-Qaeda in Iraq also had a hierarchical system of financing and administration.[17] The group had a sophisticated funds management scheme and had specialized financing units that managed resources and shared revenues between al-Qaeda in Iraq subunits. The group used tracking spreadsheets, expense reports, and standardized accounting reports.[18] Essentially, the group implemented financial management and controls with which anyone who works in a large organization would be familiar. Al-Qaeda in Iraq also used forms to track group funds and required managerial reports on finances as well as receipts for funds dispersed to members.[19]

Al-Qaeda in Iraq's successor group, the Islamic State in Iraq and the Levant (ISIL), undoubtedly learned many of its fund management strategies from it. ISIL established a financial affairs committee with a finance minister who exerted authority over all local financial councils. The finance minister also served as part of ISIL leader Abu Bakr al-Baghdadi's cabinet, and his ministry's primary responsibility was tax collection.[20] ISIL's financing strategy built on the one employed by al-Qaeda in Iraq in the 2000s but significantly expanded upon it. ISIL demonstrated the ability to learn lessons from its previous financial difficulties, resulting in enhanced financial management systems and more elaborate taxation and fund-raising mechanisms.

ISIL has also had to contend with theft and corruption within its ranks. For instance, the group detained four senior officers in Mosul in connection with the disappearance of some $4 million.[21] It is also probable that corruption was more rampant within the caliphate than reports suggest. As Hansen-Lewis and Shapiro note, ISIL's economy was based in large part on extractive industries easily subject to elite capture.[22] The group had a vested interest in ensuring that it appeared to be functioning with bureaucratic efficiency and that its members were loyal and committed to the cause. Stealing money from the group's treasury does not indicate long-term trust, loyalty, or invest-ment in the future and suggests that some of its members were motivated more by profit than ideology, a critical flaw for the long-term prospects of a terrorist group.[23]

Terrorists can also become overly ambitious when considering their ability to manage money, as ISIL demonstrated. The group introduced its own currency and attempted to manage both monetary and fiscal policy for the territory it controlled.[24] Ultimately, little came of this attempt except for some interesting collectors' items in the form of gold coins. ISIL's ambition to manage both its monetary and fiscal policy while also turning its entire economy to war-making likely hastened the group's demise.[25]

Despite ISIL's ability to raise millions of dollars, in January 2017 it was operating on a crisis budget. The group continued to levy arbitrary fines and fees, but counterterrorist financing pressures combined with internal corruption and theft left the group with dwindling resources.[26] As the group was routed, additional pilfering of the war chest by individual members was likely rampant. Some members might have done this to move funds out of the territory they were losing, but it might have also been for personal gain. The group likely hemorrhaged money during the last days of the caliphate, and no management structure could have pre-vented that as the internal systems broke down and left the group vulner-able to theft.

Groups that control significant territory are also frequently required to provide financial services and social services to local people, discussed in Chapter 6; this creates complexity in terms of financial management. Hamas, operating within the Palestinian territory and its leadership, acts as a quasistate and has many of the same responsibilities as a state. As a result, the group has a management structure, and its activities are broken down into different areas; the social and administrative branch handles funding, recruitment, and social services.[27] Similar breakdowns can be found in other terrorist groups that administer social services.

Terrorist groups that collect taxes (or engage in extortion or rent-seeking activities) often rely on advanced funds management systems, a necessity to avoid double taxation of individuals and businesses. Although many individ-uals who pay taxes to a terrorist group do so grudgingly, having to pay them multiple times can generate further ill will, unnecessarily complicating a ter-rorist organization's fund-raising strategy. For this reason, many terrorist groups that employ taxation keep extensive records and issue receipts. An example of this type of administration that evolved over time was that of Al-Shabaab. Over the course of its existence, Al-Shabaab has become effective at raising funds, managing its money, and administering payment systems.[28] The group collects taxes locally, meaning that cells raise those funds them-selves. Al-Shabaab's intelligence service, Amniyat, has also played a role in assisting in the collection of taxes.[29] Al-Shabaab's tax system is relatively efficient and free of corruption because of reliable intelligence.[30]

Terrorist groups manage their funds, but some also manage the broader economies from which they draw those funds, particularly when those funds are derived from resources highly sensitive to supply and demand. For example, the Taliban's funds management system extends to its main source of income, the poppy supply. The group has knowingly and skillfully suppressed poppy cultivation in Afghanistan to manipulate the international price. The management of supply is critical for the Taliban to maintain a high profit and ensure that its product does not become oversupplied. Few other examples of this level of restraint exist in terrorist groups. Instead, most terrorist organizations will not hesitate to flood a market if it means short-term influxes of cash. As of 2020, the Taliban was on a path toward financial independence thanks to its multiple sources of funds and new financial manager, Mullah Yaqoob. Yaqoob has focused on refining taxation methods and building export markets.[31]

Terrorist groups that enjoy a significant amount of state sponsorship or patronage have to obscure the sources and destinations of those funds. Professionals such as bankers, accountants, and lawyers can be particularly helpful in these endeavors. The Palestinian Authority (PA) and its leadership benefited from the services of a banker to manage its funds, particularly Yasser Arafat. He held accounts at the Arab Bank, run by Abdul Majid Shoman, who served as his personal banker and handled all of the PA president's investments and holdings.[32] Hamas concentrated much of its financial management in the hands of Mahmoud al-Mabhouh, a senior military wing commander of the organization. He handled the funds Iran and Hizballah provided the group and devised plans to smuggle both funds and weapons into Gaza and the West Bank.[33] Hamas also used shell companies to launder its funds in Gaza.[34] Individuals in these positions of power and knowledge can become targets for assassination (kinetic disruption), as al-Mabhouh discovered.[35] The LTTE went so far as to create its own financial institution (Eelam Bank) in Sri Lanka.[36]

Professional management of funds can also have drawbacks for terrorist organizations; like government bureaucracies, financial units can become bloated and inefficient. This can plague terrorist groups that have managed to maintain control or influence over territory for a significant period. However, to deal with the size of their bureaucracy and, in some cases, to most effectively manage their money, some terrorist groups actively seek to recruit people with the required skills. For instance, ISIL is reported to have hired an "army of accountants."[37] These individuals ensured that funds were accounted for and managed properly, and they provided useful advice on the investment and storage of funds as well as the techniques required to move money to operational theaters.

In some cases, terrorist groups are able to acquire such an extensive amount of money (often cash) that the actual management and storage of those funds become an issue. In one such example, the Lashkar-e-Taiba (LeT) acquired so much capital that it was planning to open a bank.[38] Opening a bank would have allowed the group to store the funds securely and to manage those funds more effectively, potentially also allowing them greater access to the international financial system, through which they could make diversified investments. The physical management of the funds would have been simplified because authorized individuals could have made withdrawals on accounts, and accounting would have been partially automated through the bank's systems and tracking of transactions.

Organizational management of funds is generally undertaken by terrorist groups that enjoy territorial control and a significant and consistent influx of funds. These types of groups generate more elaborate management structures and store and invest their funds in more places. These structures allow a terrorist group to avoid losing funds, ensure that payments are made on time, and prevent the population within its area of control from being double taxed, but these structures are not immune from human folly, and corruption can be rampant within terrorist organizations.

Operational Management of Funds

The more sophisticated aspects of money management are usually the purview of terrorist organizations, but cells and individuals also manage their funds. Operational management of funds has more to do with managing the day-to-day expenses of the cell, including operational requirements, than with long-term planning for the maintenance of a terrorist organization. Even cells that have acquired money and require little in the way of additional funds seek strategies to manage their finances, often diverting money from their own resources (self-financing) or taking up work to meet the needs of the group or cell, as well as looking for ways to reduce expenses.

The operational management of funds is important even for cells that receive terrorist group support for their activities. Many terrorist cells and individuals are required to finance (at least in part) their own activities, even if they are members of a terrorist organization. This is not a new trend; many PIRA active service units self-financed their local activities. Some of these units specialized in armed robberies and redirected at least a portion of the proceeds of these activities back to the finance department. The extent of their funds management was likely covering their expenses and making sure they sent the appropriate "tribute" back to the core group.[39] The Caucasus Emirate, a highly decentralized organization, required that members of each jamaat (operational unit) be responsible for raising funds for themselves.[40]

Even relatively small plots or attacks can involve money management strategies. In the 2005 failed Australia plot, the Melbourne plotters pooled their existing cash resources by making donations to a central fund. Some of the members contributed AUD 100 (roughly $75) per month, and at the time of disruption the fund was worth approximately AUD 19,000 ($14,700). One of the members of the Melbourne cell was also appointed treasurer of the fund.[41] In the foiled attack plans of the Toronto 18 terrorist cell, one individual managed the money for the group. He made the attack plans, determined their costs, and ensured sufficient funds were in place to cover those costs. He had sole responsibility for the management of the funds, and there is little indication that the other plot members paid any significant attention to the fund-raising requirements or expenditures of the group.[42]

Cash remains king for most terrorist plots and attacks. In the Toronto 18 case, the money manager for the group stored the funds in cash in a safe.[43] When he was arrested, $12,380 Canadian (about $10,000) were found at his house along with $50.[44] He also gave another cell member some of the operational funds; that member had $9,150 Canadian ($7,500) in cash in his backpack when he was arrested.[45]

The financial management activities of terrorist cells and individuals rarely involve specialized skill sets. Instead, an individual with a natural proclivity might undertake that responsibility, or the leader of the cell might control the finances. The management of the funds, and particularly the ability to estimate costs and expenses for the group, can have a direct impact on whether the plot or attack succeeds; many terrorist attacks have been hindered in their scope and scale as a result of lack of funding and poor management of existing resources.

Storing and Investing funds

Terrorist groups, particularly those that generate large profits, need to invest and store their funds, often for a long time.[46] Groups that hold territory often find themselves in need of a place to store funds, either in the form of cash, electronically, or as physical resources. How groups do this is dictated largely by their operating environment, their targeted region (where they want to conduct operations and will therefore need money), and how significant counterterrorist pressure is on the group. Storing funds, however, is rarely sufficient for groups that have acquired a significant amount of money. They need to invest those funds to protect them from the deleterious effects of inflation, hide them, or make them appear legitimate. Holding millions of dollars in a low-interest account could draw the suspicion of a financial institution as well as make the funds vulnerable to easy seizure should states determine their provenance. Without these investments, the value of the groups' money would decrease steadily and faster in areas with high inflation such as conflict zones.

Terrorist groups, cells, and individuals must store funds for differing periods. Operational cells must store excess funds before they are used for an attack, whereas organizations must store excess funds to smooth their consumption cycle. These funds can be stored as cash, as commodities or other goods, within the formal financial system, or with trusted friends. For terrorist groups with a surplus of funds, that money also has to be managed. The groups must exercise financial control, budget, and manage its funds so that they can prolong their existence. Generally speaking, terrorist groups store and invest funds, whereas operational cells and individuals store funds but only for short periods, and this rarely involves investments unless of a short duration, such as a loan.

Although less information exists regarding terrorists' storage and investment of funds compared to other elements of terrorist financing, some groups are known to have engaged in this activity. For instance, the Palestinian Liberation Organization (PLO) made investments in banks, real estate, chicken farms, estates in Africa, factories, and other businesses, and they also lent funds to states (e.g., Nicaragua).[47] These investments generated significant profits for the group: in 1987, the majority of the PLO's $500–$600 million budget came from these investments.[48] Al-Qaeda's financial network also included investments in legal and illegal companies.[49] The LTTE invested its money in stock markets and money market funds and maintained an impressive real estate portfolio.[50] These investments were likely intended first and foremost to protect the group's capital from inflationary pressures (given that it was fighting what its leaders surely knew to be a years-, if not decades-long, war) and served as a way to generate even more funds.

Terrorist organizations employ a variety of strategies to store and invest their funds, and these vary with the sophistication of the organization and the financial literacy of its members (particularly leadership). Many terrorist groups begin by storing their money in cash, but this can become onerous over time as they acquire more wealth or are required to move with any regularity. Transporting millions of dollars in cash is burdensome and opens terrorist organizations to vulnerabilities such as loss or theft. Some money storage mechanisms include bank accounts, accounts in the name of sympathizers or third parties, precious metals, stones, and other high-value goods along with accounts in countries outside their immediate area of operations.

When terrorist groups lose control of their territory, it becomes increasingly important to find other areas in which to store funds. In fact, having that money already in place in other countries is critical as well. During ISIL's retreat, the group was estimated to have smuggled around $400 million out of Iraq and Syria.[51] The group prepositioned funds outside the immediate region, preparing for the inevitable reality of being pushed out of those countries. ISIL is reported to have stored funds in "solidly reputable" bank accounts in Europe, the Middle East, and Central Asia.[52] ISIL's ability to make use of the formal financial sector means that the group will likely have the ability to preposition funds for operational activities it wishes to undertake, but this might also make the funds vulnerable to seizure should authorities be able to determine the extent of the terrorist group's connections. The group has likely used intermediaries' accounts to store their funds, and these individuals might or might not be aware of the nature of the money.

Most terrorist groups today are sufficiently financially savvy to understand the need to store funds securely and invest those funds to protect them from inflation and make them available in the long term, but not all groups employ a sophisticated strategy to manage their money. Al-Qaeda in the Islamic Maghreb (AQIM) is an example of the opposite strategy. The group stored its money by keeping its surplus funds in cash hidden throughout the desert, and it was known to store other resources such as fuel and water in this manner.[53] Storing funds in cash has costs and benefits. On one hand, the cash is readily accessible, and there is no chance of it being seized through the international financial system by state actors. On the other hand, security issues remain a concern, as does physical security, along with a more practical concern of remembering exactly where the funds are stored. This is a lesson AQIM learned: storing money by burying it in the desert has pitfalls in terms of how funds can be retrieved, particularly when there is a single point of failure. Abu al-Hamid Abu, a leader of an AQIM katiba (brigade), buried €16 million ($19,300,000) in northern Mali. He was killed in a traffic accident before he could give the GPS coordinates to another AQIM member.[54]

Terrorist groups often choose to manage their money (and store it) outside the conflict zone in which they operate. Managing and storing funds outside of a group's immediate area of operations has the benefit of removing them from the conflict zone (and potential target area for military operations), securing them from competing groups, and even keeping "sticky fingers" within the organization away from them. However, this practice also makes accessing the funds more difficult and requires a significant level of trust in the individuals with whom the funds have been deposited.

Sometimes terrorist organizations use money service businesses (MSBs) to store funds. For instance, al-Qaeda in the Arabian Peninsula (AQAP) stored funds that it acquired through taxation at the Al Omgy Money Exchange in Yemen.[55] The funds were readily available for the terrorist group's use, and the group was able to direct operatives to withdraw funds from different branches, allowing for efficient movement of funds. Al-Shabaab might also store funds with MSBs. Based on Somalia's economy, the group probably keeps a large amount of money in cash, meaning that there are likely areas in Somalia with concentrated stores of Al-Shabaab funds. The group might also keep money in some bank accounts (possibly in neighboring countries), deposit it with *hawaladars*, or use M-Pesa (a local mobile money transfer service) for short-term storage of smaller amounts.

Operational management also involves prepositioning funds in areas where they might be used for attacks, to purchase supplies and equipment, or to support the members of the terrorist organization. To position these funds accordingly, groups must move them into the area where they can be useful. After the money is there, terrorist groups need to ensure it remains secure, leaving it with trusted individuals or in accounts where the group can access it. After the funds are prepositioned, terrorist groups must maintain accurate accounts of where they are stored to avoid losing that access.

Many of the investments terrorists make also may have practical applications, such as real estate that can function as a safe haven.[56] Terrorist investments are likely more prevalent than evidence currently suggests, although they are probably constrained by the same factors that affect individual investing: funds needed in the short term are likely to be managed in cash or near-cash alternatives, whereas longer-term funds might be invested in a variety of risker vehicles. Understanding a terrorist group's longer-term objectives and financial plans might help identify potential avenues of counterterrorist efforts.

The main reasons terrorist groups have to actively invest their money is to protect it from inflation and to generate income. In many of the areas where they operate, financial sectors might be unstable, and inflation might be rampant. Therefore, if groups intend to survive for significant periods, they must invest their cash to generate interest, dividends, and other returns, protecting the capital from diminishing in value, as would happen with cash left in a safehouse or funds deposited in a low-interest (but safe) bank account.

Many groups have invested their money, including Hizballah, the LTTE, and ISIL, to name a few. Terrorist groups with significant resources and a long-term horizon for their activities tend to actively manage and invest their funds. This can be particularly true for a onetime influx of funds such as the proceeds from a bank robbery. For instance, funds the PLO acquired through its bank robbery in 1976 were invested abroad.[57] The LTTE used donations it raised, largely from the diaspora community and individuals who lived within the group's area of control, to start and grow the group's businesses. Some of these businesses were telephone services and community radio stations.[58]

In some cases, the investments themselves serve multiple purposes. Investments can be used to store cash, but they can also serve as a means of raising money for the group (above and beyond investment interest). PIRA had extensive quasilegal businesses that it used as fronts to support the organization. These businesses provided cash income and served as cover for laundering stolen funds. At one point, the group was believed to have £30 million ($42 million) in assets in pubs, hotels, and other small businesses. Reports suggest that PIRA owned at least thirty pubs in Ireland and at least one in Boston.[59] All these businesses might have been a valuable source of funds and provided other benefits. However, they might also have been a distraction because managing this complicated network would have required significant oversight.

ISIL invested in local markets in Iraq and Syria.[60] The group invested at least $250 million in legitimate businesses within the territory it controlled. Middlemen were given a lump sum to invest in businesses, and ISIL took a cut from the subsequent profits.[61] In the broader region (e.g., Turkey) they invested in construction companies, money exchanges, agricultural entities, fisheries, and real estate including hotels.[62] The purposes behind these investments are multiple: to protect terrorist funds from the costs of inflation, to hide money from foreign governments seeking to seize it, and to continue the groups' projects of state-building and control in their areas of influence.

ISIL is also reported to have made investments in foreign currency markets and garnered significant profits from this activity. The funds were returned to the group from Iraq and Jordan via the formal banking sector and provided up to $20 million.[63] ISIL financial chiefs are reported to have invested in the stock market using cash taken from the 2014 takeover of Mosul, when the group obtained $429 million from the city's central bank.[64] Although this might sound improbable, buying securities would not be impossible for a terrorist group, particularly one with ISIL's financial knowledge. The largest hurdle would be placing the funds in an account at a financial institution, but if the group were able to do that either through a cover story, a complicit or negligent banking official, or a series of transactions and corporate structures, few rules or regulations would allow the institution to detect the investment as being made by a terrorist group or individual.

Terrorist cells and individuals rarely store and invest their funds for any length of time because they are focused on operational activity, generally to be conducted in the immediate future. However, some terrorist actors have a long-term horizon for their attack plans. One interesting example of the investment of funds for operational financing was the case of Anders Breivik. He had a nine-year plan to finance the plots, started a business selling fake diplomas, and invested in the stock market specifically to raise funds for his terrorist activity.[65] He also had accounts in tax havens to avoid paying taxes and had access to anonymous credit cards provided by the banks in these jurisdictions.[66] However, Breivik's framing of his financing activities might not be entirely reliable. He wrote his manifesto shortly before the attack, long after his financing activities had started. Further, his financing of most aspects of the attack with credit card debt suggests that, in fact, he struggled to manage his finances and did not have a long-term plan to support his activities.[67]

Indeed, not all terrorists are well suited to money management and investments. In the case of the Birmingham Rucksack bomb plot of 2011, the individuals involved sought to increase the amount of money at their disposal through currency speculation but ultimately lost £9,000 (about $12,600).[68] Although terrorists might seek to generate more money through investments, many are ill suited to employ more sophisticated investment strategies; as a result, the main investments undertaken by terrorist actors are usually in real estate, existing businesses, and criminal enterprises or business models.

Terrorist groups, and to a lesser extent cells and individuals, store their funds primarily in cash, but they also invest it in the formal financial sector as well as with MSBs. They make investments to obscure their funds and hide them from authorities and to protect their windfalls from inflation. In many instances, terrorist groups store and invest their funds not in their area of operations but in easily accessible, geographically proximate locations out of the immediate line of fire of counterterrorism efforts, be they kinetic or financial in nature.

Conclusion

Although there is less direct evidence of terrorist management, storage, and investment of funds than other financing mechanisms, such as fundraising and movement, these activities remain a pillar of terrorist financing strategies. These activities vary in scope and scale depending on the level of actor involved; terrorist groups are likely to have more financial resources and act accordingly. Terrorist cells and individuals are focused on financial activities that advance their immediate activities, with some notable exceptions.

For terrorist organizations, storage of funds is primarily done with banks, although cash remains a popular choice. To help obscure the sources of their funds, they sometimes use proxies or third parties who might in fact be the account holders, masking the terrorist connection. Terrorist groups also convert funds into gold and precious metals, the rate of which is illustrated in Figure 7.1.

Empirical evidence of where terrorists choose to store their funds is limited, illustrated by the low numbers in Figure 7.1. While we know that terrorists must store their funds and the general ways they choose to do so, groups rarely reveal their storage mechanisms due to operational security concerns; the same is true for their management of funds.

Funds destined for terrorist operations are primarily stored in banks as well, although cash is a popular choice for terrorist attacks and plots. Proxies are also seen as part of the operational financial management plan, although funds are rarely, if ever, stored in gold or precious metals, as illustrated in Figure 7.2. This is logical: gold and precious metals, although relatively easy to transport, are also relatively illiquid and for the purposes of imminent terrorist attacks are unlikely to be used to store funds.

Figure 7.1 Organizational Storage of Funds

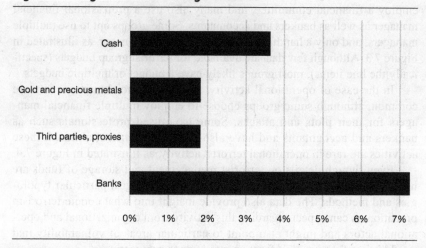

Figure 7.2 Operational Storage of Funds

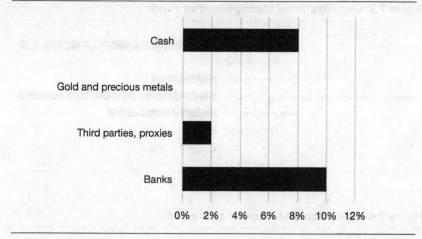

As with organizations, operational cells and individuals rarely disclose how they have stored funds for their planned attacks, illustrated by the low numbers in Figure 7.2. In addition, investigators rarely articulate how funds were stored and managed by cells and individuals, nor is this a mechanism that is widely reported. As a result, we have little detailed insight into how many cells and individuals used what particular storage mechanisms; the same is true for their management of funds.

For the management and investment of funds, terrorist groups primarily employ a financial committee, and many also use a professional financial manager as well as bankers and accountants. Some groups opt to use multiple managers, and only a handful use a single financial manager, as illustrated in Figure 7.3. Although few data are available for terrorist group budgets (specifically the line items), most groups likely have a budget or multiple budgets.

In the case of operational activity, a single financial manager is more common, although some groups choose to employ multiple financial managers for their plots and attacks. Some have used professionals such as bankers and accountants and have also made investments, although these activities are rare in operational terrorist activity, as illustrated in Figure 7.4.

Even though details on terrorist management and storage of funds are hard to come by, the available information does suggest particular typologies and methods. The data also provide insight into what counterterrorism practitioners can expect regarding this activity from organizational and operational actors and might also point to particular areas of vulnerability that would be useful to exploit from an intelligence perspective.

Figure 7.3 Organizational Management of Funds

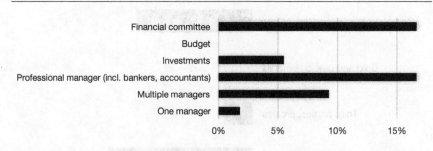

Figure 7.4 Operational Management of Funds

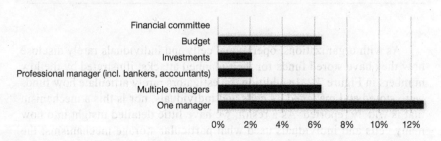

Notes

1. Basile, "Going to the Source," 171.
2. Vittori, *Terrorist Financing and Resourcing*, 68.
3. Ibid., 67–68.
4. Horgan and Taylor, "Playing the 'Green Card'—Part 1," 6, 8–16
5. Ibid.
6. Ibid.
7. Silke, "In Defense of the Realm," 350, 351.
8. Wittig, *Understanding Terrorist Finance*, 62.
9. Vittori, *Terrorist Financing and Resourcing*, 71.
10. UN Security Council, "Monitoring Team Report," November 19, 2015, 18.
11. Corley, "Liberation Tigers of Tamil Eelam," 119.
12. Ibid.
13. Vittori, *Terrorist Financing and Resourcing*, 77.
14. Ibid.
15. Ibid., 79.
16. Ibid., 77–79.
17. Bahney et al., "Economic Analysis of the Financial Records," xiii.
18. Financial Action Task Force, *Emerging Terrorist Financing Risks*, 12.
19. Vittori, *Emerging Terrorist Financing Risks*, 76.
20. Clarke and Williams, "Da'esh in Iraq and Syria," 38.
21. UN Security Council, "Monitoring Team Report," July 19, 2016, 8.
22. Hansen-Lewis and Shapiro, "Understanding the Daesh Economy."
23. Weinstein, *Inside Rebellion*, 7.
24. *BBC News*, "IS Currency Plans in 60 Seconds."
25. Hansen-Lewis and Shapiro, "Understanding the Daesh Economy."
26. UN Security Council, "Monitoring Team Report," January 13, 2017, 9.
27. Vittori, *Emerging Terrorist Financing Risks*, 72.
28. Keatinge, "Role of Finance in Defeating al-Shabaab," 4.
29. Ibid., 5.
30. Vilkko, "Al-Shabaab," 17.
31. Bezhan, "Exclusive: Taliban's Expanding 'Financial Power.'"
32. Darshan-Leitner and Katz, *Harpoon*, 89.
33. Ibid., 245.
34. *Times of Israel*, "Arab Israeli Man, Turkish Citizen."
35. Clarke, *Terrorism, Inc.*; Darshan-Leitner and Katz, *Harpoon*, 253.
36. Hess, "Substantiating the Nexus," 57.
37. Alexander and Beach, "How ISIL Is Funded."
38. Kamere et al., "Lashkar-e-Taiba," 84.
39. Vittori, *Emerging Terrorist Financing Risks*, 70.
40. Zabyelina, "Industry of Terror," 68.
41. Australian Financial Intelligence Unit (AUSTRAC), "Terrorism Financing in Australia 2014."
42. Davis, "Financing the Toronto 18."
43. *R. v. Amara.*
44. Teotonio and Mitchell, "Toronto 18 Member Pleads Guilty."
45. *R. v. Amara.*
46. Winer and Roule, "Fighting Terrorist Finance," 88.
47. Adams, "Financing of Terror," 399.
48. Ibid., 403.
49. Basile, "Going to the Source," 169.

50. Clarke, *Terrorism, Inc.*, 51.
51. Mansour and al-Hashimi, "ISIS Inc."
52. Nebenzya, "Russia Accuses Islamic State."
53. Callimachi, "Paying Ransoms."
54. Thachuk, "Gangsterization of Terrorism," 22.
55. Al-Batati and Hubbard, "Yemeni Bankers Get in Trouble."
56. Kenner, "All ISIS Has Left Is Money."
57. Vittori, *Emerging Terrorist Financing Risks*, 35.
58. Clarke, *Terrorism, Inc.*, 51.
59. Vittori, *Emerging Terrorist Financing Risks*, 68.
60. Mansour and al-Hashimi, "ISIS Inc."
61. Ibid.
62. UN Security Council, "Twenty-Second Report."
63. C. Freeman, "Islamic State 'Earning Millions.'"
64. Ibid.
65. Seierstad, *One of Us*, 107; Taylor, "Norway Gunman Claims."
66. Seierstad, *One of Us*, 107.
67. Ibid., 207.
68. Oftedal, "Financing of Jihadi Terrorist Cells," 17.

8

Moving Funds

Moving money is a fundamental component of terrorist financing.
More often than not, terrorists want to raise money in one location, store
funds in another, and use the money in yet another. Exploring their methods
of moving money, how frequently they use those methods, and the inherent
vulnerabilities of such methods can generate significant opportunities for
countering the financing of terrorism and reducing biases and assumptions
that hinder our understanding of particular fund movement mechanisms.

The ability to move funds is critical for terrorist organizations, cells, and
individuals because funds often need to flow from groups to cells, among
groups, and from donors to organizations. Terrorist groups employ a variety
of fund movement mechanisms to receive their funds from donors, patrons,
and criminal networks. Although their movement of money is often described
as an international activity, many terrorists also employ domestic money
transfer mechanisms for operational or organizational purposes within their
jurisdiction. The movement mechanisms I consider in this chapter should not
be read exclusively through an international lens. Instead, many of these
mechanisms are used within the borders of various countries.

Moving and obscuring funds are closely related aspects of terrorist
financing. In many ways, the movement of money is most vulnerable to
detection. (In money laundering models, the stage when criminals need to
place large volumes of cash into bank accounts can be highly risky, but terrorists rarely need to "place" funds or can do so over lengthier periods and
in smaller volume, reducing the possibility of detection.) When terrorist
funds cross borders or move between financial entities, they are often subject to scrutiny by banks and financial intelligence units. This creates risk

either at the national or international level from financial entities charged with detecting terrorist money. Therefore, terrorists tend to employ trade-craft when they move their money. However, not all aspects of obscuring funds relate to their movement, as I discuss in Chapter 9.

Terrorist groups use almost as many ways to move money as they do to raise it, and there is some overlap in the mechanisms employed. To move funds, terrorist groups exploit and use the following methods:

- the formal financial sector and banks
- money services businesses (MSBs), *hawala*, and informal value transfer services
- cash couriers
- cryptocurrencies, mobile payments, and financial technology
- monetary instruments
- high-value goods and precious metals and stones
- front companies
- trade-based money laundering

According to Freeman and Reuhsen, movement of funds is often over-looked in the study of terrorist financing. Scholars and policymakers tend to focus on terrorist sources of funds and uses of the money, particularly for weapons and attacks.[1] Freeman and Reuhsen argue that terrorists make decisions about movement of funds that take into consideration account volume, risk, convenience, simplicity, cost, and speed.[2] In addition to these, there are practical considerations regarding the jurisdiction in which the terrorists operate. Terrorist organizations, cells, and individuals make use of familiar fund movement mechanisms available to them in their jurisdictions, ones that do not present an insurmountable technical hurdle. Ultimately, these factors create a unique decisionmaking process for the people tasked with moving money for the terrorist groups, cells, or individuals.

Many methods of funds movement used by terrorist organizations are well illustrated by the Islamic State in Iraq and the Levant (ISIL). The group moved money across borders through a combination of hawala, MSBs, and cash couriers.[3] It selected these methods based on a number of factors, including the original form of the funds (in many cases, cash) and the ease of placing them in the formal financial sector. Willing or unwitting contacts in banks can facilitate placement and movement of funds without raising suspicions.[4] Terrorists make decisions about how to move money based on the structure of the financial sector in both the sending and receiving jurisdictions (i.e., whether MSBs, hawala, or banks are more prevalent and widely used). Using multiple transfer methods allowed the group to tailor its movement of money to the situation at hand and avoid detection, an important consideration for operational financing. The method the group chose also reflected the amount of money transferred; ISIL made use of the formal financial system to move significant funds to its affiliated groups and reportedly wired $1.5 million via banks to Mindanao, probably to support affiliate attacks in Marawi.[5]

ISIL also received funds from abroad. France determined that more than 400 people donated funds to ISIL, mostly in small amounts, some by prepaid credit card. People donated these funds to the group through humanitarian associations, financial facilitators, and unspecified online methods. These donations alerted the French authorities both to extremists abroad and to terrorist support networks in France.[6] The variation in ISIL's money movement mechanisms demonstrates the breadth and depth of the group's financial acumen and reflects the jurisdictional challenges and opportunities for a group with such international reach and supporters worldwide.

Many other terrorist groups also employ a variety of methods to move funds, partly out of financial tradecraft and partly out of necessity. Decisions about funds movement are based on a host of variables, but most important is the availability of financial services in the sending and receiving jurisdictions.

The Formal Financial Sector

The formal financial sector, composed primarily of banks, life insurance companies, investment firms, and (depending on the jurisdiction) registered MSBs, has been the target of counterterrorist initiatives since terrorist financing gained mainstream attention. The ongoing use of the sector by terrorist groups, cells, and individuals is somewhat perplexing, given international efforts against it by multilateral bodies such as the Financial Action Task Force (FATF) and similar regional groups. The Financial Action Task Force is a multilateral organization established at the G7 meeting in Paris in 1989 to combat money laundering. The Egmont Group, established in 1995, is a multilateral body of 159 financial intelligence units that provides a platform for the "secure exchange of expertise and financial intelligence to combat money laundering and terrorist financing."[7] The Wolfsberg Group is an association of thirteen global banks that aims to develop frameworks and guidance to manage financial crime risks. The United Nations, of course, also works to reduce terrorist use of the formal financial sector.[8] Despite these efforts, terrorist groups, cells, and individuals continue to make extensive use of this method to store and move funds.

Islamic banks have also been highlighted as particularly vulnerable to terrorist movement of funds. In 2005, the US Department of State wrote that "terrorist groups may also use Islamic banks" because they operate within Islamic law, and many of these banks are not subject to anti–money laundering regulations and controls normally imposed on secular commercial banks.[9]

As Abuza noted in 2003, although countries that host the majority of Islamic banks might have been slow to implement anti–money laundering and counterterrorist financing controls (for a variety of reasons, including will and technical capacity), there is no inherent vulnerability in Islamic banks that makes them more susceptible to terrorist financing.[10] The same vulnerabilities that exist within Islamic banks can also exist within Western-style banks.

Most terrorist groups make some use of the formal financial sector, although their use varies in extent and duration. The Liberation Tigers of Tamil Eelam (LTTE) had a significant amount of money in the sector, with extensive holdings in the United States, Canada, the United Kingdom, and Switzerland, as well as in offshore accounts in St. Croix and the Virgin Islands. The group also took advantage of the personal accounts of its members, supporters, and contacts to move money and prevent it from being associated with known LTTE individuals or companies.[11] Hizballah has also used banks to move funds: Al-Madina Bank and its subsidiary United Credit Bank "knowingly laundered" funds for a Hizballah arms dealer.[12] The Palestinian Islamic Jihad had dozens of bank accounts in Iran, Lebanon, and Syria as well as money in financial institutions in the West Bank and the Gaza Strip.[13] The Taliban is also reported to use the formal financial system to send and receive funds.[14]

The Lashkar-e-Taiba (LeT) moves money through a variety of mechanisms including hawala, cash couriers, and banks in the formal financial sector, which demonstrates not only a variety of methods for obtaining funds but also advanced knowledge of international systems as well as acknowledgment of the need for financial tradecraft. For instance, the group provides account numbers of some of its key fund-raising websites, presumably so that people can make direct deposits to those accounts.[15] In another example of the group's use of the formal financial sector, funds from 400,000 Pakistanis living in Britain were moved from British banks to Pakistani banks for humanitarian aid; however, of the $10 million transferred to Pakistan in 2005, more than half of it was diverted to the LeT.[16]

Some state sponsors of terrorism use the formal financial sector to move funds to their terrorist clients. For instance, information from Mossad indicates that Iran channeled money to Hamas through a European bank headquartered in Zurich.[17] Iran has also used the formal financial sector to send money to Hizballah. Iran's state-owned Bank Saderat moved $50 million from the Central Bank of Iran through its subsidiary in London to its branch in Beirut, ultimately providing the funds to Hizballah fronts in Lebanon.[18] Although this example dates from 2007, it is entirely plausible that state sponsors can and do continue to move funds to their clients through the formal financial sector, using either willing or unwitting contacts to facilitate the transactions. They might also take advantage of known anti–money laundering and counterterrorist financing program deficiencies within specific banks to help obscure the sources and destinations of their funds.

Terrorists have also used the formal financial sector to move protection money foreign businesses paid them in extortion or rent-seeking schemes to allow them continued operation. ISIL and other Syria-based terrorist groups have engaged in this practice. For example, LafargeHolcim's subsidiary in Syria is believed to have used fifty-four bank accounts and an intermediary to pay ISIL and other terrorist groups protection money to keep its cement plant open.[19]

Although significant attention has been paid to other methods of moving money, terrorists still use the formal banking sector. Despite all the effort the financial sector has put into counterterrorist and anti–money laundering practices, it remains vulnerable to abuse. By far the most profound issues arise at banks that ask too few or no questions, hire poorly vetted employees, or allow correspondent accounts or payable-through accounts, all of which can be used to facilitate terrorist financing.[20] For example, a leaked reported from the Central Intelligence Agency indicated that senior al-Rajhi family members long supported Islamic extremists and knew terrorists used their bank to facilitate their activities while HSBC in the United States maintained a correspondent relationship with al-Rajhi Bank of Saudi Arabia.[21] In this case, HSBC was vulnerable to a correspondent banking relationship with a bank co-opted by terrorists. This, of course, has not been the only issue at HSBC identified by anti–money laundering/countering the financing of terrorism (AML/CFT) regimes over the years.[22] Terrorist organizations use the formal financial sector to send and receive relatively large amounts of money because it is convenient and reliable. If or when they are able to co-opt bank employees, this mechanism of transferring funds only becomes easier and more secure for them.

Operational Financing in the Formal Sector

Terrorist cells and individuals also use the formal financial sector to store and move funds. In fact, it is rare for attacks in the West and global North to take place without funds transiting bank accounts at some point. For instance, the Sauerland cell (2007), the liquid bomb airline passenger (2006), the London underground bombings (2005), the Hofstadt group (2004), and the Madrid cell (2004) all deposited, withdrew, or moved funds through banks or financial institutions.[23]

Funds intended to finance terrorist operations have a long history of transiting the formal financial sector. In July 2000, a full year before the attacks of 9/11, SunTrust Bank in Florida opened a joint account for two of the hijackers. The bank issued them debit cards and accepted around $109,000 over the subsequent ten weeks in transfers from bank accounts in Dubai. The funds deposited into the SunTrust account sustained the attackers and paid for elements of the attack.[24] The terrorists were provided other funds in advance of their operation as well. On June 23, 2001, al-Qaeda's chief money handlers (Mustafa Ahmed al-Hawsawi and Faye Banihammad) opened accounts at the Dubai branch of Standard Chartered Bank. Al-Hawsawi provided the 9/11 hijackers funds to buy traveler's checks when they transited Dubai.[25] He also wired another $15,000 to the al-Qaeda cell in Hamburg, Germany. Ramzi bin-al-Shibh, another of the 9/11 attackers, picked up these funds. Al-Hawsawi also had power of attorney over several of the hijacker's accounts. Hours before the 9/11 attacks, he consolidated the money left in the accounts he controlled ($42,000) and withdrew it.[26] Of course, this use of the formal financial sector predates the extensive efforts to prevent its use through counterterrorist financing initiatives but provides a useful example of how operational funds have been moved for terrorist purposes.

Since the 9/11 attacks, a variety of operational terrorist activity has been financed with funds moved through the formal financial sector. The 2008 Barcelona plot also involved the movement of funds through the banking sector, with the plot leader receiving €9,000 ($11,000) through wire transfers.[27] In 2010, a suicide bomber plot in Stockholm involved donations from individuals in Glasgow deposited in cash to bank accounts.[28] Anders Breivik, perpetrator of the 2011 attacks in Norway, also made extensive use of bank accounts to move and store money for operational purchases for his attacks.[29] In 2012, Nasserdine Menni was convicted of transferring €6,725 (roughly $8,100) to a bank account of the perpetrator in the Stockholm bombing attacks of 2010; some of those funds are believed to have been used by the bomber to buy material to make pressure-cooker bombs.[30] Money for terrorist travel and small-scale attacks has also come out of the accounts of individuals in the formal banking sector. Ultimately, despite laws, regulations, and international efforts, terrorist financing through the formal financial sector is still prevalent.

Cash Couriers

Almost all terrorist groups have employed cash couriers or bulk cash smuggling to move small or large sums of money for operational or organizational financing. Cash couriers might be one of the simplest means of moving funds, but that does not mean precautions are not taken or just anyone can be employed as a cash courier. Cash couriers for terrorist organizations are trusted individuals chosen for this role with care. In some cases, they might be recruited specifically for this purpose because of their language skills or ability to move across borders, through conflict zones, into and out of specific communities. In the 1990s, al-Qaeda relied on cash couriers to move money from Pakistan into Afghanistan, having already moved it from the United Arab Emirates (UAE) to Pakistan through hawalas, or money changers.[31] As part of their operational activity, Naxalites established networks of "paid and trusted cash couriers, divided into two specialist functions." The first group was responsible for moving funds to trusted individuals, and the second used "sophisticated methods" to hide the funds. Throughout the process, meticulous records of where funds are stored, and with whom, were kept.[32]

Although cash couriers are trustworthy, having been vetted by the terrorist organization, they can also be slow.[33] As a result, they might be used by terrorist organizations only when a high level of operational security is required or there is no other way to move funds. Cash couriers use a variety of techniques to augment their operational security, such as concealing money in vehicles, packages, luggage, or anything that can hold a large physical volume of cash. Sometimes, if they are operating in a permissive environment, they do not bother to hide the cash.[34]

Although the method might be onerous, state sponsors of terrorism also use cash couriers to move money to their clients, even when relatively large sums of funds are involved. Iran's Islamic Revolutionary Guards Corps–Quds Force (IRGC-QF) used Mahan Air to move funds to Hizballah.[35] Air travel can speed up the delivery of funds through cash couriers, but because of cross-border currency controls, the amount of money that can be moved in this manner is limited, at least without employing financial tradecraft or relying on lax borders, corrupt border officials, or private airfields. The Pakistani Inter-Services Intelligence (ISI) sometimes provides cash directly to LeT members who can carry sums of money across the border into Kashmir, generating no electronic records in case of investigations.[36] Some of the money ISIL in Afghanistan (ISIL-KP) obtained was funneled from the ISIL core organization using cash couriers, alternative remittance systems, and bank transfers.[37] Cash couriers have one major advantage most other methods of moving funds lack: no electronic footprint. In today's surveillance age, that benefit likely outweighs the drawbacks of using cash couriers.

In operational financing, cash couriers offer ease of use, simplicity, and security. Rachi Ramda, the leader of the Armed Islamic Group of Algeria (GIA) in France in the mid-1990s, used lower-level members of the organization as cash couriers, moving funds to cells and individuals for a variety of activities.[38] Before the Bali bombing, Jemaah Islamiyah used two Indonesian laborers working in Malaysia as cash couriers to transfer more than $15,000 between terrorist group members. Al-Qaeda also used cash couriers in 2003 to transfer $50,000 to Jemaah Islamiyah following the Bali attack and to move $8,500 to the bombers of the Atrium mall in Jakarta in 2001.[39] Cash couriers work well for operations because smaller amounts of money are involved in terrorist attacks than in organizational support, and couriers offer greater security than many other methods of moving funds.

Money Services Businesses

Money services businesses (MSBs) and hawalas are often used by terrorist groups and by the rest of the world because their fees are often lower than those of banks, and MSBs are more widely available. MSBs, which in many jurisdictions are simply regulated or registered hawalas, also generally charge lower fees than banks to move money internationally and, in many cases, do so more quickly. It is possible that terrorist actors believe MSBs have more lax standards about gathering information and reporting it to authorities, although this likely depends on the jurisdiction and the specific MSBs. In some instances, terrorist organizations have been able to own or co-opt MSBs (or local agents or branches), making moving funds much more operationally secure. This is effectively the gold standard for any illicit financial actor: control over a money movement mechanism.

Hizballah is known to make extensive use of MSBs; Elissa Exchange and Hassan Ayash Exchange were both implicated in moving money as part of a used-car scheme Hizballah used to raise funds. After they were closed, two other MSBs quickly arose and took their place, potentially also within the terrorist financing network: Kassem Rmeiti and Hawali Exchange. These new exchange companies were designated terrorists in 2013 by the US Department of the Treasury.[40]

Hamas has also used MSBs to move money. For instance, Al Taqwa Bank (an MSB or hawala) reportedly handled as much as $60 million for Hamas.[41] Hamas also controls the Beit el-Mal holding company. The company itself holds a 20 percent stake in al Aqsa International Bank, reportedly the financial arm of Hamas.[42] Other alleged front companies used to move and hide funds are the Sunugrut Global Group and al Ajouli (MSB), both of which have been accused of money laundering for Hamas.[43]

Western Union wire transfers, travelers checks, and credit cards have all been effective means of moving funds to terrorist groups or cells, and Western Union has featured prominently in ISIL financing, in part because the company offered services in Iraq and Syria when the terrorist organization took control of the territory.[44] In one salient example, a man in Singapore was charged with providing money to ISIL to finance its propaganda efforts. He provided $450 to a man in Turkey, Mohamad Alsaid Alhmidan, via Western Union.[45] Indeed, in 2016, Alhmidan was sanctioned, along with Hussam Jamous, for providing financial services for the ISIL.[46] The amounts of money involved in each of these transactions might not be large but in quantity of transactions could amount to a significant sum of money for the group over time. Western Union has also been used by ISIL-linked militant group Jamaah Ansharut Daulah. The group received funds from people in five countries totaling $29,569. Funds were sent from Trinidad and Tobago, the Maldives, Germany, Venezuela, and Malaysia, and the money was used to purchase materials to assemble bombs later given to East Indonesia Mujahidin in Poso, Central Sulawesi.[47]

Terrorists often seek out direct control of money movement mechanisms, and ISIL was no exception. ISIL is reported to have co-opted and controlled a number of MSBs in and around the territory it controlled in Iraq, Syria, and

Turkey. According to the Central Bank of Iraq, hundreds of small, ISIL-linked exchange houses operated in Baghdad. These MSBs allowed the group to convert Iraqi dinar to US dollars and move the funds anywhere in the world with little scrutiny.[48] In March 2018, Turkish police raided a currency exchange in Istanbul with reported ties to ISIL. The raid recovered $1.3 million in currency, gold and silver, British pounds, and weapons. How much of this can be tied directly to ISIL, however, remains unclear.[49]

Terrorists exploit any technology available to finance their activities and are not targeting the MSB sector specifically because of lax regulations or reporting. Indeed, Western Union was used because of its large international presence, reliability, and relatively low fees. Terrorists also seek to hide behind volume of transfers, and the sector certainly can accommodate in that regard. Terrorists use the money movement mechanisms available in their jurisdictions, and MSBs are present in most countries around the world, offering a veritable cornucopia of options.

Hawala and Informal Value Transfer Systems

Perhaps no money movement mechanism has received as much negative coverage as hawala. In 2003, Abuza noted that the hawala sector is the "primary conduit for terrorist financing transfers," and certainly, examples of terrorist use of hawala and informal money movement mechanisms abound.[50] However, the critique of hawala as a money movement mechanism is perhaps overstated and might not reflect the data on how terrorists move funds, both for organizational and operational purposes. There are good reasons terrorists and nonterrorists alike use hawala to move money, only some of which point to inherent vulnerabilities in the sector. Some of the benefits of using hawala instead of the formal financial sector include better exchange rates, quicker transactions, avoiding limits on foreign exchange, avoiding higher fees, and avoiding complicated foreign banking procedures.[51] In other cases, these benefits might include lack of regulation and reporting.

Although the term *hawala* is used most often in literature on terrorist financing, there are in fact many different types of traditional informal financial networks: hawala or Hundi in South Asia, Fei ch'ien in China, Phoe Khan in Thailand, Door-to-Door in Philippines, and so forth. These all use traditional, geographical, cultural, and ethnic ties as part of a remittance system that transfers hundreds of millions of dollars.[52] Hawala involve the movement of money between two locations without the physical transfer of funds, and they operate both domestically and internationally.[53] Hawala are often described as a trust-based systems, but in practice, these are businesses, and the consequences for defrauding a business partner in the network likely trump trust relationships. The punishments for any such transgression would be career-ending.

Hawala transactions are used to move money in much of the world in part because they can be very fast.[54] They can be nearly instantaneous, provided that the sending and receiving parties can get to the hawaladar. In other instances, it can take days for people to pick up their money because of the infrastructure of the country in which the transfer was sent, the recipient's schedule, and a host of other factors. And despite some people's insistence that hawaladars do not keep records, this has been proven largely untrue, although the bookkeeping methods vary and can be almost entirely incomprehensible to an outside observer.[55] Instead of using banks and financial institutions, individuals find remitters or hawaladars, provide them funds, and request that the funds be transferred to another individual. Instead of moving the money physically, the hawaladar will instead contact a business associate and ask for the funds to be released to the intended beneficiary. Later, entirely independently of the original transaction (and only if or when an imbalance occurs), the two hawaladars will settle their accounts through a funds transfer (potentially through an MSB or bank) or perhaps through goods or services.

For hawaladars, settling accounts can take many forms; this is required because a hawaladar can experience more outflows than inflows or vice versa. This balancing can be done in cash transactions, merchandise, or special favors. Import/export businesses also lend themselves well to the settlement of hawala accounts because they can alter their prices on merchandise to incorporate debt payment.[56] This method of account settlement effectively uses over- and underinvoicing of goods to settle hawala accounts, not necessarily for nefarious purposes but rather to reduce the requirement to conduct a separate transaction. In other cases, hawalas use the formal financial sector to settle accounts. As de Goede notes, the principles of speed, trust, paperlessness, global reach, and fluidity claimed (and vilified) in hawala are exactly the same characteristics that globalized investment banking aspires to possess.[57]

One of the reasons hawala have been so vilified as part of the global war on terror is a common misconception that the 9/11 hijackers used hawala to finance their attacks. The 9/11 Commission explicitly states there was no evidence to suggest that the hijackers used hawala to raise or move funds. Instead, they used normal US bank accounts in their own names and received international wire transfers from al-Qaeda. The commission notes, in relation to hawala, that al-Qaeda did use this method to move money prior to 2001 and after its arrival in Afghanistan (where the banking sector was such that hawala were the only way to move funds).[58]

The vilification of hawala (and MSBs to a lesser extent) was a structural issue in the counterterrorist financing world following 9/11. Vlcek highlights some of the subsequent overreach, noting that the hawala or MSBs (depending on the jurisdiction in which they operated) were accused of "close connections" with al-Qaeda and of providing the group financial services.[59] Classified intelligence was used to justify the order to close firms, freeze assets, and place individuals on the UN sanctions list. These informal transfers have been vilified because they challenge state authority, power, and legitimacy; they can also facilitate capital flight and undermine monetary policies and controls.[60]

One of the most famous (or infamous) examples of this vilification is al-Barakaat, a Somali hawala. Al-Barakaat was accused of operating an unlicensed money transmission service and more seriously of being linked to al-Qaeda and financing terrorism. White House statements at the time of a multiagency US task force raid indicated that the network skimmed up to 5 percent off all the transactions it processed to raise funds for al-Qaeda, and the organization managed, invested, and distributed those funds on behalf of the terrorist organization. As it turns out, most of the funds seized during the raid were actually migrant remittances. The seizure of these funds, and the subsequent destruction of the al-Barakaat network, had a devastating impact on Somalia's economy and the people who worked for the company.[61] However, in the case of al-Barakaat, none of those connected with the company in the United States were ultimately charged with financing terrorism. One Somali was convicted of operating an unlicensed money transfer business in Boston, and two other Somalis operating the al-Barakaat office near Washington, DC, pled guilty to an anti–money laundering charge.[62]

Mohamed Hussein, a Somali-born Canadian citizen who ran al-Barakaat North America, was arrested during these raids. In Ottawa, his brother Liban was arrested and held for one week before being released on bail. Al-Barakaat had assets frozen in Luxembourg, the UAE, and the United States. However, by April 2002, Luxembourg had released most of the frozen money and had found no reasonable cause to keep the accounts blocked. By June 2002, a Canadian judge had also refused to extradite Liban Hussein to the United States on terrorism charges and found that US information provided no reasonable grounds on which to proceed. In a related move, Sweden also declined to press criminal charges. According to de Goede, no credible evidence of al-Barakaat's involvement in terrorist financing, or terrorism more generally, has been made public.[63] The revenues the company generated amounted to no more than $700k per year, and the links to both terrorism and terrorist financing were unsubstantiated.[64]

Although hawala have been maligned and vilified for their role in terrorist financing, there are cases where these concerns are valid, and terrorist groups do use hawala to move money. For instance, Al-Shabaab makes extensive use of MSBs and hawala to move money into Somalia from international donors. Al-Shabaab supporters in Missouri used licensed MSBs with offices in the United States to remit money to Somalia intended for the general support of Al-Shabaab fighters.[65] (Many Somalia hawala are in fact registered as MSBs in other countries.) In Somalia, Al-Shabaab moves money through local money transfer agencies or by direct bank deposits when those financial institutions are available. The accounts are maintained in the names of Al-Shabaab finance officials.[66]

Terrorist groups tend to use the existing money-moving means available to them in the territory in which they operate, and this is not always done with the support of the population. If hawala are prevalent in the area, they use hawala; however, if other, more formal mechanisms exist, they also use those. When al-Qaeda in the Arabian Peninsula (AQAP) took control of towns and villages in the south and east of Yemen, most banks closed. As a result, the terrorist group (and people in its area of control) turned to MSBs to move funds. In particular, the Al Omgy Money Exchange was used. The exchange held accounts for the national oil company, disbursed salaries for the Yemeni government, and also provided accounts for al-Qaeda members. The exchange has ninety-five offices across Yemen that essentially work like banks.[67] The Al Omgy Money Exchange was later designated as a terrorist entity by the United States for providing financial services to AQAP. The owner of the money exchange described his relationship with AQAP as a business relationship in which he had no choice.[68] The forced use of hawala is another form of exploitation in which terrorists engage when they are able to control or influence territory, and often little can be done by the local population to prevent it.

Hawala have been used to move money for operational purposes, although specific examples are limited. One example includes the individual involved in the Times Square terrorist attack in May 2010, Faisal Shahzad. He had handlers in Pakistan in the Tehrik-i-Taliban Pakistan (TTP) who arranged for $4,900 to be sent to him via hawala.[69] In another example, money moved through the hawala system from Gulf countries to LeT cells was used to finance the Mumbai 2008 attacks as well as the Bangalore bombing in July 2008.[70] LeT is also believed to have used hawala networks to move funds before the 2000 Red Fort attack in Delhi, and hawaladars are also believed to have knowingly moved funds for Iraqi insurgent groups during the first war in Iraq, making them targets of coalition counterterrorist operations.[71] Hawala have been used to move funds for groups across the political and ideological spectrum. Their trust and anonymity might be a driver, but in many parts of the world, this is simply the only way (or at least the cheapest way) to move funds.

Financial Technology, Cryptocurrency, and Social Media

Financial technologies that move, manage, and store funds have proliferated significantly over the past decade and now feature prominently as applications on cell phones, as websites, and generally as part of the information technology infrastructure of the twenty-first century. Financial technologies include ways to manage and invest money, methods to move it internationally, peer-to-peer lending platforms, crowdfunding platforms, payment systems, and many other services. Terrorist groups exploit modern communication and financial technology including cell phones, social media, and encrypted applications to move money securely.

Terrorist groups primarily use cryptocurrencies, mobile payment systems, and other financial technologies to move and obscure funds. Although some reports have indicated that terrorist groups "finance" their activities in this manner, actually raising funds through cryptocurrencies and new technologies is rare. Terrorist groups solicit donations through cryptocurrencies, mobile payment systems, and financial applications and use that technology to send the funds where they are needed, obscuring their sources and destinations depending on the technology. For instance, in 2016, the Mujahideen Shura Council active in the Gaza Strip, considered a terrorist organization by the United States since 2014, launched a campaign for donations. The group was specific in how it wanted those donations, asking for them in Bitcoin and stating that they would use the money for the purchase of weapons.[72]

Terrorist groups such as ISIL might have also been using Bitcoin and other digital or cryptocurrencies to move funds since 2014. In that year, ISIL fighters in Raqqa, Syria, indicated that they prefer to make long-distance transactions using digital currencies such as Bitcoin.[73] This use of Bitcoin, even before significant counterterrorism pressure was exerted on the group and MSBs in Syria, demonstrates that terrorist groups can and do adopt new technologies well before they are forced to do so by counterterrorist measures. The scope and scale of that adoption does, however, shift with external pressures. In 2019, Hamas might have adopted Bitcoin as a fund-raising method. The Gaza-based Izz el-Deen al-Qassam brigades, proscribed by the United States and European Union, called on supporters to donate using Bitcoin in a fund-raising campaign. The group generated a new digital wallet with every transaction, making it harder to keep tabs on its financing. Between March and April 2019, the campaign was estimated to have raised around $7,400.[74] In later years, ISIL solicited money through a website, asking individuals to donate money using Bitcoin and giving the address of a Bitcoin wallet for deposit. The website instructed individuals to use Local-Bitcoins in Helsinki, Finland, and noted that the donations would be used to fund the "activities of the website."[75]

The adoption of financial technologies and mobile payment systems can be particularly rapid in countries and areas traditionally underbanked. For instance, Somalia has primarily used hawala for international money movement, but few individuals had bank accounts or used any form of fund movement other than cash transactions. Somalis had a need to be able to send small amounts of money throughout the region quickly and efficiently. To cater to this need, mobile payment systems were created and widely adopted in the horn of Africa. These systems, such as M-Pesa, are relatively common in East Africa and allow users to send funds directly to each other for low fees and with little oversight. Of course, as with all fund movement mechanisms, they can also be exploited for terrorist financing purposes, and some Al-Shabaab supporters have moved funds for the group through mobile payment systems.[76]

More established financial technologies are also popular with terrorist groups. For instance, ISIL used PayPal to obtain funds from its supporters. In 2018, the group was facing financial pressures, so it sold some of its minted coins as collectors' items. The purchases of the coins were done via PayPal.[77] Terrorists adopt new financial technologies when they have widespread acceptance; have proven reliability; can handle a significant volume of transactions; and can ensure anonymity, usability, and security.[78] Some of these criteria might not be inherent in the technology but can be achieved through basic tradecraft (such as false identities or proxies).

Terrorist groups frequently combine social media calls for funds with financial technologies to collect and move those funds.[79] They use social media platforms to reach followers and then direct them to provide their donations through financial applications. In 2017, the al-Sadaqah website (an allegedly al-Qaeda-linked website), used Facebook and Telegram to solicit donations from its supporters via Bitcoin.[80] Separately, Hajjaj al-Ajmi was sanctioned by the United Nations in 2014 for using Twitter to solicit funds for Nusra Front.[81] Saad al-Kaabi, listed by the United Nations as a terrorist in 2015, posted solicitations for donations on Facebook and WhatsApp in order to arm, feed, and treat fighters in Syria.[82] Terrorists use these mechanisms to raise funds because of the reach they can have in a short period and, correspondingly, the amount of money they can raise, even though they risk exposure.

The effectiveness of these campaigns is questionable, of course. For example, the Mujahideen Shura Council was only able to raise $500 through an online campaign asking for donations in cryptocurrencies.[83] Many campaigns might raise relatively small amounts of money because people are not generally supportive of the terrorist organization, because they are unable to overcome the technological obstacles to creating and maintaining a Bitcoin or cryptocurrency wallet or account, or because they are avoiding the transfer mechanism out of operational security concerns, given that cryptocurrency is nowhere near as anonymous as has been claimed, particularly without the use of tumblers, exchanges, and other services that make using Bitcoin more challenging.

Increasingly, neo-Nazis, white supremacists, white nationalists, and other ideologically motivated violent extremists use Bitcoin, cryptocurrencies, and new financial technologies to solicit donations from their supporters and to move funds. Bitcoin has become the "preferred payment method for Stormfront, the oldest and largest white supremacist website on the internet."[84] To move money, right-wing terrorist organization National Action relies on peer-to-peer transactions such as PayPal and bank transfers.[85] Increasingly, white supremacists and right-wing extremists are being financially deplatformed from other payment services because of pressure from groups dedicated to exposing their activities.[86] They are turning to alternative payment processors and mechanisms for their fund movement needs.

Although useful for money transfers, cryptocurrencies are rarely used by terrorist organizations to purchase goods and services. Terrorists adopt cryptocurrencies to manage, transfer, and use funds, although full terrorist adoption of cryptocurrency might be restricted because of the limited acceptability and usability of cryptocurrency in regions where they operate.[87] In the future, that might change as terrorist groups can increasingly use Bitcoin to pay for services such as website hosting, as ISIL reportedly did using Bitcoin.[88]

As with any new technology or technique terrorists can use, there is often significant discussion around whether it is permissible to use the technology, a trend specifically seen with Islamist extremist groups. In February 2018, the "Tech Talk" section of *Al-Haqiqa*, a pro-al-Qaeda English-language magazine, examined the permissibility of using Bitcoin and other cryptocurrencies to fund terrorist activities.[89] Although terrorist groups, and specifically al-Qaeda- or ISIL-affiliated or -inspired groups, often seek religious justification or permissibility for their actions, they are also not beholden to their ideology; if a technology or financing method becomes available, terrorist groups, cells, and individuals frequently use it, even if it is not a widely accepted or condoned method.

Terrorist cells and individuals have also received funds for attacks and operational activities through Bitcoin and cryptocurrency. Individuals seeking to raise funds to send fighters abroad to join ISIL received donations for this purpose through Bitcoin and other cryptocurrencies. In June 2015, US authorities convicted Shukri Amin of helping ISIL supporters travel to Syria through the use of social media sites where supporters were encouraged to contribute Bitcoin.[90]

Although Bitcoin and other cryptocurrencies get the bulk of the media coverage on terrorist use of financial technologies, older, more established methods are commonly used among terrorists to move funds. In 2015, a would-be suicide bomber, Mohamed Rehman, and his wife were found guilty of plotting a terrorist attack to take place on the anniversary of the 7/7 London attack.[91] Rehman set up a PayPal account and used it to purchase from eBay the ingredients, components, and equipment to build an improvised explosive device.[92] Given the widespread use of PayPal, it is unlikely that it was a deliberate attempt at obfuscation; instead, it was likely the simplest way to purchase the goods available to the couple. Similarly, Bahrun Naim, the mastermind of the Jakarta attack in 2016, used Bitcoin to transfer funds to the militants and fund other terrorist activities. He also reportedly used PayPal to move funds.[93] Avoiding the formal financial sector and its diligence with regard to identifying terrorist financing might have been one of the reasons operational cells have moved funds through new financial technologies. In some cases, their choice to move funds in this manner might also be a function of lack of banking or financial infrastructure or simply a desire to pay lower fees.

The use of cryptocurrencies by terrorist organizations is not widespread but is likely to increase as adoption of the technology becomes more widespread. In 2020, a US civil case sought to freeze hundreds of thousands of dollars allegedly raised for terrorist groups.[94] As the barriers to use of financial technology decrease and make it more user friendly, terrorist groups, cells, and individuals increasingly use them to move funds. However, this adoption might be less out of an interest to obscure terrorist activity than it is to move funds with low fees. The ability to obscure transactions might simply be a positive side effect of some of these technologies. Many terrorists increasingly understand the limitations of privacy in the digital space and use multiple methods to obscure their activities instead of relying on the existing anonymity provisions of the technology.

Precious Metals and Stones

Terrorists do not just use new technologies to move funds; they also rely on older methods, such as moving value through precious metals and stones. However, as mechanisms for moving funds have proliferated, particularly with the increase in the number of inexpensive options generated by financial technologies, this method of moving value and funds has decreased. As with any terrorist money movement mechanism, the use of precious metals and stones is dependent on the sending and receiving jurisdiction and the prevalence of this particular method of value transfer among the populations in those jurisdictions.

Transmitting value through precious metals and stones might sometimes be preferable to sending money through formal or informal networks. This might be because of concern about counterterrorist financing surveillance, but it might also serve as a way to diversify money movement schemes to prevent losses in case of detection or accidents. This mechanism is also a good way to move high value without drawing attention, and it can function similarly to a cash courier. Gold remains popular with terrorist groups; it is reliable and easily disguised, and tracing its origin is nearly impossible.[95] Further, depending on where the terrorist group or cell operates, gold might be highly valued and widely used, making it easy to exchange for goods or services. For instance, gold has been used by the Taliban to move funds, specifically from Saudi donors. The Taliban flew gold bullion directly from Dubai to its unofficial capital in Kandahar.[96]

Diamonds have also frequently been cited by analysts and researchers as a way terrorist groups move funds. Hizballah is believed to have been involved in the diamond business, likely as a business venture, and al-Qaeda and some of its affiliates are believed to have used diamonds to store and move value.[97]

Operationally, the storage and movement of value or funds in precious metals and stones is less common; some cases of cells and individuals using this method exist, but in these instances, the individuals involved had prior access to and knowledge of the sector. Value transfer using precious metals and stones remains largely the purview of terrorist groups and, even then, is somewhat restricted as a general financing method.

Trade-Based Funds Movement

Sophisticated terrorist organizations and those with connections in the business community can take advantage of existing trade networks to move money. To do this, terrorist actors generally require (1) the use of a legitimate or front business, (2) plausible goods to trade, and (3) enough business acumen to create false invoices. Several schemes exist to move money in this way. In an overinvoicing scheme, the originator ships goods but invoices the recipient for more than was shipped or more money than the goods are worth. The differences, after the recipient has paid the invoice, can be allocated to a terrorist group, cell, or individual. In an underinvoicing scheme, the originator ships more goods than are invoiced or underprices the goods shipped. The beneficiary of the transaction can then sell the goods and pay the invoice, creating a profit that can be diverted to terrorist purposes. Other variations on these themes exist; in some, no goods are shipped at all, and the ignorance of customs officials is exploited to facilitate the movement of funds between companies with a plausible cover story.

In one variation of this scheme, a terrorist organization can supply another group "funds" or value by sending them goods that can be sold without requiring the recipient to pay for them. Al-Shabaab is believed to have received large-scale overseas support from al-Qaeda donors through this method. Goods were brought into Somalia by Al-Shabaab-linked businessmen and sold, with the revenues provided to the group.[98] In the case of Al-Shabaab and Somalia, goods might be brought into Somalia instead of cash or transfers because the goods can be sold for an increased profit in Somalia compared with their origin country. At the same time, it might also be a way for the groups to avoid using Somalia's MSB or hawala network, which they might assume is monitored by counterterrorism officials.

The LTTE also used misinvoicing of goods (either over- or underpricing the goods in question) to move funds under a plausible cover, effectively obscuring terrorist funds through commercial mechanisms.[99] Chechen groups also moved funds through goods; they used stolen cars they could sell for cash or barter to move funds, and sometimes the cars were ransomed.[100] LeT also engages in a variety of illegal activities, including underinvoicing.[101] For instance, Kashmiri carpet dealers reduce the value of exports to Gulf countries on a shipping invoice. The difference between the true value and the value of the invoice returns to India through hawala transfers.[102] Hamas has also moved funds and value through trade-based money laundering mechanisms. In August 2017, Israel's domestic intelligence service, Shin Bet, announced that it had disrupted a Hamas money laundering ring. The scheme involved funneling hundreds of thousands of dollars from officials in Gaza to the West Bank city of Hebron via Turkey. Goods were purchased in Turkey and imported to Hebron using international shipping companies. Funds from the sale of the goods were given to Hamas operatives in Hebron, effectively moving them from Gaza to the West Bank through a series of intermediaries and trade activity.[103]

Moving money through trade-based mechanisms involves taking advantage of the varying (and in many cases, unknowable) prices of goods in two jurisdictions. The prices depend on what the exporting and importing parties agreed to and could be affected by shifting market prices.[104] False invoicing is particularly convenient if a group already has companies established to conduct transactions. The risk of detection is low, although with the establishment of trade transparency units around the world, it is increasing.[105] Trade-based mechanisms are primarily used by terrorist groups, although it remains possible that cells and individuals could use these mechanisms as well.

Conclusion

Many terrorism analysts assume that terrorists seek to operate outside the formal financial and banking system and specifically point to the informal and underground systems as a means of moving funds.[106] In practice, a variety of methods are used to move money, and the formal financial system features prominently. Terrorist groups, cells, and individuals all employ a variety of mechanisms to move money to and from the areas in which they operate or aspire to operate.

Operationally, cells and individuals have more limited requirements for money movement, but the stakes are higher. When they are involved in the movement of funds, it is often either to kickstart their attack plan or to settle their affairs just prior to the attack. Banks have played a significant role in moving money for terrorist attacks and other operational activities, but other money mechanisms are also frequently employed by terrorist organizations, cells, and individuals. Terrorist networks in Europe used a variety of means to move funds.

Figure 8.1 illustrates the prevalence of each mechanism of money movement used by terrorist groups. The most widely used mechanisms are banks, trade-based methods, hawala, and cash couriers. It is important to recall that these data represent reported methods in open source information; reporting biases might exist (particularly regarding the use of hawala), and many mechanisms might be significantly underreported, such as the use of credit cards or mobile payment methods, because of the small amounts of money involved or lack of access to information detailing these methods.

In Figure 8.2, the methods used by terrorist cells and individuals in plots and attacks are outlined. Cash couriers are used most often, followed by banks and MSBs. Financial technologies are relatively popular, as are credit cards

Figure 8.1 Organizational Movement of Funds

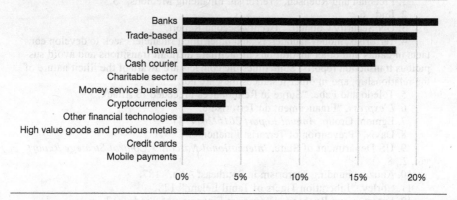

Figure 8.2 Operational Movement of Funds

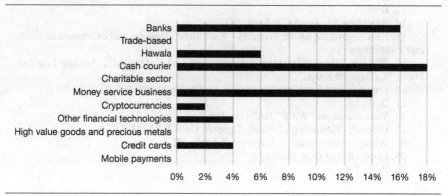

and cryptocurrencies. These more contemporary methods of money movement are likely to increase in the future as globalization and digitalization take further hold on the global economy and cash transactions become abnormal.

Terrorists ultimately use these methods to move money at their disposal in the jurisdictions in which they operate, but they also pay attention to other factors, such as volume, risk, convenience, simplicity, cost, and speed. Despite the vilification of hawala, banks remain a popular method for moving funds for both operational and organizational activity. Although cryptocurrency and financial technologies are increasing in popularity, the increase in their use by terrorist actors has not been explosive but is likely to continue growing, albeit not exponentially. Old methods that promise security and anonymity remain popular for terrorist actors, although global trends might shift the availability of these methods.

Notes

1. Freeman and Ruehsen, "Terrorism Financing Methods," 5.
2. Ibid., 6.
3. UN Security Council, "Twenty-Second Report."
4. Terrorists, money launderers, and other illicit financiers seek to develop contacts in banks and other institutions to facilitate difficult transitions and avoid suspicious transaction reports. Sometimes the contacts are aware of the illicit nature of the relationship, and in other instances they are not.
5. Toledo and Fabe, "Surge in Remittances Preceded IS Attack."
6. *L'express*, "Financement du Terrorisme."
7. Egmont Group, *Annual Report 2016/2017*, 11.
8. Davis, "Prevention of Terrorist Financing."
9. US Department of State, *International Narcotics Control Strategy Report*, vol. 2., 8.
10. Abuza, "Funding Terrorism in Southeast Asia," 187.
11. Corley, "Liberation Tigers of Tamil Eelam," 128.
12. Freeman and Ruehsen, "Terrorism Financing Methods," 17.
13. Darshan-Leitner and Katz, *Harpoon*, 41.
14. Financial Action Task Force, *Emerging Terrorist Financing Risks*, 20.
15. Kamere et al., "Lashkar-e-Taiba," 83.
16. Ibid.
17. Bergman, *Rise and Kill First*, 551.
18. US Department of the Treasury, "Fact Sheet: Designation of Iranian Entities and Individuals."
19. Waldie, "How a Desmarais Investment Got Entangled"; Agence France-Press, "Lafarge en Syrie."
20. Freeman and Ruehsen, "Terrorism Financing Methods," 17.
21. Ibid., 18.
22. Viswanatha and Wolf, "HSBC to Pay $1.9 Billion."
23. Oftedal, "Financing of Jihadi Terrorist Cells," 22–23.
24. Wittig, *Understanding Terrorist Finance*, 62.
25. Farah, *Blood from Stones*, 2.
26. Ibid., 2–3.

27. Oftedal, "Financing of Jihadi Terrorist Cells," 60.

28. Ibid., 62.

29. Seierstad, *One of Us*, 225.

30. *BBC News*, "Stockholm Bomb Funder Nasserdine Menni."

31. Freeman and Ruehsen, "Terrorism Financing Methods," 7.

32. Ridley and Alexander, "Combating Terrorist Financing."

33. Ibid., 9.

34. Ibid., 7.

35. US Department of the Treasury, "Treasury Designates Iranian Commercial Airline."

36. Kamere et al., "Lashkar-e-Taiba," 84.

37. UN Security Council, "Monitoring Team Report," July 19, 2016, 10.

38. Oftedal, "Financing of Jihadi Terrorist Cells," 22.

39. Freeman and Ruehsen, "Terrorism Financing Methods," 9.

40. US Department of the Treasury, "Treasury Identifies Kassem Rmeiti & Co."

41. Vittori, *Terrorist Financing and Resourcing*, 43.

42. US Department of the Treasury, "Shutting Down the Terrorist Financial Network."

43. Vittori, *Terrorist Financing and Resourcing*, 73.

44. Freeland, "How Can Sound Customer Due Diligence Rules Help?" 45.

45. Channel News Asia, "Singaporean Charged for Supporting Publication."

46. US Department of the Treasury, "Memorandum for Department of Defense Lead Inspector General."

47. *Jakarta Post*, "Police Track Foreign Funding."

48. Mansour and al-Hashimi, "ISIS Inc."

49. *Daily Sabah*, "Turkish Police Discover Around $2M," as cited in Bauer, "Survey of Terrorist Groups and Their Means of Financing."

50. Abuza, "Funding Terrorism in Southeast Asia," 184.

51. Jamwal, "Hawala," 188–189.

52. Ibid.

53. Jamwal, "Hawala," 183.

54. Freeman and Ruehsen, "Terrorism Financing Methods," 11.

55. Ibid.

56. Feldman, "Fund Transfers," 358.

57. de Goede, *Speculative Security*, 102.

58. National Commission on Terrorist Attacks upon the United States, *Final Report*, 169–173.

59. Vlcek, "Hitting the Right Target."

60. Passas, "Fighting Terror with Error," 319.

61. de Goede, *Speculative Security*, 103–110.

62. Vlcek, "Hitting the Right Target," 282.

63. de Goede, *Speculative Security*, 103–110.

64. Ibid., 108–111.

65. Financial Action Task Force, *Emerging Terrorist Financing Risks*, 22.

66. Hiraal Institute, "AS Finance System," 6.

67. Al-Batati and Hubbard, "Yemeni Bankers Get in Trouble."

68. Ibid.

69. Ibid., 10.

70. Kamere et al., "Lashkar-e-Taiba," 84.

71. Freeman and Ruehsen, "Terrorism Financing Methods," 10.

72. McCoy, "Is ISIS Being Funded by Anonymous Bitcoin Donations?"

73. Ensor, "Fourth British ISIL Kingpin Unmasked."

74. Wilson and Williams, "Hamas Shifts Tactics."

75. Meir Amit Intelligence and Terrorism Information Center, "Funding Terrorism."

76. Foundation for Defense of Democracies, *Al-Shabaab*.

77. Meir Amit Intelligence and Terrorism Information Center, "In View of Its Financial Problems."

78. Dion-Schwarz, Manheim, and Johnston, *Terrorist Use of Cryptocurrencies*, 23.

79. Davis, "New Technologies but Old Methods in Terrorism Financing."

80. Malik, "How Criminals and Terrorists Use Cryptocurrency."

81. UN Security Council, "Narrative Summary of Reasons for Listing: Hajjaj bin Fahd al Ajmi."

82. UN Security Council, "Narrative Summary of Reasons for Listing: Sa'd bin Sa'd Muhammad Shariyan al-Kabi."

83. Knutson, "Terrorists Trying Multiple Times."

84. Ibid.

85. Keatinge, Keen, and Izenman, "Fundraising for Right-Wing Extremist Movements," 16.

86. Davis, "New Technologies but Old Methods in Terrorism Financing."

87. Dion-Schwarz, Manheim, and Johnston, *Terrorist Use of Cryptocurrencies*, 13.

88. Financial Action Task Force, *Financing of Recruitment for Terrorist Purposes*.

89. Hasbi and Mahzam, "Cryptocurrencies."

90. Malik, "How Criminals and Terrorists Use Cryptocurrency."

91. Stubley, "Wife of Suspected ISIS Terrorist."

92. Ibid.

93. Hasbi and Mahzam, "Cryptocurrencies?"

94. *United States of America, Plaintiff, v. 155 Virtual Currency Assets, Defendants*.

95. Freeman and Ruehsen, "Terrorism Financing Methods," 19.

96. Farah, *Blood from Stones*, 113.

97. Freeman and Ruehsen, "Terrorism Financing Methods," 20.

98. Hiraal Institute, "AS Finance System," 5.

99. Corley, "Liberation Tigers of Tamil Eelam," 128.

100. Wittig, "Financing Terrorism Along the Chechnya-Georgia Border," 258.

101. Kamere et al., "Lashkar-e-Taiba," 82–83.

102. Ibid.

103. Ahronheim, "Israeli Spy Agency."

104. Freeman and Ruehsen, "Terrorism Financing Methods," 19.

105. Ibid.

106. Rider, "Weapons of War," 19.

9

Obscuring Funds

Terrorist groups, cells, and individuals use a variety of methods to obscure the sources and destinations of their funds. They do this to prevent detection of their movement of funds, hide what they are purchasing, circumvent sanctions, and prevent counterterrorism practitioners from identifying where they store their money (so it will not be seized). Terrorists also work to hide their management structures, budgets, and financial plans. They use financial tradecraft, which involves methods to obscure terrorist funds, throughout the financing process, and many of their techniques have multiple purposes.[1] For instance, they raise funds using charitable causes because moving money through charities can obscure the source and destination of those funds. Similarly, terrorists might move money using cryptocurrencies to hide the sources and destinations of funds and to profit from any increase in price.

Some elements of terrorist financing are not necessarily financial tradecraft but can still obscure funds because of deficiencies in the international systems designed to detect and deter this activity. For instance, moving funds across jurisdictions is often necessary for terrorist actors to achieve their aims but not necessarily part of their attempts to obscure the transfer. This kind of money movement can also have the unintended effect of hiding its origin or at least complicating the money trail. In other cases, deliberate efforts are made to obscure funds by moving them across jurisdictions. For instance, kidnappings for ransom might occur in one jurisdiction, but payments are made in another to avoid the funds being tracked.[2]

Terrorist actors tend to spend most of their efforts to obscure money movement when they want to move funds internationally. This is because

175

domestic movement of funds often takes place in areas controlled or influenced by the terrorist organization. These are essentially permissive environments for them. Also, local sums can be so small as to be difficult to detect as terrorist financing activity. In terrorists' main areas of operations, they can be more assured of the security and safety of their transactions because they are better positioned to co-opt business owners and bribe or threaten local financial service providers. Domestic transactions are also rarely subject to as much scrutiny as international ones. International movement of funds often requires them to go through jurisdictions with anti–money laundering/combating the financing of terrorism (AML/CFT) regimes. To move funds internationally, terrorist groups employ the highest level of tradecraft.

Regardless of whether they are moving, using, storing, managing, or raising funds, terrorists use a variety of techniques and technologies to obscure their funds:

- cash
- cryptocurrencies, financial technologies, and online procurement
- control or co-option of a financial entity
- intermediaries, third parties, false identities, and proxies
- exploitation of gender bias by the use of female financial facilitators
- organizations (charities and businesses)
- money laundering to hide funds
- specialist financial facilitators and money launderers

Although quantifying these financial tradecraft activities of terrorist actors would be extremely beneficial from a counterterrorism perspective, few data exist on them. As a result, in this chapter I rely on a handful of case studies and examples to illustrate how terrorists engage in financial tradecraft.

Cash

The use of cash is often a base component in financial tradecraft. Cash can be used for purchases, donations, and money movement through cash couriers. Using cash effectively stops the money trail because there are no effective ways to track even small amounts of it. Cash couriers also have an important role in financial tradecraft: they are critical facilitators in the movement of funds that circumvents the financial sector. In some cases, the use of cash couriers is not primarily to obscure the funds; instead, it is a function of the financial sector in which the terrorists operate. Regardless, keeping funds out of the formal financial sector makes transactions much more difficult to track using conventional financial intelligence mechanisms.

In other instances, the use of cash couriers is a deliberate form of financial tradecraft. For instance, prior to the Bali bombing, Jemaah Islamiyah used two Indonesian laborers as cash couriers to transfer more than $15,000 between terrorist group members, hide the funds from authorities, and ensure the money was easily available.[3]

The Lashkar-e-Taiba (LeT) also makes extensive use of cash, but this is dictated both by the financial sector in which the group operates and its desire to avoid creating a money trail between the group and its supporters. For example, Jamaat-ud-Dawa (JuD) members collect donations and return to their home bases with cash, leaving no electronic record of this money being raised, transiting JuD's hands, and then being delivered to the LeT.[4]

Cash is also one of the main ways terrorist groups, especially those that control territory, accrue funds. When terrorist groups engage in rent-seeking activities or sell commodities, they can insist on receiving the funds in cash. For instance, in territory controlled by the Islamic State in Iraq and the Levant (ISIL), oil managers demanded cash payments from traders and were warned against transferring funds through banks for fear that Western intelligence agencies could intercept the financial information.[5] ISIL also insisted on being paid in dollars (rather than Syrian pounds) because this made it easier for the group to transfer funds abroad and pay for imported goods.[6]

Cryptocurrencies, Financial Technologies, and Online Procurement

Financial technologies are increasingly used by terrorist groups, cells, and individuals to obscure their funds. Terrorists use a variety of financial technologies not only because of their efficiency and simplicity but also in some cases because they are perceived as more secure or anonymous. This is because they are thought to be subject to less scrutiny or have laxer anti–money laundering and counterterrorist financing protocols. Two of the technologies widely adopted by terrorists are Bitcoin and Monero, the latter of which has a much stronger privacy reputation than does Bitcoin.

Indeed, one of the main attractions of Bitcoin is its perceived anonymity. In 2014, an article released by an ISIL supporter detailed how Bitcoin can limit an individual's exposure to the Western financial system and recommended using it to donate funds to ISIS and to individuals who aspired to travel to Syria to join the group.[7] Terrorists are, however, increasingly cognizant of the limitations of Bitcoin's privacy and anonymity and have adopted additional financial tradecraft to prevent their transactions from being traced. One of these limitations is that Bitcoin's foundational technology, the blockchain ledger, is public and can be viewed and analyzed by anyone.[8] This means that in and of itself, Bitcoin is not untraceable. However, combined with other techniques (such as using proxies, multiple wallets, etc.), Bitcoin transactions can be difficult to track, not unlike cash. Bitcoin is particularly useful for crowdfunding campaigns or quick donation schemes in which terrorists can solicit funds, share their Bitcoin wallet addresses, and then quickly transfer funds out of the wallet into other wallets, hiding much of their money trail by using exchanges or tumblers. Although these campaigns might be limited in duration, they can be effective at providing terrorists quick infusions of money. In a clear example of a terrorist group attempting to hide the sources and destinations of its funds, Hamas has increasingly turned to cryptocurrencies to achieve this end while raising funds. In March 2019, Hamas urged supporters to donate money through Bitcoin. The group's request directed prospective donors to a website that generated a unique Bitcoin address for each user, increasing the operational security of the transactions.[9]

Prepaid credit cards are also popular with terrorists because they can be used to buy goods and services in a relatively anonymous manner. Multiple money movement methods were used for the Paris and Brussels attacks: the plotters moved money and purchased items using cash, prepaid cards, and debit cards.[10] The attackers used cash extensively to purchase supplies and equipment and to sustain themselves. The attackers also used PayPal for some purchases and payments.[11] The complexity of the financial trail in this case was also a function of France's technologically advanced financial sector, which the terrorists could exploit to obscure the sources, destinations, and uses of funds in the lead-up to the attack. These techniques are particularly useful in economies where cash has gone out of style, and extensive use of cash would in and of itself potentially raise suspicions. In another case from 2020, the US Department of Justice filed a civil suit to seize the cryptocurrency assets of a number of terrorist actors and noted that some of these funds were used to buy and trade prepaid credit cards online.[12] These examples demonstrate some sophistication at financial tradecraft. Combining financial tradecraft methods increases anonymity and operational security for the terrorists and makes it more difficult for authorities to identify the sources, destinations, and uses of funds.

The internet and online marketplaces and the financial technologies that underpin the payment mechanisms associated with them have made procurement for terrorist purposes much easier than it used to be. Historically, terrorists would have to create ties to businesses (or a plausible cover story), identify the goods they wanted, and ensure they did not arouse suspicion. In the case of the Toronto 18, the plotters created a cover story of being student farmers to explain their purchases of fertilizer. They went as far as to purchase shirts and business cards with "student farmers" on them.[13] Interacting face-to-face with clerks in brick-and-mortar retailers increased the likelihood of someone raising suspicions about what the individuals were doing.[14] In today's context, terrorists can use a distributed network of operatives to obtain the goods and services they want, to a large extent through online retailers and marketplaces. For instance, ISIL-affiliated individuals are reported to have created front companies to facilitate their procurement of unmanned aerial vehicles (UAVs) and related material. This is illustrated by the case of Yunus Emre Sakarya, who owned or controlled Profesyoneller Elektronik, a company involved in purchasing UAV-related equipment for ISIL worth more than $500,000.[15]

For operational activity, cells and individuals rarely need to create a procurement network to acquire the goods and services they want. Instead, they can simply exploit online retailers and marketplaces to obtain their goods and materials and avoid the kind of scrutiny that might come from purchasing the goods in a brick-and-mortar store. An example of this type of online procurement activity involves a Canadian, Abdulrahman el-Bahnasawy. In 2016, el-Bahnasawy was arrested in the United States on charges of conspiracy to conduct a terrorist attack. He purchased bomb-making materials online and shipped them to an individual in the United States he thought was a coconspirator but who actually turned out to be a Federal Bureau of Investigation (FBI) employee. El-Bahnasawy shipped approximately forty pounds of hydrogen peroxide, a key ingredient for triacetone triperoxide (TATP; the same explosive used in Manchester bombing). El-Bahnasawy also sent Christmas lights, batteries, battery holders, thermometers, and aluminum foil, all goods that can be used for bomb-making. Bahnasawy used his personal funds to finance the plot, but he also sought monetary contributions from other members of the cell and the core organization of ISIL. In the plot, Bahnasawy acted as a financial facilitator, putting his coconspirator in touch with the FBI employee to provide funds so more materials could be produced. Several hundred dollars were sent for these purposes, likely through bank accounts.[16] The low dollar amounts of the transactions were unlikely to have aroused any suspicions, and the purchases online also did not appear to have raised any alarms, despite the combination of goods procured by Bahnasawy. Using the online retailer allowed Bahnasawy to avoid interacting face-to-face with any employees, thus reducing the chances of someone reporting him and his purchases as suspicious. Of course, online purchases are also logistically easier, as people around the world have found out through their adoption of Amazon and other regionally specific retailers to make purchases.[17]

Terrorist organizations have not widely adopted cryptocurrencies or other financial technologies as main methods of obscuring their funds, but the groups have increased their use of these activities over the past decade. Ultimately, terrorists will continue to adopt new technologies as they become available in the areas in which they operate. A technology that appeals to terrorist actors is relatively simple, widely available, has good security features, can easily be converted to cash, can be easily used to purchase goods, and can be combined with other financial tradecraft practices to increase the security of a financial transaction.

Controlling or Co-opting a Financial Entity

For any terrorist actor, one of the best ways to avoid detection is by co-opting or controlling individuals who work in financial entities. By having trusted insiders, terrorist actors can avoid having their transactions reported, use false identities and identifying information (even if not particularly convincing), and combine a host of other financial tradecraft practices to avoid detection. This practice is largely the purview of terrorist groups because at that level they want to invest in long-term financial operations.

To move funds internationally, some terrorist groups work to control or co-opt money services businesses (MSBs) or employees at banks or other financial entities. These organizations can strip out identifying information from transactions, omit reports, or add an extra layer of anonymity by avoiding reporting the transaction to authorities. Al-Shabaab is a good example of this: one of the main organizers of a Missouri-based group of Al-Shabaab supporters worked at an MSB. This individual helped to structure transactions below the US reporting threshold and provided false identification information in the transaction records, including fictitious names and phone numbers. The MSB worker hid the nature of the transactions as well as the sender and beneficiary of the transfers.[18]

Complicit bankers are useful for terrorist organizations seeking to obscure the sources and destinations of their funds, as illustrated by Hizballah's use of Lebanese Canadian Bank (LCB). LCB was a Beirut-based institution formed in 1960 as Banque des Activities Economiques SAL. The bank operated as a subsidiary of the Royal Bank of Canada's Middle Eastern operations. The North American office was in Montreal; total assets for the bank had a value of nearly $5 billion.[19] The bank held accounts for MSBs laundering money and earning commissions for Hizballah. One of the senior bank managers structured cash deposits, and employees received funds from Hizballah couriers, including bulk cash brought directly from the airport and deposited into a nearby branch.[20] In fact, the terrorist group's extensive use of the bank bordered on control. LCB was fined $102 million by the United States for its money laundering and terrorist financing activities on behalf of Hizballah.[21] LCB also worked with its correspondent bank, American Express (Amex), to conduct transactions in dollars.[22] Amex executed millions of dollars' worth of wire transfers. The name on the account was Martyrs, so investigators believe there was little question that Amex knew it was executing wire transfers on behalf of Hizballah.[23] This complicity allowed Hizballah to access the international financial system and move money worldwide.

In more recent years, ISIL has demonstrated significant financial trade-craft in its operations, including through the control and co-optation of financial entities. To establish a truly global financial network outside of the scrutiny of the international community, ISIL co-opted a network of money movers and financial facilitators known as the al-Rawi network.[24] The network was headquartered in Iraq with offices in Sudan, Syria, Turkey, and the Gulf region. Turkey acted as a central node in the network.[25] The owner of the network was described by the US Department of the Treasury as an ISIL financier.[26] He operated the Hanifa Currency Exchange in Syria, an MSB that could move money internationally. The network did not originate with ISIL, however. Al-Rawi resuscitated a money movement network active during Saddam Hussein's regime that had primarily been used for sanctions evasion. As part of his work for ISIL, al-Rawi facilitated financial transactions, stored large amounts of cash for the group, controlled the exchange rate for US dollars in Abu Kamal, and facilitated payments to ISIL fighters. The al-Rawi network also included a Kenyan woman who facilitated transactions in Central Africa, Libya, and Syria.[27]

Terrorist groups able to control or co-opt financial entities have an extensive ability to employ advanced tradecraft and effectively hide the sources and destinations of their funds. The financial entities provide access to the international financial system, cover stories for the terrorists' money movement, accept false names and documentation, and a variety of other benefits. However, these bankers or entities can also be a singular point of vulnerability for the terrorist group; after they have been identified, they can lead to a significant illumination of a terrorist financing network and expose actors with varying levels of complicity.

Intermediaries, Third Parties, False Identities, and Proxies

Terrorist organizations, cells, and individuals use intermediaries, third parties, false identities, and proxies (sometimes called nominees in financial crime circles) to obscure their financial footprint, and as Ryder notes, these practices are particularly relevant when they raise funds through criminal activity.[28] Many terrorists are reluctant to use their own names in transactions. Freeland argues that they instead seek to use anonymous accounts, fronts, trusts, charities, corporate vehicles, and professional intermediaries to hide the individuals conducting the transactions.[29] However, examples of many of these activities in actual cases of terrorist financing are difficult to find. Instead, only a few examples of this are available, in particular the use of proxies. They can be willing or unwitting and might be found through close friends, associates, or in the broader community. Indeed, the use of proxies has a long history in terrorist financing. Members of the Irish diaspora allowed their bank accounts to be used as repositories for PIRA funds, effectively obscuring the money from any authorities who might have attempted to freeze or seize the funds.[30]

Reports have suggested that ISIL's affiliates outside of Iraq and Syria use "clean" individuals (likely proxies or third parties) to carry out transactions in the formal financial sector.[31] These individuals have had little to no interaction with law enforcement in the jurisdictions in which they operate and are also unlikely to have significant connections to the terrorist organization. Instead, they are likely to be selected by one individual with connections to ISIL and encouraged to help the group move funds. In some cases, they might be provided modest compensation for their services. The individuals might have no knowledge or even inclination that they are facilitating financial transactions on behalf of a terrorist organization. However, in some cases they might be fully cognizant of the cause for which they are working, and this is their way of advancing it.

Terrorists also used proxies for their operational activities, as was illustrated by Operation Crevice. A key member of the plot to bomb the United Kingdom, Momin Khawaja, was arrested in Ottawa, Canada, in 2004 for his role. Khawaja used a young woman in Ottawa to move money for the planned attack. Khawaja explained to her that it was hard for men to conduct transactions, but women did not raise suspicion.[32] On January 13, 2003, she wired $5,180 via Western Union to one of the UK plotter's wives. Four days later, she opened a Bank of Montreal account in her own name and provided Khawaja the debit card, later found in the possession of one of the UK plotters. On January 28, she deposited a total of $2,000 into this account.[33] Presumably, these funds were provided by Khawaja and deposited by his proxy into the account to facilitate the movement of funds overseas.[34] Although this plot was disrupted, there was no indication in the court proceedings that any of this activity had been deemed suspicious by the financial sector.

Terrorist organizations, cells, and individuals all use proxies, fake names, third parties, and intermediaries to conduct their financial transactions. Most of the time, these individuals have some connection to the terrorist actors, although that relationship might not be obvious and could be difficult to detect during the course of an investigation. Terrorist actors might also seek to exploit inherent or perceived biases in reporting entities and investigative authorities by using the names of women or other "nonsuspect" individuals to conduct transactions.

Exploiting Gender Bias Through the Use of Female Financial Facilitators

A commonly overlooked aspect of terrorist financing is gender. Women play important roles in terrorist financing and facilitation of operations. However, their role is often subsumed in the broader organizational movement because of the attention paid to those in kinetic (i.e., bomb-throwing) roles, who have predominantly been men. However, even kinetic activity is beginning to be seen as less male-dominated than people once assumed. Recent research has demonstrated that women account for approximately 23 percent of membership in terrorist organizations, based on an estimate of their involvement in attacks.[35] However, this estimate is likely low given that women often hold "invisible" roles in terrorist organizations, and financing is one of those roles. In one estimate, 40 percent of jihadists received money raised or contributed by women.[36]

Women work as financiers in many terrorist organizations, but this activity is often underreported or seen as terrorist support activity rather than terrorism writ large. However, financial support for terrorist activities is a principal enabler of that activity. As a result, women's roles in terrorist financing are likely critical to the success of many terrorist organizations' activities. One such example involves the Israel-Palestinian conflict. During the Al Aqsa intifada, approximately twenty-five Palestinian women were arrested during a six-month period for smuggling more than $25,000 each over the border from Jordan to Israel for use by terrorist groups. They were used to smuggle the funds because the terrorists anticipated that they would be scrutinized less than men.[37] Osama bin Laden's sisters were also used as transit points in the United Arab Emirates (UAE) for moving cash to him in Afghanistan.[38]

Female Hizballah members have worked as fund-raisers for the group and have sold clothing, arranged community dinners, and created a sponsor-a-fighter program.[39] Al-Shabaab is also no stranger to female financiers: one of the primary roles for women in the group is as fund-raisers.[40] In Kismaayo, female Al-Shabaab members have collected funds for the group, convincing men and women to donate money and goods such as jewelry.[41] In the Somali diaspora community, women have also worked to support the terrorist organization. In 2016, two female Al-Shabaab supporters created a support network for the group that included women from Canada, Egypt, Kenya, the Netherlands, Somalia, Sweden, the United Kingdom, and the United States.[42] Female Kurdish refugees have also acted as terrorist financiers for Kurdish extremist groups, including the Kurdistan Workers' Party (PKK).[43] One such example was Hanan Ahmed Osman, who was granted refugee status in Canada in 1984 and became a key PKK fund-raiser. Another woman in Canada, Zehra Saygili, helped raise and smuggle money for the PKK in the late 1990s as part of the Kurdish Cultural Association in Montreal.[44] When women are involved in operational activity, they sometimes take on the role of "managers" of the plot, including its financing, and provide logistical support. For example, in June 2002, six individuals in Morocco were arrested for plotting to attack US and British ships in the Straits of Gibraltar. Al-Qaeda was behind the plan, and the wives of the operatives collected and transferred funds, purchased small boats, and acted as couriers for the al-Qaeda cell.[45]

For terrorist organizations, encouraging women to support the cause in this way has several benefits. It allows women to become involved in the group without undertaking operational roles, which many terrorist groups would prefer to avoid. Also, women are believed to attract less scrutiny from law enforcement and security services, so using women in financial transactions (or at the very least female names) is a form of operational security that can enhance the terrorist groups' ability to obscure the sources and destinations of funds. For operational cells, women can be key contributors in areas such as financing and procurement and might in fact attract less attention than their male counterparts. However, this does not exclude the possibility of women taking on more kinetic roles in plots and attacks.

Organizations

One of the ways terrorist groups obscure their funds is by commingling them with legitimate funds.[46] Indeed, this is often the case when terrorists use charities and other organizations (including legitimate companies) to move funds. They deposit the funds into the legitimate organization's accounts, move the funds to the destination country or region as part of a project or investment, then divert some of those funds toward terrorist purposes. In this way, all the funds appear legitimate and related to the organization that moved them, when in reality some of the funds were illicit. The charitable sector, specifically nonprofit organizations, are often exploited in this way. For instance, charities are believed to have been used by al-Qaeda in the Arabian Peninsula (AQAP) to obscure the source of funds coming from its support networks abroad.[47] Other terrorist groups such as the Liberation Tigers of Tamil Eelam (LTTE) likely also exploited this feature of charitable organizations among their other attractive features for terrorist financing, discussed in detail in Chapter 3.

Terrorist groups also use corporate structures to obscure the sources, destinations, uses, and movement of their money. Two terrorist groups in the Philippines, the Moro Islamic Liberation Front (MILF) and the Moro National Liberation Front (MNLP), established commercial businesses to hide their financial dealings. They were also linked to a trading company network through al-Qaeda and Jemaah Islamiyah and used companies such as Pyramid Trading, ET Diton Travel, and Khalifa Trading Industries to hide their procurement activities and movement of funds.[48]

Financial tradecraft is also used to divert funds from legitimate businesses to support members (and their families) of terrorist organizations. To do this, businesses add "ghost" employees to their payroll.[49] Fake employees of a company receive regular "salary" payments. This allows terrorist groups to move money to individuals without implicating itself in the financial transaction. However, this requires that the business, or at least its financial controller, be complicit in the activity.

Although the use of organizations to obscure their financial footprint is largely the domain of terrorist groups, financial tradecraft is also increasingly used in small plots by cells and individuals. The Sydney plotters (in the failed 2005 Australia plot) used false names to register mobile phones and establish front companies to order and purchase chemicals.[50] The use of organizations provided a veneer of legitimacy to their transactions and likely prevented the companies shipping the goods from raising suspicions, although the extent to which many companies would report particular procurement activities remains questionable.[51]

Specialist Financial Facilitators and Money Launderers

Although much of the terrorist financing literature references money laundering, it often overstates the extent of such activities taking place. Money laundering techniques are usually applied by terrorists only in a limited sense—in some cases to make money for the organization and in other cases to obscure the money trail. Terrorist obscuring of funds has a different purpose than money laundering, and therefore other techniques are used. In many cases, because the sources of the funds are legal, money laundering techniques are not required. In some rare cases, terrorists might use sophisticated money laundering techniques, particularly when the funds are derived from criminal activities. However, for the most part, basic financial tradecraft is sufficient for terrorists; detecting terrorist money (in advance of an attack, in particular) is difficult, and after the fact, many terrorists are not concerned about having their accounts and methods exposed.

The more established a terrorist group, the more likely it uses money laundering techniques. This is particularly true if the group has established businesses, employs criminal business models, owns semilegitimate businesses, is involved in holding territory, or has complex financial structures. For instance, Hizballah maintains a portfolio of businesses it uses to obscure funds, and unlike most other terrorist organizations, because of the extent of its criminal activities, the group engages in money laundering. The group is also known to operate front companies and employ agents in Dubai, presumably to facilitate international financial transactions.[52] Hizballah is not alone in using sophisticated money laundering techniques and employing specialists. The Ulster Defence Association (UDA) and Ulster Volunteer Force (UVF) also drew on the assistance of accountants and businessmen for financial advice on sources of funds and how to launder money.[53]

Allegations are frequently made about professionals being involved in hiding the sources and destinations of funds for terrorist groups. For instance, in 2005, the US Department of State noted that criminal organizations and terrorists employ the services of professionals such as accountants and lawyers to help move and hide funds.[54] Although this is a logical claim, only a few examples support it. This might be because of little actual use of accountants or lawyers in this activity, or alternatively, that their use is effective at obscuring the funds and their terrorist connections.

Groups that have a surplus of funds are more likely to use money laundering techniques, and a case in point is the Taliban. The Taliban uses money laundering techniques not only to launder funds but also to invest them for future management. To launder the funds it obtains through the drug trade, the Taliban invests in commodities; moves funds through hawala money transfers; overprices goods for export and trade; and invests in real estate, shell businesses, and the stock market. The group has also been known to engage in trade-based money laundering through overvaluing products purchased, making the payment appear legitimate, and keeping the "extra" money, a technique that is largely undetectable by the authorities.[55] The combination of these techniques is reminiscent of advanced money laundering schemes and is likely effective at complicating the money trail.

In some cases, terrorist groups specifically designate people to serve as financial facilitators. These individuals generally serve as intermediaries between groups, cells, or individuals and have little role in the actual operations of the terrorist organization. That, however, is not to say they are not aware of their activities; instead, they are likely fully cognizant of the terrorist nature of their work, and financial facilitation is the way they choose to serve the cause or simply make money. Financial intermediaries can play an important role in obscuring the sources or destinations of funds. To do this effectively, terrorist organizations can use a variety of individuals, organizations, or companies (which might be real or might be shell companies). Using multiple entities for a financial transaction makes following the flow of funds and proving the ultimate use of the funds more difficult. For instance, funds coming to al-Mourabitoun from the Middle East passed through a number of intermediaries to obscure their origin and their destination.[56] This activity likely required the services of a financial facilitator to ensure the funds made it to their destination and did not arouse suspicion.

Using specialized financial facilitators to move money to terrorist organizations is not a new technique for terrorists; it has been used for decades, particularly in state funding of terrorist groups. For instance, funds are transferred to Hizballah through the financial officers of Iran's Islamic Revolutionary Guard Corps Quds Force (IRGC-QF).[57] These specialized individuals have skills to move funds through the international financial system with minimal risk of detection; have a series of front, shell, and shelf companies; and can effectively obscure the sources and destinations of funds.

When terrorist groups engage in patronage of other groups, they sometimes employ specialized individuals to transfer and obscure the funds. For example, Myrna Mabanza, a US-designated ISIL facilitator based in the Philippines, was involved in the transfer of up to $107,000 to Insilon Hapilon. She also served as an intermediary between Insilon Hapilon and ISIL in Syria, coordinating money transfers and sometimes facilitating travel between terrorist groups as well.[58] Mabanza might have been selected for this role because of her existing knowledge of the financial sector; because of personal connections in the financial services industry; and because of her gender, which terrorists assume will arouse less suspicion in reporting entities as well as law enforcement and security services.

Another example of an ISIL financial facilitator involved in terrorist patronage is Abdulpatta Escalon Abubakar, who facilitated transactions between ISIL and ISIL in the Philippines. In July 2016, $20,000 was sent through Abubakar to ISIL elements in the Philippines. The next month, he facilitated a transfer of $50,000 to ISIL's network in the Philippines. The following year, in July 2017, Abubakar worked with an ISIL member in the Philippines to facilitate the transfer of $5,000. Some of these funds might have been used to purchase weapons.[59] Yet another financial facilitator for ISIL was Waleed Ahmed Zein, later designated a terrorist by the US Department of the Treasury. Zein developed an international financial network to facilitate money transfers for ISIL. He used hawalas and intermediaries to conduct and obscure the transactions. His network had links in Europe, the Middle East, the Americas, and East Africa. Between 2017 and 2018, he moved more than $150,000 through the network and sent funds to Central Africa, Libya, and Syria. His financial tradecraft included using intermediaries to obscure the actual senders and recipients of the funds.[60]

ISIL has employed a network of financial facilitators who provide a variety of services. They store money on behalf of the group, and they also receive money on behalf of people without identification cards or the ability to receive funds. In some cases, they bring money directly into a combat zone for the benefit of a combatant.[61] Some of these financial facilitators might be deeply implicated in the banking sector. According to a French report, France has identified between 150 and 200 secret bankers who facilitate the flow of money for ISIL in Lebanon and Turkey.[62]

Terrorist groups (and to a lesser extent cells and individuals) rely upon financial facilitators to access difficult to reach places, such as underbanked areas or those in which surveillance of the banking system is high. Financial facilitators are also used to move money into and out of conflict zones, employing a variety of means to do so, including smuggling networks and cash couriers.

Financial tradecraft is largely the purview of terrorist organizations, but cells and individuals also demonstrate financing tradecraft. In one instance, the Strasbourg cell (which planned to bomb Christmas markets in 2000) divided purchases for the plot among its members and bought small amounts of chemicals in forty-eight different pharmacies all over Germany to avoid drawing attention to it activities.[63] Although operational financial tradecraft is less common than tradecraft employed by organizations, simple measures can be effective at helping prevent the detection of financial activity.

Conclusion

Terrorist groups, cells, and individuals all use varying levels of financial tradecraft to obscure the sources, destinations, and uses of their funds. They use cash, couriers, organizations, financial technologies, cryptocurrencies, and specialized financial facilitators. In some cases, they might also seek to exploit counterterrorist practitioners' biases in order to move funds.[64] These techniques are generally less sophisticated than the money laundering techniques organized crime groups use, although there is a certain cross-pollination of ideas and use of money laundering techniques. Although difficult to quantify, terrorist actors' use of financial tradecraft is a critical element of their financing methods and can, with little effort, complicate counterterrorism practitioners' efforts to follow the money trail.

Notes

1. Davis, "New Technologies but Old Methods in Terrorism Financing."
2. Financial Action Task Force, *Emerging Terrorist Financing Risks*, 18.
3. Freeman and Ruehsen, "Terrorism Financing Methods," 9; Shelley, *Dirty Entanglements*, 35.
4. Kamere et al., "Lashkar-e-Taiba," 84.
5. Coker, "Rise and Deadly Fall of Islamic State's Oil Tycoon."
6. Ibid.
7. Hasbi and Mahzam, "Cryptocurrencies?"
8. Fanusie, "Terrorist Networks Eye Bitcoin."
9. Fanusie, "Jihadists Upping Their Bitcoin Game."
10. Lormel, "Lessons Learned from the Paris and Brussels Terrorist Attack."
11. La, "Comment les Terroristes."
12. *United States of America, Plaintiff, v. 155 Virtual Currency Assets, Defendants.*
13. Davis, "Financing the Toronto 18."
14. Counterterrorism Police, "Multiple Bombings."
15. Office of the Lead Inspector General, "Operation Inherent Resolve," 113.
16. *United States of America v. Abdulrahman El Bahnasawy.*
17. Davis, "How Terrorists Use the Internet."
18. Financial Action Task Force, *Emerging Terrorist Financing Risks*, 22.
19. Darshan-Leitner and Katz, *Harpoon*, 213.
20. Freeman and Ruehsen, "Terrorism Financing Methods," 17.
21. Raymond, "Lebanese Bank to Pay U.S. $102 Million."
22. Darshan-Leitner and Katz, *Harpoon*, 221.
23. Ibid., 226.

24. Joscelyn, "US Designates Members of Rawi Network."

25. UN Security Council, "Hanifa Money Exchange Office."

26. US Department of the Treasury, "Counter Terrorism Designations: Fawaz al-Rawi."

27. Soufan Center, "Intel Brief."

28. Rider, "Weapons of War," 18.

29. Freeland, "How Can Sound Customer Due Diligence Rules Help?" 43.

30. Vittori, *Terrorist Financing and Resourcing*, 55.

31. Levitt, "Introduction," 9.

32. Ontario Superior Court of Justice, "Reasons for Judgement," 14.

33. Ibid.

34. Ibid., 15.

35. Davis, *Women in Modern Terrorism*.

36. Dean, "Draining the Ocean," 63.

37. Cragin and Daly, *Women as Terrorists*, 25.

38. Winer, "Globalization, Terrorist Finance, and Global Conflict," 25.

39. Davis, *Women in Modern Terrorism*, 50.

40. Ibid., 114.

41. Donnelly, "Women in Al Shabaab."

42. Whitcomb, "Two Women Convicted."

43. Cragin and Daly, *Women as Terrorists*, 25.

44. Ibid., 26.

45. Ibid., 28.

46. Clarke, "Overview of Current Trends."

47. UN Security Council, "Monitoring Team Report," January 13, 2017, 11.

48. Germann et al., "Terrorist Financing in the Philippines," 153.

49. Clarke, *Terrorism, Inc.*, 35.

50. Australian Financial Intelligence Unit (AUSTRAC), "Terrorism Financing in Australia 2014."

51. Davis, "How Terrorists Use the Internet."

52. Clarke, *Terrorism, Inc.*, 73.

53. Silke, "In Defense of the Realm," 353.

54. US Department of State, *International Narcotics Control Strategy Report*, vol. 2, 8.

55. Clarke, *Terrorism, Inc.*, 116.

56. Mémier, "AQMI et Al-Mourabitoun," 34.

57. Al-Othaimin, "How Iran Finances Hezbollah."

58. Joscelyn, "Treasury Sanctions ISIS Facilitator."

59. Office of the Lead Inspector General, "Operation Inherent Resolve," 113.

60. US Department of the Treasury, "Treasury Sanctions East African Facilitator."

61. TracFin, "Tendances et Analyse."

62. *Asharq Al-Awsat*, "200 'Secret Bankers' Facilitate Money."

63. Oftedal, "Financing of Jihadi Terrorist Cells," 31.

64. Davis, "Future of the Islamic State's Women."

PART 3

New Frontiers

10

Stemming the Flow of Funds

Prior to the terrorist attacks of September 11, 2001, countering the financing of terrorism was a nascent aspect of counterterrorism in the international community.[1] Following those attacks, the United States and its allies led the international community in creating norms and regulations to counter the financing of terrorism, including encouraging countries to criminalize terrorist financing, creating or expanding financial intelligence units to include investigation and prosecution of terrorist financing offenses, creating mechanisms for freezing terrorist assets, and adopting existing international gray and black lists to punish states for lack of action on terrorist financing, among other measures.[2]

Counterterrorist financing was adopted as a main pillar of counterterrorism because money provides terrorists the ability to purchase goods, acquire materials, pay for training, and conduct terrorist attacks. Reducing the amount of money terrorists have access to curtails the scope and scale of their activities. To prevent the funding of terrorism, the international community has developed tools to seize terrorists' funds, prevent them from raising money in the first place, and encourage the use of financial intelligence to illuminate terrorist networks. At its core, countering terrorist financing is a collective action problem that suffers from free riders who benefit from the increased public good of less terrorism but who do not incur the costs associated with preventing terrorists from using their jurisdiction.[3] Although having an international counterterrorist financing system without free riders would provide the most benefit, some benefits can still be realized using a variety of approaches to counter terrorist financing, even if some states defect from international agreements to do so.

Approaches to Counterterrorism Financing

Like terrorist financing, counterterrorist financing has been conceptualized too narrowly in much of the academic and practitioner literature, focusing almost exclusively on how to stop terrorists from raising and moving funds by criminalizing these activities and enforcing counterterrorism financing laws. Although these tactics are obviously an important part of countering terrorist financing, other approaches address some of the mechanisms of financing more effectively than criminalization. There are five main approaches to countering the financing of terrorism:

- criminalization and policing of terrorist financing activities at the international and domestic levels
- use of military force, including targeted strikes, control of territory, and capture of key individuals
- exploitation of financial intelligence and use of financial information for surveillance
- exclusion of terrorist financing actors through application of international and domestic sanctions and asset seizure
- regulation of the private sector assigning some responsibility for preventing terrorism to financial institutions and the private sector

These approaches are not mutually exclusive and, in fact, work best when used in combination and adjusted to specific circumstances. Each approach has counterterrorism utility in disrupting both organizational and operational terrorist financing. Some of these approaches are rarely available (such as use of military force), whereas others (such as criminalization and policing) are standard and considered international best practices. There is also significant overlap between the approaches and tools used. For instance, the exploitation of financial intelligence approach feeds into both the law enforcement and military approaches, and the regulation of the private sector approach clearly feeds the intelligence and law enforcement approaches. However, classifying counterterrorist financing approaches in this manner allows for a more nuanced discussion of the options as well as the development of more pointed critiques about their utility.

Criminalization and Law Enforcement

The most common approach to countering terrorist financing involves its criminalization. This approach is an international norm but in practice often falls short in terms of implementation and enforcement.[4] Both the United Nations and the Financial Action Task Force (FATF) have led the criminalization of terrorist financing approach; both international bodies have called on states to criminalize the activity and investigate and prosecute cases of it. The criminalization approach has long been touted as a means to tackle terrorist financing and draws on law enforcement efforts against organized crime.[5]

This approach focuses on enacting and enforcing laws that make a variety of the financial and support activities of terrorist groups illegal. Some laws also make any financing activity related to a terrorist attack illegal. These laws are enacted at the national level, meaning that they vary between jurisdictions. Some states also make membership in terrorist organizations illegal. As with many terrorist offenses, making financing illegal is designed to be preventative.[6] In some cases, terrorist financing offenses are levied against members of a cell or group that assisted an individual or group to conduct terrorist activity but were not involved in the attack itself. This approach primarily addresses how terrorists raise and move funds, although in some cases it also seeks to criminalize the use or management of funds.

The application of counterterrorist financing laws, in addition to their content, also varies widely across jurisdictions. Because these are still relatively new laws in many countries, prosecution of individuals for terrorist financing offences is relatively rare, with a few notable exceptions in France, the United Kingdom, and the United States. However, the lack of enforcement of these laws leads to questions about their utility and the will or capability of law enforcement to investigate and prosecute terrorist financing offenses.

Writ large, many aspects of terrorist financing (and specifically fundraising) are countered by effective laws and enforcement of those laws. For instance, terrorist organizations that engage in rent-seeking activity do so most effectively in countries without a monopoly on the use of violence, where terrorists can control or influence territory. However, even in countries with relatively strong rule of law, terrorists can engage in extortion. As I illustrated in prior chapters, some terrorist groups have extorted money from diaspora communities by threatening the safety of friends and family members back in their home countries; these rent-seeking activities remain pernicious. In these cases, the local rule of law is less effective because few states can assure a diaspora community that they can maintain the safety of their friends and family. Even outlawing the transfer of funds to these organizations will often result in the displacement of funds to a criminal organization or alternative means of paying the "safety tax." Consideration should be given to identifying the individuals involved in the extortion activity and prosecuting them for criminal activity (including terrorist financing). Consideration should also be given to using the extortion networks as intelligence sources: by exploiting the financial network of extortion, key players within the organization and opportunities for meaningful disruption can be identified. Allowing the networks to continue to operate for a short period might expose the players involved through financial intelligence. Providing that information to partner countries where similar networks might be operating, as well as the state "hosting" the terrorist group, might facilitate the prosecution of key individuals or disruption of the extortion network.

Some of the limitations of the criminalization approach to countering terrorist financing are lack of relevant laws, lack of prioritization, and lack of expertise. In some cases, failure to see terrorist financing as a threat has led to a lack of investigative prioritization. This might also be compounded by a lack of understanding of the importance of financing for enabling terrorist attacks. Lack of investigative expertise about financial crimes, and more specifically terrorist financing, might also hinder the criminalization approach. Few states have more than a handful of investigators assigned to terrorist financing, and even fewer have specialized investigators, which profoundly affects their ability to understand and ultimately detect and disrupt the activity. States might also choose not to disrupt terrorist financing activity for fear of blowback from the groups, shifting their utility to a terrorist entity from passive sponsor to target of attack. Unfortunately, terrorist groups, movements, cells, and even individuals become more costly to disrupt over time, and failing to do so when a group is primarily using the territory for support purposes might allow it to develop more sophisticated networks, recruitment pathways, and ultimately entrenchment in a jurisdiction.

Military Force

The war in Iraq and Syria reinforced that military forces have a key role to play in countering terrorist financing. Some of the actions military units can undertake include bombing of cash storage sites or sites from which significant funds are derived (such as oil refineries), killing or capturing key terrorist financiers, and of course collecting intelligence on terrorist financing. Military actions to counter terrorist financing primarily focus on targeting the methods terrorists use to raise and store funds but, in some cases, might also target their management and movement of funds, as in the case of strikes against cash shipments. In the short term, these strikes appear effective at reducing the financial resources and competencies of a terrorist group, but the longer-term effects and whether this type of terrorist decapitation (of a skill set, if not leadership) are unknown.[7]

The military approach to counterterrorism is applicable only when terrorists control or influence a significant portion of territory or there is armed conflict. Although the use of military force to counter terrorist financing might be limited, to do it effectively in times of conflict, militaries have to establish and maintain a capacity for counterterrorist financing analysis. During military confrontation with terrorist groups, it is also not sufficient to simply identify individuals to capture or kill. Second- and third-order effects of terrorist activity have to be considered, as is the case with nonmilitary actions. In some instances, although a target might be acquirable, delaying action and "letting the network run" might be the preferred course of action to expose targets and collect more intelligence on the financing and associ-ated functions such as operational planning.

The US military has largely led the military approach to countering ter-rorist financing, specifically using US special forces.[8] The US government has innovated the use of financial power as warfare to play a central role in international security strategies.[9] In Afghanistan and Iraq, the United States developed cells responsible for the collection, analysis, and dissemination of financial intelligence; these "fusion" cells built on the success of an existing intelligence group in US Central Command (CENTCOM), the Threat Finance Exploitation Unit.[10] The 2006 *US Army Field Manual* helped to bridge the gap between counterinsurgency and counterterrorist financing, which led to the development of counterthreat financing and highlighted the importance of defeating finance networks in counterinsur-gency operations.[11] In the United States, a number of government depart-ments and agencies, including the Defense Intelligence Agency, have a role or mandate to counter the financing of terrorism.[12]

The military approach to counterterrorist financing has also been used against criminal business models, specifically narcotics trafficking. This approach, as Felbab-Brown notes, is flawed. Terrorists, insurgents, and criminal actors gain political legitimacy and popular support from their involvement in the trade by providing social services and employment to the local population. To counter this, the interdiction of illicit shipments, destruction of labs, and capture of key traffickers are far more effective strategies than the destruction of local resources in an attempt to eradicate illicit material (thus increasing the terrorists' political capital by directly threatening the livelihoods of local populations).[13] Other options include licensing the illicit economy, although in many cases, terrorist actors might simply insert themselves into the newly legal aspects of the economy.

The military approach to countering the financing of terrorism largely relies on kinetic action to achieve its objectives, using capture or kill mis-sions to target key financial leaders, destroy cash shipments and storage sites, destroy or damage infrastructure or resources used to raise funds, and use intelligence (including defense intelligence) to illuminate terrorist financing networks. While limited in application, in specific circumstances, this may be an effective way to counter the financing of terrorism and reduce the overall threat of terrorism emanating from a particular region, although little empirical evidence is available on the longer-term impacts.

Exploitation of Financial Intelligence

Financial intelligence is intelligence collected on the financial activities of individuals, cells, and organizations. The financial intelligence approach to countering terrorist financing combines with other types of intelligence to achieve a variety of objectives. This approach is most readily combined with military, law enforcement, or security service action against terrorist actors. Critiques of counterterrorist financing have argued that efforts to criminalize terrorist financing have yielded few results; conversely, the emerging financial intelligence approach is often cited as a benefit of counterterrorist financing frameworks and presented as a counterpoint to these critiques. Since 9/11, the use of financial intelligence has grown substantially: most countries now have a financial intelligence unit, and many law enforcement and security services make regular use of this kind of intelligence in their counterterrorism activities.

Financial intelligence is not produced only by such units; it is any intelligence of a financial nature and can therefore be collected from a variety of sources, including bank records, corporate documents, human intelligence, and so forth.[14] Over time, counterterrorist financing strategies have been recalibrated to place increasing emphasis on the strategic and operational value of financial intelligence.[15] However, some practitioners have also noted that the raw data they get from financial intelligence units in the form of suspicious transaction reports have "no immediate value to law enforcement investigations."[16] Clearly, it is important to differentiate between financial intelligence and financial data: the former is analyzed and contextualized, whereas the latter is not. Most banks (and even national financial intelligence units) have an abundance of financial data and little in the way of actual financial intelligence or capability to produce it.

Covert action, part of the practice of intelligence, can also be undertaken against terrorist financing activities.[17] Most terrorist financing mechanisms are vulnerable to covert action, but particularly attractive targets are the storage methods. One example of covert action targeting the management and storage of funds is the Israeli intelligence targeting Hizballah finances. In the late 2000s, Hizballah and its leadership fell prey to a Ponzi scheme. Salah Ezzedine, a wealthy businessman, became embroiled in the scheme and encouraged those around him to invest as well. The investors included senior Hizballah leaders and financial managers. Ultimately, when the Ponzi scheme collapsed, the terrorist organization not only lost significant funds but also experienced a political crisis.[18] The Ponzi scheme targeted Hizballah's storage and management of funds as well as the group's desire to increase profits on its investments. In the end, Hizballah forfeited millions of dollars.

Financial intelligence is not immune from criticism. For instance, de Goede argues that financial data are useful for creating social network analysis, which she describes as an imaginative method that works by mining and mapping terrorist networks. Practices such as this, enabled in the name of the war on terrorist financing, now far exceed their original objectives and produce extrajudicial security actions.[19] Parker and Taylor argue that financial intelligence collection is intrusive but a necessary consequence of the changing security environment, and effective measures come at a price.[20]

The intelligence approach also includes the creation of terrorist financing "indicators" and typologies.[21] Many of these indicators lack specificity, however; they generate false positives and in many cases are so generic as to be useless. In other cases, they are so specific as to be obvious. Many financial intelligence experts recognize that there are real limits to the utility of indicators; for instance, account profiling is unlikely to identify a terrorist customer.[22] At the same time, financial intelligence can be used for leads in investigations because it allows investigators to track movements and expenditures—critical components of attack preparations.[23] Financial transactions can also reveal connections between known and unknown parts of a network, and changes in the patterns of financial activity can signal changes in terrorist plans.[24]

Financial intelligence can also facilitate financial surveillance. The practice helps outline the patterns of life and activities of a subject of investigation and can occasionally identify the locations of subjects of interest. However, the use of basic tradecraft can limit the utility of financial surveillance. For instance, financial surveillance might be collected on a suspect's accounts, but if the subject uses prepaid cards provided by someone not under investigation, it might be difficult for investigative agencies to discover transactions. The use of cash can also complicate financial surveillance and instead might force investigators to rely on more traditional surveillance techniques.

The utility of financial intelligence in dealing with terrorist organizations is obvious but might be less apparent when dealing with small cells and individual terrorists plotting attacks. Much of the financial activity in the lead-up to small cell or lone-actor attacks is difficult to perceive as terrorist financing because it is relatively indistinguishable from everyday use of funds unless the potential terrorist context is understood. However, financial intelligence can be critical in determining when terrorists start to act on their ideas, that is, mobilize to violence.[25] Their terrorist intent involves purchases in support of their attack plans or potentially acquiring material or travel documents. Using financial intelligence to determine where someone is on the mobilization trajectory can help identify key points for intervention and help to establish a criminal case. Financial intelligence can also help in the assessment of an individual terrorist's or cell's capabilities and possible courses of action—that is, what is financially viable for them.

There are challenges for the effective, efficient, lawful, and ethical use of financial surveillance.[26] The practice requires timely and structured access to financial data, which some financial institutions are unwilling or unable to provide. Encouraging all financial and reporting entities (including, as applicable, financial technology companies and social media companies) to provide timely, structured data should be an international requirement to effectively combat terrorist financing and to enable counterterrorism investigations. In other cases, lawful access to financial data has proven difficult to obtain, given strong protections for personal financial information, which hinders counterterrorism efforts.

How terrorists use funds lends itself well to financial intelligence and analysis. This information is largely derived from financial intelligence unit disclosures, such as information from the Financial Transactions and Reports Analysis Centre of Canada (FINTRAC), the Financial Crimes Enforcement Network (FinCEN) of the US Department of the Treasury, and others. In some cases and jurisdictions, financial intelligence can also be collected directly from banks or other financial entities by court order. It can also be collected through other intelligence collection mechanisms such as human sources and signals intelligence.[27] Before undertaking operational activity, terrorist cells and individuals have to develop capabilities (such as weapons handling skills and the ability to build improvised explosive devices), undertake planning, and make preparations for their attacks. Much of this has a financial component in the form of purchases and preparations terrorists conduct in advance. These activities can provide significant insight into how advanced a plot is and how viable it might be. Financial intelligence can be extremely useful in understanding and disrupting crimes, even those not motivated by profit, such as terrorism.[28]

Over the past several years, there has been an increase in low-sophistication, small-scale, and lone-actor attacks across North America, Europe, Australia, and elsewhere. These attacks might or might not be directed by international terrorist organizations, but they are most certainly inspired by them. Understanding how these attacks were financed can enhance the ability to detect and deter terrorist activity. This approach involves conceptualizing terrorist financing at its lowest levels and recognizing that traditional counterterrorist financing mechanisms (such as large-cash transaction reports) might not assist in detecting this activity. Instead, financial intelligence can be used at a more tactical level to determine the state of intent, planning, preparation, and capability of a terrorist cell or individual.

A small-scale plot or attack is one relatively low in sophistication, usually involving only a few people at most. For instance, most stabbings and truck-ramming attacks constitute small-scale terrorism, whereas the Paris attacks of 2015 and the Brussels attacks of 2016 constitute more traditional terrorist events, given their higher complexity, their use of relatively sophisticated explosive devices, and number of people involved in their planning and perpetration. According to the Royal United Service Institute (RUSI), in Great Britain, small-scale and lone-actor attacks consist of "the threat or use of violence by a single perpetrator (or small cell) not acting out of purely personal-material reasons, with the aim of influencing a wider audience, and who acts without any direct support in the planning, preparation and execution of the attack, and whose decision to act is not directed by any group or other individuals (although possibly inspired by others)."[29]

Detecting and deterring small-scale attacks through financial intelligence can be challenging because the amount of money involved is limited. However, these attacks still require financing and almost all involve some financial activity that can potentially provide valuable intelligence.[30] As with all operational financing and terrorist activity, context is everything. Without additional information that suggests links to terrorism, the people planning small-scale attacks would be nearly impossible to identify, such as when they purchase knives, rent vehicles, or even rent a second apartment, seemingly everyday activities.

Despite the fact that the financial requirements for these types of attacks can be minimal, individuals do make purchases directly in support of their plots and outside of their usual pattern of activity. They might also get money from outside sources, such as obtaining loans from banks or friends, using their credit card more than usual, or potentially committing theft. Even for unsophisticated, simple, lone-actor attacks, the terrorists usually buy weapons or material specifically for the attack. For instance, the London Bridge attack in June 2017, which left seven people dead and forty-eight injured, involved knives purchased at £4 ($6) each.[31] For the Toronto Incel van attack, the van rental likely cost less than $100 CAD ($75).[32] Ultimately, absent alternative explanations, these financial transactions on their own do not indicate that a terrorist attack is imminent, but for law enforcement or security services monitoring potential terrorists, a purchase of knives or van rental could indicate such activity. Terrorists involved in small-scale attacks might also use financial tradecraft to obscure their activities from law enforcement and security services, primarily by using cash.

The detection of other terrorist activity, such as travel to participate in a terrorist training camp, can be enhanced by using financial intelligence. For example, although travel to certain regions has been relatively cheap (although the costs involved increase substantially if international flights are required), "aspiring fighters still need money to pay for the journey and to sustain themselves en route, even if they are assured that all needs will be taken care of once they arrive in Syria."[33] As Keatinge noted, individuals traveling to Syria used automatic teller machines (ATMs) and debit and credit cards, which left a financial footprint of their activities.[34] Even if these activities are not detected in advance of departure, this information can be used to geolocate terrorists, support terrorist financing prosecutions at a later date, or establish patterns of life for financial surveillance.

Not all financial intelligence used to detect the timing of an attack involves purchases. In one instance, the day before attackers traveled to Copenhagen, two of the cell members emptied their bank accounts.[35] This might have been the plotters' attempt to remove traces of their activities from the financial sector (a form of terrorist tradecraft), or it might have been "settling affairs" by taking money out of the accounts and leaving it with friends or family members for later use or to give their desired beneficiary the funds in case of their death. In 2010, a Swedish cell also had two members empty their bank accounts just before they attacked.[36] Again, although this activity might not fall within the definition of terrorist financing absent information on its intent, such financial activity could potentially indicate to law enforcement or security services that an attack was in the final stages of its preparations. In another case, the Manchester bomber withdrew £250 ($350) in cash in the days before the attack. Then, three days prior to the attack, he transferred £2,500 ($3,500) to his brother, who is believed to have known about the attack in advance.[37] These withdrawals likely constituted changes in the terrorist's financial activity in preparation for the attack.

One of the easiest pieces of financial intelligence to decipher is the purchase of weapons or components for improvised explosive devices, although in recent years, some of the procurement of materials for terrorist attacks has taken place online. Terrorists increasingly use online global merchants such as Amazon, eBay, and others migrating online and facilitating online purchases and delivery.[38] One example of this trend was the plot of Abdurahman el-Bahnasawy. He purchased many of the components for an improvised explosive device online and had them shipped to a "coconspirator" (who was, in fact, an FBI undercover employee).[39] Online purchases preclude any interaction with in-person salespeople who might identify the combination of goods purchased suspicious or identify other behaviors as concerning.[40] Online procurement of materials to be used in terrorist attacks is likely to increase over the coming years as more jurisdictions are served by global merchants such as Alibaba, Amazon, and others. Obtaining such goods quickly, cheaply, and from a variety of merchants can be effective terrorist operational tradecraft.

In the lead-up to a terrorist attack, changes in financial patterns of behavior can be significant and may also help detect intention among previously identified individuals who have adopted an extremist mindset. As Keatinge notes,

> The key to effective transaction monitoring is thus knowledge of typical account activity against which deviations and inconsistencies can be mapped. Just as financial institutions undertake this analysis to protect themselves and their account holders from fraudulent activity based on this historical analysis, so, it would seem, could they conduct such analysis to identify activity that might be consistent with the financial footprints left by those travelling to fight with designated terrorist organisations.[41]

Although identifying suspicious or anomalous account activity is desirable, counterterrorist financing intelligence suffers from a small-data problem. Money laundering is relatively easily detected because of the scope of the activity; this allows patterns to be detected, algorithms to be programmed, and anomalous activity to be identified. In terrorism, tactics are always changing, and the scope and scale of the problem is such that it requires a bespoke-data solution rather than a big-data solution.

Although many financial behavior changes would not, at face value, make reporting entities think "terrorist financing," they could be alerted to behavior inconsistent with the individual's usual pattern of activity. Of course, these changes have to be analyzed and interpreted in the context of a significant body of other information that suggests terrorist activity is potentially underway for these relatively innocuous activities to indicate an imminent threat. These activities, considered in the context of an extremist mindset, can provide insight into an individual's readiness to act, amount of money he or she can dedicate to a plot or attack, and any final preparations he or she might be making.[42] These activities are unlikely to be identified by financial entities and reporting institutions; instead, they are largely the purview of law enforcement or security services already monitoring suspect individuals. Awareness of these activities by reporting entities might help them identify similar changes in behaviors for individuals of whom they might already be suspicious and therefore can help them file suspicious transaction reports or identify the activity to appropriate authorities.

Financial intelligence does not directly counter terrorist financing, but it can enable other counterterrorist financing operations and responses. For instance, to stop terrorist fund-raising by extortion, states have few viable options other than establishing effective rule of law and trusted national governments.[43] However, it might be possible to exploit the financial intelligence generated through the rent-seeking activity to help these states, particularly where the terrorist organizations have a foothold, to counter the activity within their borders, or to enable other counterterrorist financing operations. Although this might seem like an unappealing option to many in law enforcement and security services, it offers a realistic counterterrorism financing opportunity for international collaboration to detect and ultimately disrupt these activities.

The intelligence approach to countering terrorist financing involves exploiting financial intelligence (and other intelligence, for an all-source approach) to understand how terrorists raise, use, move, store, manage, and obscure their funds. The intelligence approach also helps to balance other strategies that focus solely on cutting off financial flows, instead suggesting a more comprehensive approach that uses financial intelligence to understand terrorist networks, cells, and lone actors.[44] This intelligence can then be leveraged to support other approaches, including law enforcement and military action, and to enhance legislative and regulatory approaches, implement financial exclusion mechanisms, and refine private sector approaches.

Financial Exclusion, Sanctions, and Asset Freezes

Another approach to countering terrorist financing involves excluding their organizations, cells, and individuals from the financial system through sanctions, national and international listings, and freezes. This approach addresses financing mechanisms such as raising, storing, and moving funds. Financial sanctions are part of the so-called smart sanctions developed in response to the acknowledgment that comprehensive sanctions cause high levels of suffering among populations.[45] The multilateral efforts to freeze assets and suppress terrorist raising and movement of funds were among the first priorities after 9/11.[46] On their own, these efforts have had limited success.[47]

International sanctions are frequently implemented to counter terrorist financing by states. Byman proposes that outside governments should try to raise the costs for regimes that passively support terrorism through economic pressure as well as technical assistance aimed at enhancing their security capacity.[48] However, achieving international consensus and implementing sanctions at the level of the United Nations can be challenging because sharing of sensitive intelligence at this forum is limited. Other approaches include unilateral or coordinated multilateral sanctions (frequently led by the United States), but their efficacy at stopping the flow of funds, instead of simply displacing it, remains questionable. In many cases, sanctions and financial exclusion can cause disruption to a terrorist group's operating budget. However, most terrorist organizations are diversified in their funding sources. Cutting off state sponsorship, or significantly reducing it, can have organizational costs in terms of salaries, but operationally, it might not have an immediate impact.

Financial exclusion as a counterterrorism financing method is often separate from the criminalization and law enforcement approach. Many jurisdictions use a civil standard, or noncriminal standard, to establish listing procedures and enforce forfeiture of cash.[49] Indeed, critiques of the financial exclusion approach note that often intelligence (rather than evidence) is used to justify the exclusion of persons or entities, with no requirement to link specific property to terrorism.[50] Other critiques of the approach point out that in many jurisdictions there is no legal recourse if people have been excluded from the financial sector and had their assets frozen.[51] Some jurisdictions might also have a reverse onus, in that individuals must prove their assets were acquired through legal means to regain access to them. Regarding funds managed and stored by terrorist actors, one of the main counterterrorism financing objectives is to freeze and seize these assets, ultimately using the evidence acquired to convict them for terrorist financing or other offenses.[52]

Financial exclusion mechanisms, particularly at the international level, are being applied less frequently. Fewer submissions for the designation of terrorists are being made to the United Nations, and Gurulé argues that this is because of lack of enforcement.[53] This might also result from an increase in legal challenges to these regimes, most notably in the European Union.

Private Sector Regulatory Measures

Perhaps the biggest shift in financial crime management following the terrorist attacks of 9/11 was in measures designed to regulate the private sector and force banks, money services businesses, and other financial entities to report possible terrorist financing activity. States drafted (or redrafted) laws against terrorist financing and money laundering, and one of the main objectives was to create a regulatory and mandatory reporting framework for financial entities in the private sector. These efforts varied from jurisdiction to jurisdiction but primarily consisted of the requirement to report "suspicious activity" to financial intelligence units or law enforcement. These regulations co-opted private entity actors and made them partners in national and international security, whether they wanted to be involved or not.

The private sector regulatory approach focused on establishing a de facto requirement for private entities to partner with security services and law enforcement through mandatory reporting. In many jurisdictions, this meant registering with the state, keeping records of financial transactions, and enforcing customer identification standards. This approach targets how terrorists raise, move, store, and manage their funds and seeks to address how they obscure their funds.

The private sector regulatory approach has been strongly criticized by the private sector as well as by governments. The private sector has resisted increased regulation in part because of the increased costs these requirements impose on them. However, this approach has also allowed for cross-pollination between the private sector and the financial services sector because many former law enforcement and security service officers find second careers with financial entities, helping them to counter terrorist financing and prevent money laundering.

In response to these increased costs and the questionable efficacy of the regulations implemented to detect terrorist financing, entities in the private sector have called on financial intelligence units, as well as law enforcement and security services, to share information with them to help them identify this activity. One of these methods is the development of "indicators" of terrorist financing, as I previously discussed. Although this approach was initially well received, it soon became clear that many "red flags" were of little practical utility.[54] A response to these critiques has been the development of public-private partnerships.

The financial sector is an important partner for countering terrorist financing. Around the world, along with the criminalization of terrorist financing, states have adopted mandatory reporting from the financial sector on money laundering and terrorist financing activities. Although jurisdictions require their own unique level of reporting, from basic suspicious activity reports to electronic funds transfers exceeding a particular threshold (or no threshold, in some cases), states rely on the private sector for these reports. This regulatory approach has extended the reach of the states and made private sector institutions an arm of state security.

Public-Private Partnerships

Public-private partnerships are increasingly being undertaken between banks and other financial entities and law enforcement, financial intelligence units, and security services to address the issue of financial crime, including terrorist financing. Some have argued that these partnerships are critical for detecting, deterring, disrupting, and denying terrorist and criminal organizations.[55] Others have called for enhanced cooperation between the public and private sectors to reinforce national and private capabilities to fight financial crime.[56] One of the driving factors behind the establishment of these partnerships is a concern that financial sector institutions are failing to meet their obligations to counter terrorist financing.[57] These partnerships are driven by the idea that public-private collaboration on counterterrorism financing is more likely to lead to positive outcomes.[58]

To date, more than twenty national governments have committed to developing public-private partnerships to share financial information.[59] The members of these partnerships share operational financial intelligence, including identifying information on individuals of concern. These partnerships might also involve sharing strategic intelligence, such as indicators, as Canada's financial intelligence unit, FINTRAC, does.[60]

Although the structure of these partnerships varies among (and even within) jurisdictions, the partners aim to facilitate the proactive exchange of information between intelligence agencies and banks and to enhance the effectiveness of the anti–money laundering and countering the financing of terrorism (AML/CFT) regime.[61] Recognizing the utility of these arrangements, FATF and other international bodies are increasingly advocating the establishment of public-private partnerships.[62]

In most states, little is known about the actual structure of these partnerships and their governing principles. For instance, in Canada, little is known about public-private partnerships particularly as they relate to counterterrorism initiatives.[63] In a recent Security Intelligence Review Committee report, allusion was made to a possible public-private partnership between the Canadian Security Intelligence Service (CSIS) and the private sector, but there is minimal information on how or why these partnerships have developed, how information-sharing is controlled, what guidelines are in place for the protection of privacy, and how information is being shared with financial institutions.[64] CSIS's review agency raised questions about whether CSIS was abiding by the "strictly necessary" principle in ingesting information of a financial nature.[65]

De Goede has also raised issues with public-private partnerships. Banks' and other financial institutions' political and moral requirement to comply (and be proactive) in detecting illicit financing is in tension with "their profit motive and their obligations for client confidentiality."[66] Although public-private partnerships give the illusion of an alignment between commercial and security interests, in reality, the relationship is one of "friction, tension, and contradiction."[67]

Public-private partnerships have yielded impressive results in the area of financial crimes, although few examples of successes in counterterrorist financing have come to light. Despite the ethical and privacy concerns about these partnerships, they present a possible template for engaging with other types of companies with a stake in counterterrorist financing activity, such as social media companies.[68] Indeed, social media platforms are exploited by terrorist actors to raise funds by soliciting donations, particularly as these platforms are increasingly incorporating funds movement mechanisms. As social media companies increasingly move into providing financial services, they have access to data that can support "know your customer" programs, and this might have significant privacy implications. Not all social media companies have a stellar track record of taking action to counter terrorism or protecting the privacy of their users. A significant challenge for many social media companies will be in identifying illicit crowdfunding campaigns or solicitations for funds and shutting them down before they can generate significant funds.

The private sector regulatory approach to counterterrorist financing is gaining momentum with public-private partnerships, and these partnerships are being expanded to include social media companies and financial technology companies. Although these efforts might yield better relationships and, ideally, more timely and relevant information, they also come with risks and costs. The private sector regulatory approach to countering terrorist financing overlaps with several other approaches, and the implications of this augment the potential risks (and benefits) of these partnerships.

The "Cost of Terrorism" Problem

One of the most common critiques of efforts to counter the financing of terrorism is that terrorism is cheap.[69] The implication of this critique is that efforts to prevent terrorists from acquiring funds have failed and are thus wasted.[70] This critique misses the mark by conflating terrorist organizational and operational financing and ignoring the variety of counterterrorism approaches that can be used. The "cost of terrorism" critique focuses on the cost of individual terrorist attacks, which, admittedly, can be low, and argues that efforts to "stop the flow of funds" to these types of attacks waste resources.[71] However, most terrorists, even so-called lone actors, are inspired by broader organizations that require significant funds to sustain themselves. This critique also focuses on the interdiction of terrorist funds, ignoring the other approaches (such as the intelligence approach) that can use financial intelligence to identify networks and imminent activity. The critique also ignores the possibility that one of the reasons terrorists have adopted cheap attacks is because efforts to stop them have reduced their financial resources and forced them to focus on low-complexity, low-sophistication, and low-cost attacks.[72] This is not to suggest that financial intelligence and countering terrorist financing are some sort of counterterrorism panacea—far from it. In fact, propositions about the utility of countering the financing of terrorism have received little in the way of critical evaluation, a lacuna that diminishes the field.

The "cost of terrorism" problem suffers from another fallacy: that low-complexity attacks are always cheap. Certainly, a simple stabbing attack can have a small financial footprint. However, other attacks, such as those involving firearms, can increase in cost significantly. In many cases, terrorists will seek specific weapons for these attacks, thus raising the costs. The majority of firearms attacks cost a minimum of $1,000 when factoring in the weapons purchase as well as ammunition. Costs can rise substantially if terrorists also train for their attacks (e.g., by visiting shooting ranges) or employ operational security measures (e.g., acquiring burner phones). Although individual costs involved in attacks seem small, they add up.

This of course also raises questions about the subjective definitions of "low cost" and "cheap." Whether something is high or low cost is entirely relative. For individuals earning a low salary, a few hundred dollars might be considered high cost or even prohibitively expensive. For others earning tens of thousands, or even hundreds of thousands, of dollars, a portion of their salary could be considered either high or low cost depending on their personal circumstances. The jurisdiction where terrorists seek to conduct operations also plays a role in the relative cost of a terrorist attack. For instance, acquiring a firearm in the United States is far less expensive (in many cases) than obtaining one in Europe; in contrast, acquiring a firearm in a conflict zone might be less expensive. Jurisdictional costs matter, and to truly assess and compare the cost of terrorism, they have to be held constant.

The subjective nature of costs, jurisdictional impacts on costs, and the conflation of organizational and operational financing have all contributed to confusion about the true cost of terrorism and its supposed cheapness.[73] Certainly, some attacks will always have a low absolute cost, whereas other, hidden costs might make what appears at first glance a simple, low-cost attack relatively expensive. Ultimately, the "cost of terrorism" argument is something of a red herring: it attacks the surface of counterterrorist financing practice without delving deeper into the actual mechanisms of terrorist financing, understanding the different approaches to counterterrorist financing, or considering the subjective nature of "low cost" or "cheap."

For counterterrorist financing actors, detecting and deterring self-funding of terrorist organizations and cells' operational activity requires paying attention to small amounts of money. For many law enforcement and security organizations, this is a significant paradigm shift because terrorist financing has often been conceptualized as relatively large scale (i.e., costing $10,000 or more) and international in nature (hence the emphasis on cross-border and international transaction reports within many financial intelligence units). This conceptualization of terrorist financing has been proven wrong on numerous occasions and might have contributed to the lack of terrorist financing charges and interdictions, such as in the case of the Toronto 18 terrorist plot.[74] Reconceptualizing terrorist financing as any amount of money, and acknowledging that even small amounts can enhance terrorist capacity, is critical for all counterterrorist actors. This is particularly relevant in the policy and legislative realm, in which laws and reporting requirements on terrorist financing might be mismatched to the actual methods and trends in the activity.

Emerging Challenges: Lone Actors and Terrorist Movements
One of the main challenges facing counterterrorist financing is the development of terrorist movements (rather than structured organizations).[75] Counterterrorism practitioners are no strangers to individuals inspired by a terrorist group (rather than direct members of it) who take action on their violent ideas. The development of extremist movements that lack any kind of real structure, such as QAnon, Incels, and Boogaloo Bois, is the latest evolution of the terrorist threat and might challenge the ability to use existing tools.[76] Certainly, there is much to learn from the attacks perpetrated by individual actors who were inspired by ISIL that occurred throughout much of the world in the mid- to late 2010s. Those attacks involved little movement of money, meaning that one of the main approaches to countering terrorist financing, preventing financial flows, had limited utility.[77] Many of the lessons learned about how individual terrorist attacks occur can be used to identify and thwart acts of violence perpetrated by individuals associated with extremist movements. However, the lack of formal structure (and significant financing activity) of these new terrorist movements mean many of the tools and approaches developed to counter the financing of terrorist organizations will have limited utility against them.[78]

Conclusion

Counterterrorist financing in the twenty-first century not only faces a number of challenges but also benefits from a number of approaches. Although there is an abundance of terrorist and extremist actors ranging from movements, groups, cells, and individuals across the political spectrum, there are also numerous well-developed approaches to countering their financing. Combining these approaches provides the maximum benefit. Criminalization, which will remain a pillar of counterterrorist financing, is most effective when combined with an intelligence approach. For its part, the intelligence approach supports military counterterrorist financing actions as well as the financial exclusion approach. Underpinning all these approaches are, of course, regulation of the private sector and partnerships with financial entities and, increasingly, social media companies. Of course, this is not to suggest that counterterrorist financing approaches are a complete solution or have been optimized for the current threat environment. In fact, the ongoing changes to that environment in terms of terrorist and extremist actors, the abundance of financing mechanisms available, and the limited capacity of many states to take full advantage of these approaches severely limits the effectiveness of counterterrorist financing, as does the lack of prioritization by states. New tools, approaches, and technologies will need to be continually developed to meet the challenges of modern terrorist financing, and ultimately states will need to prioritize the investigation, prosecution, and disruption of terrorist financing mechanisms and networks.

Notes

1. Whereas the United Nations adopted the International Convention for the Suppression of the Financing of Terrorism in 1999, the Financial Action Task Force (established in 1989) did not formally include terrorist financing until after the 9/11 attacks. http://www.un.org/law/cod/finterr.htm and http://www.fatf-gafi.org/about/.

2. Shortly after the attacks of 9/11, President George W. Bush issued Executive Order 13224, ordering the freezing of assets and blocking of transactions by individuals and entities associated with or supporting al-Qaeda, Osama bin Laden, and other listed groups. Davis, "Prevention of Terrorist Financing."

3. Bogers and Beeres, "Burden Sharing in Combating Terrorist Financing," 2993–2994; Clunan, "Fight Against Terrorist Financing," 569.

4. Davis, "Prevention of Terrorist Financing."

5. Official of the Northern Ireland Office, "Tackling Terrorist Finance," 1482–1485.

6. West and Nesbitt, "Proscribing Far Right Terrorism."

7. Jordan, "Attacking the Leader, Missing the Mark."

8. McKiernan et al., *Counterterrorism and Threat Finance Analysis*, 2.

9. Zarate, *Treasury's War*.

10. McKiernan et al., *Counterterrorism and Threat Finance Analysis*, 5.

11. Ibid., 33.

12. Pagan et al., *SOF Role*, 97.

13. Felbab-Brown, *Shooting Up*, 7.

14. Davis, "Rethinking Global Counterterrorist Financing."

15. Parker and Taylor, "Financial Intelligence."

16. Maxwell and Artingstall, "Information-Sharing Partnerships," 5.

17. Warner, "Wanted: A Definition of 'Intelligence.'"

18. Darshan-Leitner and Katz, *Harpoon*, 162–172.

19. de Goede, "Risk, Preemption, and Exception," 99.

20. Parker and Taylor, "Financial Intelligence."

21. Irwin, Choo, and Liu, "Modelling of Money Laundering."

22. Freeland, "How Can Sound Customer Due Diligence Help?" 44.

23. Williams, "Warning Indicators, Terrorist Finances, and Terrorist Adaptation," 8.

24. Ibid.

25. Canadian Security Intelligence Service, "Mobilization to Violence."

26. Parker and Taylor noted the emergence of financial surveillance in 2010. Parker and Taylor, "Financial Intelligence," 949.

27. Davis, "Rethinking Global Counterterrorist Financing."

28. Richard Riley, director for economic crime, cyber, and anticorruption at the British home office. Dutton, "Sharing Financial Intelligence May Reduce Organized Crime."

29. Keatinge and Keen, "Lone-Actor and Small Cell Terrorist Attacks," 7.

30. This was recognized in the recent review of 2017 terrorist attacks in the United Kingdom. Anderson, "2017 Terrorist Attacks."

31. Harper, "From London Bridge to Ariana Grande."

32. Herhalt, "Minassian Described Planning."

33. Keatinge, "Identifying Foreign Terrorist Fighters," 24.

34. Ibid., 3.

35. Oftedal, "Financing of Jihadi Terrorist Cells," 43.

36. Ibid., 62.

37. Mendick, Evans, and Ward, "Exclusive: Manchester Suicide Bomber."

38. Davis, "How Terrorists Use the Internet."

39. *United States of America vs. Abdulrahman El Bahnasawy.*

40. Davis, "How Terrorists Use the Internet."

41. Keatinge, "Identifying Foreign Terrorist Fighters," 26.

42. Ibid., 3.

43. Keatinge, "Role of Finance in Defeating Al-Shabaab," 27.

44. Keen, "Public-Private Collaboration," 8.

45. Léonard and Kaunert, "Combating the Financing of Terrorism Together?" 112.

46. Biersteker, "Targeting Terrorist Finances," 78.

47. FitzGerald, "Global Financial Information."

48. Byman, "Passive Sponsors of Terrorism," 117.

49. Bell, "Confiscation, Forfeiture, and Disruption of Terrorist Finances," 114.

50. Ibid., 115.

51. de Goede, "Risk, Preemption, and Exception," 101.

52. Although the freezing of terrorist funds can be effective at reducing the terrorism threat, there are also significant loopholes in the current regime. Terrorist financiers with frozen assets have been able to access thousands of dollars per month for basic necessities. Given the costs of terrorist attacks, a small portion of these funds would be more than enough to finance operational terrorist activity. Talley and Hope, "Accused Terrorists Use Loopholes."

53. Gurulé, "Demise of the UN Economic Sanctions," 62.

54. Pieth, "Editorial: The Financing of Terrorism," 2.

55. Forman, "Combating Terrorist Financing," 9.

56. Hardouin, "Banks Governance and Public-Private Partnership."

57. Keen, "Public-Private Collaboration," 6–7.

58. Ibid., 12.

59. Maxwell and Artingstall, "Information-Sharing Partnerships in the Disruption of Crime," 1.

60. Financial Transaction and Reports Analysis Centre of Canada (FINTRAC), "Project PROTECT."

61. Ridley and Alexander, "Combating Terrorist Financing."

62. Financial Action Task Force, *AML/CFT and Public-Private Sector Partnership.*

63. Outside of terrorist activity financing, private-public partnerships have been established and are more widely known. FINTRAC, "Project PROTECT."

64. Security Intelligence Review Committee, *SIRC Annual Report 2016–2017.*

65. Canadian Security Intelligence Service, "Access to Information Request."

66. de Goede, "Chain of Security," 26.

67. Guittet and Jeandesboz, "Security Technologies," 235–237, as cited in de Goede, "Chain of Security," 26.

68. Keatinge and Keen, "Social Media and Terrorist Financing," 2.

69. Williams, "Warning Indicators, Terrorist Finances, and Terrorist Adaptation," 6.

70. Neumann, "Don't Follow the Money," 4.

71. Ehrenfeld, "Funding Evil," 27.

72. Acharya, "Small Amounts for Big Bangs?" 285.

73. Ibid.

74. Davis, "Financing the Toronto 18."

75. Davis, "Rethinking Global Counterterrorist Financing."

76. Amarasingam and Argentino, "The QAnon Conspiracy Theory"; Davis, "Incel-Related Violence Is Terrorism"; Kriner and Clarke, "How the Boogaloo Bois."

77. Napoleoni, "Terrorist Financing," 60.

78. Hoffman and Ware, "Assessing the Threat of Incel Violence."

11

Old Methods,
New Technologies

Terrorists finance their activities in many ways; the exact mechanisms depend on a number of factors, including where they are operating, the structure of the financial sector in their jurisdictions of operations (the "financial terrain"), the nature of their activities, and their preexisting capabilities, to name a few. Terrorists want to raise, use, move, store, manage, and obscure their funds to engage in their desired activities. These financing mechanisms vary in scope and scale along a number of variables, most notably whether the financing is occurring for operational or organizational purposes. Beyond raising funds, terrorists also use that money to support their organizational and operational activities, including on small-scale and individual attacks. Funds have to be managed, stored, and invested to protect from inflation. Funds also have to be moved to and from areas where the terrorists are operating, and those funds must be hidden from authorities. To do that, terrorists employ a variety of money movement mechanisms using the formal financial sector, money services businesses, the charitable sector, cash couriers, financial technology, trade-based activities, and precious metals and stones. Cryptocurrencies are also useful for hiding the sources and destinations of funds, as are other financial tradecraft techniques, including financial facilitators. Terrorists keep their funds available for both short-term operational needs and long-term organizational ones, which can involve professional money managers, financial committees, and investments in an assortment of sectors.

The ways terrorists finance their activities depend in large part on whether they are involved in organizational or operational financing. For terrorist organizations, the main purpose is to obtain funds that can sustain and build a terrorist group over the medium to long term. For operational financing, the purpose is principally to finance terrorist attacks. These different goals often result in variations in the scope and scale of the financing activity and which mechanisms are chosen. In essence, terrorist organizations seek out longer-term, stable sources of funds that can help with their sustenance, whereas operational actors such as cells and individuals seek financing mechanisms to help them achieve their immediate goals, usually plots and attacks. Although organizational financing often involves criminal networks and business models, it can also involve small amounts of money from individual donors. For cells and individuals planning operations, the amount of money involved is usually more constrained, and efforts to obscure the use of funds tend to be more elaborate to avoid detection.

To systematically analyze the main methods of terrorist financing, the data created for this analysis have been broken down and summarized in the figures below. Each financing method has been ordered by rank within each element of the terrorist financing framework. It is important to keep in mind that this ordering is based on open source, available information and captures only the prevalence of the technique. The importance of each technique might be quite different depending on how much money it generates or involves; however, given the paucity of reliable information across terrorist actors in this regard, a rank ordering of observed activity is currently the best assessment of importance.

Terrorists raise funds in a variety of ways, as illustrated in Figure 11.1. At the organizational level, the main methods used by groups include state sponsors; businesses and investments; taxation, extortion, and protection rackets; kidnapping for ransom; and robbery and theft. At the operational level, terrorists engage primarily in self-financing to raise funds but also obtain funds from terrorist patrons, support networks, and financial crimes.

Terrorists use their funds primarily for terrorist attacks, including weapons and component procurement, as illustrated in Figure 11.2. However, organizationally, terrorists also have significant expenses in terms of social services and member salaries; propaganda and recruitment; and corruption, lobbying, and political activities. Although these are the most frequently observed terrorist uses of funds, the actual amounts spent might differ significantly from this rank order. Operationally, terrorists have two main categories of expenses: attacks (including weapons and components) and operational security.

Terrorists, regardless of whether they are involved in a group or are preparing for operational activity, primarily move money through banks. Other methods are also commonly used, as illustrated in Figure 11.3. Terrorist organizations also use trade-based money movement techniques, along with hawala and cash couriers, to move funds. Operationally, terrorists also move

Figure 11.1 Main Methods of Fund-Raising

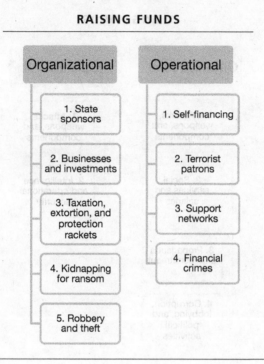

RAISING FUNDS

Organizational

1. State sponsors

2. Businesses and investments

3. Taxation, extortion, and protection rackets

4. Kidnapping for ransom

5. Robbery and theft

Operational

1. Self-financing

2. Terrorist patrons

3. Support networks

4. Financial crimes

money in cash. Of course, depending on the type of activity in which the terrorists engage, the scope and scale of funds moved differ dramatically.

Terrorist financing mechanisms vary between organizational and operational activity, and in most cases there is only cursory overlap. However, terrorists usually store funds in banks or in cash regardless of whether the actor is a group, cell, or individual, as illustrated in Figure 11.4. Despite concerns that terrorist financing is increasingly taking place outside the formal financial sector, and therefore reporting requirements are an unnecessary burden on that sector,[1] my research demonstrates that banks remain a primary means of funds movement for both operational and organizational financing. Terrorists store their funds in banks and cash for two simple reasons: liquidity and safety. Over the long term, terrorists might store their funds in less liquid investments, but this is primarily to generate more money and protect it from inflation. For everyday expenses and operational planning, nothing beats storage of funds in banks (which are often state-backed or state-insured) or cash.

Figure 11.2 Main Uses of Terrorist Funds

Terrorist management of funds is an overlooked but important aspect of their financing. Organizationally, terrorist groups employ professional managers and financial committees; they sometimes use multiple managers, as illustrated in Figure 11.5. At the operational level, most terrorist cells planning attacks have one manager for the group; in some cases they employ more than one manager and split the tasks between them. Many cells and individuals also plan their purchases to determine the costs and establish a budget to calculate the funds required to execute their plans. Of course, terrorist groups also employ budgets, although evidence of this, despite some notable work on the topic,[2] is less readily available than for some of the attacks and plots.

Terrorists also seek to obscure their funds. They do this by using third parties, proxies, and false names. Terrorists use a variety of methods to obscure funds, but little information is available about this financing mechanism, resulting in a lack of data for developing a rank order of techniques.

The financing mechanisms and techniques I have outlined suggest areas in which counterterrorism policies and practices should be focused;

Figure 11.3 Main Funds Movement Techniques

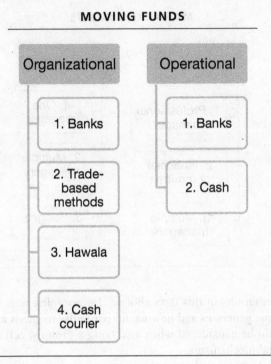

Figure 11.4 Storage of Funds

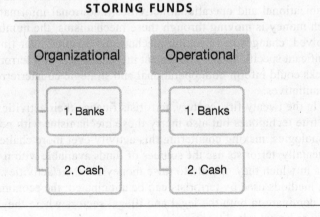

Figure 11.5 Management of Funds

however, limitations in this data abound. Determining how much money each technique generates and how useful particular methods are to terrorist groups should be considered when analyzing a group's, cell's, or individual's financial mechanisms.

These data suggest that in some instances, assumptions about which sectors might be used most by terrorists are wrong, whereas in other cases, some sectors might be used to a significant extent despite the international community's efforts to exclude terrorists from them. Although the formal and near-formal financial sectors continue to be used by many groups for organizational and operational activities, additional information on how much money is moving through these mechanisms, the number of actors involved, changes in financing mechanisms adopted over time, and how significant specific money movement mechanisms are for terrorist plots and attacks could inform both operational and strategic counterterrorist financing initiatives.

In the twenty-first century, terrorists finance their activities using tried and true techniques but also marry those mechanisms with new tools and technologies, making countering this activity ever more challenging. Fundamentally, terrorists use the sources of funds available within the jurisdictions in which they operate to raise money for their activities. Because of this, methods used by terrorists can be anticipated: the economic activities that dominate in both the legal and illegal sectors where they operate are likely to be exploited by terrorist actors.

Terrorist Financing Framework

The framework presented over the course of this book is meant to assist counterterrorism practitioners in understanding and analyzing financing mechanisms for terrorist and extremist groups and movements, as well as for cells and individuals. The framework also emphasizes the need for a detailed understanding of the economic terrain of the jurisdictions in which terrorists operate. That analysis should consider economic and criminal activity, the structure of the financial sector, and terrorist activity, as illustrated in Table 11.1. Combining these two forms of analysis can yield a powerful tool for understanding the financing activities of groups, cells, and individuals in specific jurisdictions and anticipating future areas of expansion of terrorist activity.

Regarding terrorist activity, consideration should be given to groups and movements that have articulated a threat against the jurisdiction or its allies and that operate in neighboring jurisdictions or have an interest in exploiting a specific jurisdiction because of lax regulations, particularly appealing financing mechanisms, or logistical opportunities (e.g., access to weapons and components).

The analytic framework describing terrorist financing mechanisms and methods (illustrated in Table 11.2) outlines all the known financing mechanisms, specific methods within each, and the prevalence of their use.

The framework outlined in Tables 11.1 and 11.2 is an overview of the factors that should be considered in terrorist financing analysis. Although the various methods terrorists have used to finance their activity cannot be listed, these broad categories provide a base from which to evaluate possible activities, to identify leads for further investigation, to develop proactive relationships and contacts with important sectors, and to hypothesize about terrorist actors' potential capabilities.

Table 11.1 Terrain Analysis Considerations

Economic and criminal activity
- Legal economic activity (industries, sectors, services, etc.)
- Illegal economic activity (theft, drugs, smuggling, etc.)
- Informal and cash-based economy
- Social services and supports

Financial sector structure
- Banks, money service businesses
- Informal value transfer services
- Financial technologies and cryptocurrencies
- Frequency of cash use
- Other

Terrorist and extremist activity
- Movements, groups, cells, and individuals in jurisdiction
- Intent in jurisdiction (financing, operational activity, safe haven, transit area, etc.)

New Frontiers in Terrorist Financing

To identify emerging trends in terrorist financing, I looked at how new technologies and methods have been adopted over time by terrorist organizations, cells, and individuals. Although the data are limited to the sample size of this study, I was able to augment this analysis with my experience as a counterterrorism practitioner. Some trends were evident in the data, whereas others are based on examples shared with me through my work. To augment this analysis, I looked at other financial and finance-related criminal activities that have taken place over the past few years and combined those observations

Table 11.2 Financing Mechanisms, Methods, and Organizational and Operational Use

Mechanism	Method	Organizational	Operational[a]
Raise	Businesses, investments, cryptocurrencies, and cultural activities	38	10
	Charitable sector	2	4
	Counterfeiting and pirated goods	13	0
	Financial crimes	13	16
	Identity-based support networks	27	16
	Kidnapping for ransom	36	0
	Maritime piracy, gambling, and prostitution rackets	29	2
	Resource exploitation	13	4
	Robbery and theft	33	8
	Self-financing	7	36
	Smuggling and trafficking: drugs, goods, and people	29	6
	State sponsors	45	2
	Taxation, extortion, and protection rackets	38	0
	Terrorist patrons	27	3
	Wealthy donors	27	4
Use	Attacks, weapons, components, and training	33	52
	Corruption, lobbying, and political activities	16	2
	Intelligence and operational security	13	10
	Propaganda and recruitment	18	0
	Social services, sustenance, salaries, and support activities	49	2
	Terrorist group patronage	13	0
Store	Banks	7	10
	Cash	4	8
	Gold, precious metals	2	N/A
	Third parties, proxies	2	2
Manage	Budget	N/A	6
	Financial committee	16	N/A
	Investments	5	2
	Multiple managers	9	6
	One manager	2	12
	Professional manager (incl. bankers, accountants)	16	2

continues

Table 11.2 Continued

Mechanism	Method	Organizational	Operational[a]
Move	Banks	22	16
	Cash courier	16	18
	Charitable sector	11	0
	Credit cards	0	4
	Cryptocurrencies	4	2
	Hawala	18	6
	High-value goods and precious metals	2	0
	Mobile payments	0	0
	Money services businesses	5	14
	Other financial technologies	2	4
	Trade-based	20	0
Obscure	Financial facilitators	N/A	N/A
	Third parties, proxies	N/A	N/A
	Cash	N/A	N/A
	Compartmentalization	N/A	N/A
	Money laundering	N/A	N/A
	Charitable sector	N/A	N/A
	Gender bias	N/A	N/A
	Online procurement	N/A	N/A

Note: a. The numbers represent a percentage of time each method was observed in the author's dataset.

with other trends in the terrorist sphere to determine where potential new areas, or areas of growth and opportunity, exist for terrorists.

Financial Technology and Social Media

In recent years, two emerging trends have had significant interplay for terrorist financing: financial technologies (including cryptocurrency) and social media. Terrorist financiers use social media to solicit donations and then use financial technologies including cryptocurrency to transfer the funds internationally.[3] These fund-raising campaigns are easy to set up, can reach hundreds or thousands of people almost instantaneously, and enable funds to be transferred within minutes or hours.

Adding to this complexity are many international companies offering financial services, and these are sometimes localized or specific to a region or country. Counterterrorist financing professionals must familiarize themselves with the financial technologies in the area in which they conduct operations or analyze terrorist organizations. For instance, M-Pesa is widely used in East Africa. Understanding the mechanisms involved in transferring money this way can help to identify the vulnerabilities and strengths of this technology, leading to the ability to detect terrorist use of it and counter it. As another example, Qi cards, a method of salary transfer, was exploited by the Islamic State in Iraq and the Levant (ISIL).[4]

Many social media companies used to promote terrorist causes have encrypted chat functions that allow for secure communication between terrorists including account information, payment instructions, and so forth. Some of the most widely used platforms are chat platforms such as Telegram, but social media companies are increasingly incorporating encrypted chat functions into their platforms. This means terrorists' calls for funds might not be sent publicly—they might be sent to select individuals but can still reach hundreds, if not thousands, of prospective donors. Social media companies are also embedding methods for transferring funds in their sites rather than redirecting users to external payment processors. Facebook aspires to make it "as easy to send money to someone as it is to send a photo."[5] As of 2019, "Facebook already allows peer-to-peer transfers but only in existing currencies and between accounts linked to bank-issued payment cards."[6] Signal and Telegram are also planning to launch their own forms of digital currency.[7] These services could be exploited by terrorists to launch a fund-raising campaign; circulate it quickly through their friends, colleagues, and other members of groups (perhaps using a cover story for why they need the funds); reach hundreds, thousands, or even tens of thousands of people quickly; and have the money in their accounts within hours, if not minutes. The onus will be on the social media companies to ensure money is not being raised for terrorist purposes. However, given the speed at which these terrorist campaigns could be launched, this monitoring must be proactive and ongoing rather than a retrospective review of an account or process. Incentivizing social media companies to devote the dedicated resources required to get ahead of these trends will require a creative combination of rewards and meaningful punishments (likely significant and possibly criminal).

Much has been made of terrorist use of Bitcoin and cryptocurrency; although terrorists have certainly been adopting this financial technology since 2015, there has been no widespread sea change away from other fund movement mechanisms. Terrorist actors continue to use older, more well-established methods to send funds and are constrained by the realities of the financial systems in the areas where they operate, particularly for purchasing goods, equipment, components, and weapons. Although terrorist use of cryptocurrency is increasing, the scope and scale of this activity is difficult to quantify. Certainly, terrorist organizations have launched fund-raising campaigns and are actively soliciting donations from their supporters in Bitcoin and digital currencies. However, the focus on digital and cryptocurrencies has eclipsed the actual trend, which is the increased use of financial technologies by all levels of terrorist actors to finance their activities. Although concerns exist about the anonymity of many of these technologies, it remains critical to note that only a few terrorist organizations, cells, and individuals have the technical capability to employ the advanced financial tradecraft that make these transactions truly anonymous.

The future of countering terrorist financing must be proactive, predictive, and in real time rather than historical, based on reporting a transaction to a financial intelligence unit days, if not weeks after the fact. Instead, companies will increasingly have to prevent or shut down the transfer of funds in real time, requiring ongoing monitoring and up-to-date information about the nature of the terrorist threat wherever they are operating or have reach. A significant challenge will be how to establish regulations around this and ensure effective enforcement and information-sharing with these companies.

All terrorist financing methods have evolved with technology. Terrorists, both at the organizational and at the operational level, do not hesitate to embrace newer technologies that can facilitate their financial activity or provide them enhanced security. In fact, many terrorists are early adopters of these technologies. Counterterrorist financing practitioners must respond by also becoming early adopters to determine how these technologies can be used for the various elements of terrorist financing and how those uses can be countered, disrupted, or exploited for intelligence purposes. This will require increased analytic capabilities in all departments and agencies as well as information-sharing and outreach to the private sector. These requirements could become onerous for small, less well-resourced jurisdictions, which might necessitate a centralized information-sharing mechanism to develop expertise on new financial technologies that can be deployed internationally on an as-needed basis.

Financial technology is at the forefront of new trends in terrorist financing, but this does not mean it will be widely adopted and used exclusively by all terrorist organizations, cells, and individuals. Terrorists are likely to continue to use a smorgasbord of methods to raise, use, move, store, manage, and obscure their funds. Many of these methods will predate modern technology. The use of cash is likely to remain important as well as the misuse of loans and welfare benefits to finance terrorist activity. State sponsorship is also likely to remain a significant source of funds for terrorist organizations. Financial technology will be adopted by some terrorists, including organizations, cells, and individuals, but is unlikely to displace the existing methods terrorists use. The most sophisticated terrorist actors will adopt new technologies but will also combine those technologies with older methods to make tracing the sources and destinations of funds more challenging for law enforcement and security services.

Cyber Crime

Terrorists increasingly rely on developing cyber capabilities, including cyber crime, to finance their activities. For instance, ISIL's cyber caliphate recruited hackers whose responsibilities included targeting the West.[8] Although the group did manage to execute some relatively high-profile attacks, it was not sophisticated enough to compromise systems, exfiltrate data, or steal money from a bank. Over time, terrorist organizations might devote more resources to these activities both for raising money and plotting attacks.

In the future, terrorists might make more significant use of cyber crime to fund their activities and might aspire to large-scale thefts. One potential template for this activity was the 2015–2016 SWIFT banking hack, in which millions of dollars were stolen. The attacks were conducted by APT 38 and were attributed to North Korea. The first attack involved a $101 million theft from the Bangladesh central bank from its account at the New York Federal Reserve Bank; shortly after, another attack was reported against a commercial bank in Vietnam.[9] Both attacks involved malware that issued unauthorized SWIFT messages, similar to malware developed by the Lazarus group, believed to be linked to North Korea.[10] Although these hacks generated a significant amount of media attention and likely involved the theft of hundreds of millions of dollars, the group(s) that perpetrated the attacks were likely state sponsored, meaning that they had significant resources at their disposal. Whether terrorist groups currently have, or will have in the near future, the capability to conduct this type of attack does not appear to be the case. However, that does not mean this is not a desired capability for terrorist groups, cells, or individuals. One individual, or a handful of individuals with specialized knowledge and skills, could join a terrorist group or movement and engage in criminal activity along these lines, if not necessarily on this scale. At the same time, were terrorist groups such as ISIL or Hizballah to recruit and fund research and development in this area, this type of large-scale and highly lucrative hack might be within their reach. This type of theft would be akin to bank robberies in the amount of funds that could be stolen and how that might affect the organizational development of a terrorist actor.

Other cyber crimes that might appeal to terrorist entities are the use of ransomware and identity theft to raise money or move it surreptitiously. These criminal skill sets would likely be adopted either from individuals already proficient in these activities or specifically developed by already computer-savvy individuals within terrorist entities. Some limited examples of this type of activity undertaken for the benefit of terrorist actors exist; however, it is important to remember that much of this remains in the realm of the hypothetical for the time being. For how much longer, however, remains to be seen.

An assessment of the immediate threat suggests that terrorist actors will likely seek to use cyber crime for more small-scale funding opportunities closer to the areas in which they operate, taking advantage of the distinct nature of their financial sector to perpetrate cyber frauds and thefts. Of particular concern are terrorist actors using cyber crime to steal money from individuals in countries that lack the investigative abilities to detect and prosecute the perpetrators. Encouraging the development of skills to investigate cyber crime in all financial sectors internationally would provide a complementary tool for detecting and deterring terrorist financing.

Over time, terrorist financing has not changed to a significant extent, although it is common to hear the refrain of "unprecedented" terrorist activity. One such example is ISIL. In recent years, ISIL has been described as an unprecedented terrorist organization for the amount of money the group raised through territory control and extractive activities. However, as I have demonstrated throughout this book, the work of ISIL was actually highly precedented. The group did not employ any truly new or unique funding strategies; instead, it used tried-and-true methods of raising funds and exploited other known financing methods to move, store, manage, and obscure those funds. The scale might have been bigger than that of other groups, although perhaps not as significant as assumed, particularly when one considers the amount of money terrorist groups such as Hizballah have access to and the failure to control for inflation in most analyses and comparisons of terrorist financing.

Despite being able to challenge some of the assumptions about terrorist financing using the data I gathered for this analysis, there is still a long way to go to truly understand terrorist financing. There will be many challenges to understanding the nuanced changes in the terrorist financing landscape over the past few decades, how terrorists finance their activities, and what terrorism actually costs in organizational sustenance and operational activities. Further, detailed descriptions of specific terrorist groups and their financing strategies will be important for building understanding of terrorist financing. Additional effort should be directed toward understanding the costs and activities associated with financing terrorist plots and attacks. The baseline data I developed for this study is just a starting point; more detailed data are required to really understand the scope and scale of terrorist financing and identify changes over time. Data-driven economic models of terrorist financing methods could be useful, as could more detailed, on-the-ground analyses of the costs of terrorist attacks based on local conditions. Without this information, empirical knowledge of terrorist financing will remain stunted, and efforts to combat terrorist financing will be based on assumptions rather than fact and might therefore lack effectiveness and efficiency.

The Future of Counterterrorist Financing

Counterterrorist financing involves five main approaches: criminalization and law enforcement, military force, intelligence, financial exclusion (including sanctions and asset freezes), and regulation of the private sector. These approaches work best when used in combination, depending on specific situations, but many states have adopted the first one and neglected the rest. Worse, many countries have the laws required to prosecute terrorist financing offenses but lack the ability to understand, investigate, and preempt the activity.

This is a result, in part, of the complexity of terrorist financing investigations. Although many can be straightforward, they require a certain level of competence with financial information; financial literacy; understanding of technical information (electronic funds transfer reports, for instance, or the somewhat technical information in suspicious transaction reports); and the ability to properly analyze, integrate, and act on this information. The complexity of investigations is unlikely to diminish in coming years, particularly as the terrorist financing landscape becomes further integrated into cyberspace and more online activity occurs across a far broader number of actors ranging from financial services companies to social media companies.

Terrorism is not a local phenomenon, and neither is terrorist financing, although some financing mechanisms might occur in the jurisdictions in which terrorists operate or seek to operate. Even though the march of globalization might have been slowed by the Covid-19 pandemic, the overarching trend of increased interconnectivity and businesses operating internationally will also increasingly lead terrorists to act internationally and finance their activities through mechanisms that interact with many countries and sectors. Terrorists will increasingly engage in jurisdictional arbitrage—seeking more lax jurisdictions for their financing activities.[11] Indeed, Napoleoni identified this issue in 2013, noting that when the United States enacted stricter counterterrorist financing laws and practices after 9/11, these laws displaced terrorist financial activity to Europe.[12] In many cases, this will take place in weak or failed states but might also occur in states where implementation of anti–money laundering or countering the financing of terrorism (AML/CFT) legislation and regulation have been slow or nonexistent.

Nevertheless, the move online by terrorists can help to create some elements of a data trail that should enable prosecutions and other disruptions of terrorist activity, including financing. Of course, some basic terrorist tradecraft can obscure this trail, but this will likely be the purview of particularly competent organizations, cells, and individuals rather than the norm.

The future of counterterrorist financing will be a space for specialists, but they should not work in a silo. Instead, they must be aware of and use the expertise of other specialists in adjacent areas of investigation and keep an eye on the broader terrorist landscape to ensure that their techniques are correctly identifying the threat, emerging issues, and financing mechanisms. Having complementary areas of expertise, such as cyber investigation or detailed terrorist organizational knowledge, will be essential to successfully investigating, detecting, disrupting, and prosecuting terrorist financing activity.

The current landscape presents a number of unique challenges for countering terrorist financing, including of course the different levels of actors involved in the activity and the significant range of activities these actors can undertake, from large-scale, high-capacity attacks to small-scale or lone-actor attacks. Detecting and deterring the financing activities associated with these actors and types of activity is a significant challenge, but opportunities exist to leverage existing infrastructure, networks, skill sets, and legislative frameworks to exploit financial intelligence to its maximum advantage and prevent and detect terrorist financing.

Researchers, academics, and practitioners are increasingly making the distinction between operational and organizational financing and recognizing its implications for counterterrorist financing practices (and evaluations of those activities). What has yet to happen is a distinction in the responses to counterterrorist financing. International guidance from the Financial Action Task Force continues to conflate these two issues. States are not encouraged to prioritize their particular risk. Some countries face the risk of local terrorist attacks and need to focus on operational financing, whereas other countries face more of a risk of organizational financing and therefore need to focus their efforts there. Prioritizing in such a manner will allow states, particularly those with weak AML/CFT regimes, to enact the most efficient solutions first, then address the "nice to haves" later. Ideally, all states would have resilient counterterrorist financing regimes tailored to their economic terrain that make the distinction between those two types of financing and have systems in place to detect such activity by groups, cells, and individuals, as well as effective policy and regulatory tools to respond to changes in those risks and threats.

Understanding the nuanced differences between organizational and operational financing and the specific mechanisms of terrorists can help states develop evidence-based counterterrorist financing practices. This understanding can also help to identify what mechanisms terrorist organizational and operational actors might use to finance their activities, allowing law enforcement, security services, and other counterterrorist financing actors to develop proactive practices and policies to detect and deter such financing.

Beyond these challenges, other issues remain regarding counterterrorist financing policies and practices. For instance, there are few empirical analyses of the effects of counterterrorist financing practices. It remains unclear what these policies and approaches actually achieve, which ones are most effective and in which circumstances, which practices might create unintended harms (and what those might be), and how they can be enhanced to better achieve their stated aims. It is critical to understand what counterterrorism policies and practices achieve, particularly as we adapt to a shifting threat environment with increasing levels of actors (movements, groups, cells, and individuals) from a variety of ideologically and politically motivated violent extremists and ultimately a more diverse risk environment that will challenge existing counterterrorist financing approaches.[13]

Terrorists today have at their disposal a great range of skills, methods, and techniques they can use to finance their activities. The lesson from terrorist financing in the early years of the twenty-first century is that it is increasingly complex with a high number of actors. There are many terrorist groups, cells, and individuals and different styles of terrorism that require diverse responses to counter their financing. Terrorist financing mirrors the overall increase in complexity in international financial systems, markets, and emerging technologies. Terrorist and extremist movements, groups, cells, and individuals, in terms of their financing, are part of a continuous cycle of adaptation and counteradaptation. This will not change in the future, and yet our responses must evolve to leverage counterterrorist financing tools and adapt them to our new realities.

Notes

1. Dean, "Draining the Ocean," 71.
2. Clarke et al., "Financial Futures of the Islamic State."
3. Davis, "New Technologies but Old Methods in Terrorism Financing."
4. US Department of the Treasury, "Treasury Designates Key Nodes."
5. *Economist*, "Facebook's Planned New Currency."
6. Ibid.
7. Ibid.
8. Graham-Harrison, "Could ISIS's 'Cyber Caliphate.'"
9. Corkery, "Once Again, Thieves Enter."
10. Pagliery and Riley, "North Korea–Linked 'Lazarus' Hackers."
11. Williams, "Warning Indicators, Terrorist Finances, and Terrorist Adaptation," 6.
12. Napoleoni, "Evolution of Terrorist Financing Since 9/11," 15.
13. Davis, "Rethinking Global Counterterrorist Financing."

Bibliography

Abuza, Z. "Funding Terrorism in Southeast Asia: The Financial Network of Al Qaeda and Jemaah Islamiya." *Contemporary Southeast Asia* 25, no. 2 (2003): 169–199.

Acharya, Arabinda. "Small Amounts for Big Bangs? Rethinking Responses to 'Low Cost' Terrorism." *Journal of Money Laundering Control* 12, no. 3 (2009): 285–298. https://doi.org/10.1108/13685200910973655.

Adams, J. "The Financing of Terror." In *Contemporary Research on Terrorism*, edited by Paul Wilkinson, 393–405. Aberdeen: Aberdeen University, 1987.

Agence France-Presse. "Lafarge Charged with Complicity in Syria Crimes Against Humanity." *Guardian*, June 28, 2018. http://www.theguardian.com/world/2018/jun/28/lafarge-charged-with-complicity-in-syria-crimes-against-humanity.

———. "Lafarge en Syrie: Possible déclassification des documents secret-défense." *Le Monde*, May 7, 2018. https://www.lemonde.fr/international/article/2018/05/07/lafarge-en-syrie-des-documents-secret-defense-peuvent-etre-declasses_5295762_3210.html.

Ahmad, Jibran. "Taliban Video Shows Sons Born to Kidnapped US, Canadian Couple." Reuters, December 20, 2016. http://web.archive.org/web/201707111 60328/http://www.reuters.com/article/us-afghanistan-hostages-idUSKBN 1490I4.

Ahronheim, Anna. "ICYMI: Iran Pays Hezbollah Much More Than You Previously Thought." *Jerusalem Post*, September 15, 2017. https://www.jpost.com/Middle-East/Iran-News/Iran-pays-830-million-to-Hezbollah-505166.

———. "Israeli Spy Agency Uncovers Gaza-Turkey-Hebron Money Trail." *Jerusalem Post*, August 3, 2017. https://www.jpost.com/Arab-Israeli-Conflict/Israeli-spy-agency-uncovers-Gaza-Turkey-West-Bank-money-trail-501506.

Al-Batati, Saeed, and Ben Hubbard. "Yemeni Bankers Get in Trouble over a Customer, Al Qaeda." *New York Times*, November 15, 2016. https://www.nytimes.com/2016/11/16/world/middleeast/yemen-al-qaeda-bank.html.

Alexander, Dean C. *Business Confronts Terrorism: Risks and Responses*. New York: Terrace, 2004.

Alexander, Harriet. "New York Woman Charged with Sending $85,000 in Bitcoin to Support ISIL." *Telegraph*, December 14, 2017. https://www.telegraph.co.uk/news /2017/12/14/new-york-woman-charged-sending-85000-bitcoin-support-isil/.

Alexander, Harriet, and Alistair Beach. "How ISIL Is Funded, Trained, and Operating in Iraq and Syria." *Telegraph*, August 23, 2014. https://www.telegraph.co.uk /news/worldnews/middleeast/iraq/11052919/How-isil-is-funded-trained-and -operating-in-Iraq-and-Syria.html.

Allard, Tom. "Exclusive: Looted Cash, Gold Help Islamic State Recruit in Philippines." Reuters, January 22, 2018.. https://www.reuters.com/article/us -philippines-militants-islamicstate-ex/exclusive-looted-cash-gold-help-islamic -state-recruit-in-philippines-idUSKBN1FC0E2.

Al-Othaimin, Ibrahim. "How Iran Finances Hezbollah." *Saudi Gazette*, March 15, 2018. http://saudigazette.com.sa/article/530471/Opinion/OP-ED/How-Iran -finances-Hezbollah.

Amarasingam, Amarnath, and Marc-André Argentino. "The QAnon Conspiracy Theory: A Security Threat in the Making?" *CTC Sentinel*, 2020.

Anderson, Christina. "Former Hostage Helped by Al Qaeda Describes 6-Year Ordeal in the Sahara." *New York Times*, September 24, 2017. https://www .nytimes.com/2017/09/24/world/africa/sweden-mali-qaeda-gustafsson.html.

Anderson, David. "2017 Terrorist Attacks MI5 and CTP Reviews Implementation Stock-Take Unclassified Summary of Conclusions." UK Government, June 11, 2019. https://assets.publishing.service.gov.uk/government/uploads/system/uploads /attachment_data/file/807911/2017_terrorist_attacks_reviews_implementation _stock_take.pdf.

Anthes, William L. "Financial Illiteracy in America: A Perfect Storm, a Perfect Opportunity." *Journal of Financial Service Professionals* 58, no. 6 (2004): 49–56.

Arena, Michael P. "Hizballah's Global Criminal Operations." *Global Crime* 7, no. 3 (2006): 454–470. https://doi.org/10.1080/17440570601073186.

Arnold, Michael, and Saud Abu Ramadan. "Hamas Calls on Supporters to Donate to Group in Bitcoin." Bloomberg, January 30, 2019. https://www.bloomberg.com /news/articles/2019-01-30/hamas-calls-on-supporters-to-donate-to-group-in -bitcoin.

Asal, Victor, Shawn Flanigan, and Ora Szekely. "Doing Good While Killing: Why Some Insurgent Groups Provide Community Services." *Terrorism and Political Violence* (2020): 1–21. https://doi.org/10.1080/09546553.2020.1745775.

Asharq Al-Awsat. "200 'Secret Bankers' Facilitate Money Flow to ISIS." December 13, 2017. https://english.aawsat.com//home/article/1111796/200-secret-bankers -facilitate-money-flow-isis.

Associated Press. "Pakistan Begins Seizing Charities Linked to US-Wanted Cleric." *New York Times*, February 14, 2018. https://www.nytimes.com/aponline /2018/02/14/world/asia/ap-as-pakistan-radical-cleric.html?smid=tw-share.

Australian Financial Intelligence Unit (AUSTRAC). "Terrorism Financing in Australia 2014." 2014. Accessed July 24, 2017. https://www.austrac.gov.au/business /how-comply-guidance-and-resources/guidance-resources/terrorism-financing -australia-2014.

———. "Terrorism Financing Regional Risk Assessment for South-East Asia 2016." 2016. https://www.austrac.gov.au/sites/default/files/2019-07/regional-risk -assessment-SMALL_0.pdf.

Azami, Dawood. "How Does the Taliban Make Money?" *BBC News*, December 22, 2018. https://www.bbc.com/news/world-46554097.

Bahney, Benjamin W., Radha K. Iyengar, Patrick B. Johnston, Danielle F. Jung, Jacob N. Shapiro, and Howard J. Shatz. "Insurgent Compensation: Evidence from Iraq." *American Economic Review* 103, no. 3 (2013): 518–522. https://doi.org/10.1257/aer.103.3.518.

Bahney, Benjamin W., Howard J. Shatz, Carroll Ganier, Renny McPherson, and Barbara Sude. "An Economic Analysis of the Financial Records of al-Qa'ida in Iraq." Santa Monica, CA: RAND Corporation, 2010.

Baidawi, Adam. "Ex-Federal Worker in Australia Accused of Financing ISIS." *New York Times*, January 23, 2019. https://www.nytimes.com/2018/01/23/world/australia/federal-worker-isis-financing.html.

Bantekas, Ilias. "The International Law of Terrorist Financing." *American Journal of International Law* 97, no. 2 (2003): 315–333.

Basile, Mark. "Going to the Source: Why Al Qaeda's Financial Network Is Likely to Withstand the Current War on Terrorist Financing." *Studies in Conflict and Terrorism* 27, no. 3 (May 2004): 169–185. https://doi.org/10.1080/10576100490438237.

Basra, Rajan, and Peter R. Neumann. "Criminal Pasts, Terrorist Futures: European Jihadists and the New Crime-Terror Nexus." *Perspectives on Terrorism* 10, no. 6 (2016): 25–40.

Bauer, Katherine, and Matthew Levitt. "Al Qaeda Financing: Selected Issues." In *How Al-Qaeda Survived Drones, Uprisings, and the Islamic State*, edited by Aaron Y. Zelin, 93–105. Washington, DC: Washington Institute for Near East Policy, June 2017. https://www.washingtoninstitute.org/policy-analysis/how-al-qaeda-survived-drones-uprisings-and-islamic-state.

BBC News. "IS Currency Plans in 60 Seconds." Accessed January 25, 2021. https://www.bbc.com/news/av/world-middle-east-30053006.

———. "Profile of Jakarta Suspect Bahrun Naim." January 14, 2016. https://www.bbc.com/news/world-asia-35316915.

———. "San Bernardino Shooting: Who Were the Attackers?" December 11, 2015. https://www.bbc.com/news/world-us-canada-35004024.

———. "Sheffield Men Jailed for Funding Jihadists in Syria." January 11, 2019. https://www.bbc.com/news/uk-england-south-yorkshire-46842932.

———. "Stockholm Bomb Funder Nasserdine Menni to Be Freed." June 10, 2014. http://www.bbc.com/news/uk-scotland-glasgow-west-27778594.

———. "Terror Plot: Jail Terms for Birmingham Bomb Plotters." Accessed August 17, 2017. http://www.bbc.com/news/uk-22290927.

Bell, R. E. "The Confiscation, Forfeiture, and Disruption of Terrorist Finances." *Journal of Money Laundering Control* 7, no. 2 (2004): 105–125.

Bell, Stewart. "Massive RCMP Probe Stopped Al-Qaeda-Linked Conspiracy to Derail Passenger Train: Newly Released Documents." *National Post*, January 11, 2014. https://nationalpost.com/news/canada/massive-rcmp-probe-stopped-al-qaeda-linked-conspiracy-to-derail-passenger-train-newly-released-documents.

Bergman, Ronen. *Rise and Kill First*. New York: Random House, 2018.

Bergman, Ronen, and David D. Kirkpatrick. "With Guns, Cash, and Terrorism, Gulf States Vie for Power in Somalia." *New York Times*, July 22, 2019. https://www.nytimes.com/2019/07/22/world/africa/somalia-qatar-uae.html.

Bezhan, Frud. "Exclusive: Taliban's Expanding 'Financial Power' Could Make It 'Impervious' to Pressure, Confidential Report Warns." Radio Free Europe/Radio Liberty, September 16, 2020. https://www.rferl.org/a/exclusive-taliban-s-expanding-financial-power-could-make-it-impervious-to-pressure-secret-nato-report-warns/30842570.html.

Bhagat Singh BRAR and Canada (Minister of Public Safety and Emergency Preparedness), No. T-669-16 (Federal Court December 23, 2019).

Biersteker, Thomas J. "Targeting Terrorist Finances: The New Challenges of Finan-
cial Market Globalisation." In *Worlds in Collision: Terror and the Future of
Global Order*, edited by Ken Booth and T. Dunne, 74–84. London: Palgrave
Macmillan, 2002.

Bogers, M., and R. Beeres. "Burden Sharing in Combating Terrorist Financing."
*International Journal of Social, Behavioral, Educational, Economic, and
Industrial Engineering* 7, no. 12 (2013): 2992–2998.

Braun, Michael. "Drug Trafficking and Middle Eastern Terrorist Groups: A Growing
Nexus?" Washington, DC: Washington Institute for Near-East Policy. July 25,
2008. http://www.washingtoninstitute.org/policy-analysis/view/drug-trafficking
-and-middle-eastern-terrorist-groups-a-growing-nexus.

Brennan, David. "Nut Jihad: Taliban Makes Millions from Pistachio Farms."
Newsweek, March 26, 2018. http://www.newsweek.com/funding-terror-snacks
-taliban-rake-millions-pistachio-profits-860393.

Brisard, Jean-Charles, and Kevin Jackson. "Islamic State's External Operations and
the French-Belgian Nexus." *CTC Sentinel* 9, no. 11 (2016).

Brisard, Jean-Charles, and Gabriel Poirot. "Le Financement des Attentats de Paris
(7–9 Janvier et 13 Novembre 2015)." Centre d'Analyse du Terrorisme, October
2016. http://cat-int.org/wp-content/uploads/2017/03/Financement-des-attentats
-2015-VF.pdf.

Butt, Shelby, and Daniel Byman. "Right-Wing Extremism: The Russian Connection."
Survival 62, no. 2 (March 2020): 137–152. https://doi.org/10.1080/00396338
.2020.1739960.

Byman, Daniel. "Outside Support for Insurgent Movements." *Studies in Conflict
and Terrorism* 36, no. 12 (2013): 981–1004. https://doi.org/10.1080/1057610X
.2013.842132.

———. "Passive Sponsors of Terrorism." *Survival* 47, no. 4 (December 2005): 117–
144. https://doi.org/10.1080/00396330500433399.

———. "Understanding, and Misunderstanding, State Sponsorship of Terrorism."
Studies in Conflict and Terrorism (2020): 1–19. https://doi.org/10.1080/1057610X
.2020.1738682.

Byman, Daniel, and Sarah E. Kreps. "Agents of Destruction? Applying Principal-
Agent Analysis to State-Sponsored Terrorism." *International Studies Perspectives*
11, no. 1 (2010): 1–18.

Byman, Daniel, Peter Chalk, Bruce Hoffman, William Rosenau, and David Brannan.
Trends in Outside Support for Insurgent Movements. Santa Monica, CA: RAND
Corporation, 2001.

Callimachi, Rukmini. "Paying Ransoms, Europe Bankrolls Qaeda Terror." *New
York Times*, July 29, 2014. https://www.nytimes.com/2014/07/30/world/africa
/ransoming-citizens-europe-becomes-al-qaedas-patron.html?_r=0.

Callimachi, Rukmini, and Sewell Chan. "Hostage Held by Al Qaeda in Mali for 5
Years Is Freed." *New York Times*, August 3, 2017. https://mobile.nytimes
.com/2017/08/03/world/africa/mali-stephen-mcgown-south-africa-al
-qaeda.html?referer=.

Canadian Security Intelligence Service. "Access to Information Request: Public Private
Partnerships in Canada (Information Sharing)." 2019.

———. "Mobilization to Violence (Terrorism) Research—Key Findings." 2018.
https://www.canada.ca/en/security-intelligence-service/corporate/publications
/mobilization-to-violence-terrorism-research-key-findings.html.

Casey, Liam. "Van Attack Suspect Alek Minassian Was Searching for Job, Set to Graduate College." Global News, April 26, 2018. https://globalnews.ca/news /4170290/toronto-van-attack-alek-minassian-background/.

Castner, Brian. "Exclusive: Tracing ISIS' Weapons Supply Chain—Back to the US." *Wired*, December 12, 2017. https://www.wired.com/story/terror-industrial -complex-isis-munitions-supply-chain/.

Chalk, Peter. "The Liberation Tigers of Tamil Eelam Insurgency in Sri Lanka." In *Ethnic Conflict and Secessionism in South and Southeast Asia: Causes, Dynamics, Solutions*, edited by Rajat Ganguly and Ian Macduff, 128–165. Thousand Oaks, CA: Sage, 2003.

Channel News Asia. "Singaporean Charged for Supporting Publication of Islamic State Propaganda." April 15, 2019. https://www.channelnewsasia.com/news /singapore/singaporean-charged-for-supporting-publication-of-islamic-state -11446836.

Chauhan, Satender. "Terror Module with Links to Canada, Pakistan Busted; 2 Terrorists Arrested." *India Today*, May 21, 2017. https://www.indiatoday.in/india /story/terror-module-canada-pakistan-khalistan-terrorists-arrested-978377 -2017-05-21.

Chelin, Richard Philippe. "From the Islamic Maghreb of Algeria to the Economic Caliphate of the Sahel: The Transformation of Al Qaeda in the Islamic Maghreb." *Terrorism and Political Violence* (2019).

Chew, Amy. "Why a Resurgent Jemaah Islamiah in Indonesia Is Also Bad News for Malaysia and Singapore." *South China Morning Post*, July 7, 2019. https://www.scmp.com/week-asia/society/article/3017465/why-resurgent -jemaah-islamiah-indonesia-also-bad-news-malaysia.

Clarke, Colin P. "ISIS Is So Desperate It's Turning to the Drug Trade." *Fortune*, July 24, 2017. http://fortune.com/2017/07/24/isis-mosul-defeated-news-territory -islamic-state-drugs/?utm_content=buffer1dd3c&utm_medium=social&utm _source=twitter.com&utm_campaign=buffer.

———. "An Overview of Current Trends in Terrorism and Illicit Finance." Santa Monica, CA: RAND Corporation, September 7, 2018. https://www.rand.org /pubs/testimonies/CT498.html.

———. "Small Arms and Light Weapons (SALW) Trafficking, Smuggling, and Use for Criminality by Terrorists and Insurgents: A Brief Historical Overview." The Hague: International Centre for Counterterrorism, July 2020.

———. *Terrorism, Inc.: The Financing of Terrorism, Insurgency, and Irregular Warfare*. Santa Barbara, CA: Praeger, 2015.

Clarke, Colin P., and Phil Williams. "Da'esh in Iraq and Syria." In *Terrorist Criminal Enterprises*, edited by Kimberley L. Thachuk and Rollie Lal, 27–62. Santa Barbara, CA: Praeger, 2018.

Clarke, Colin P., Kimberly Jackson, Patrick B. Johnston, Eric Robinson, and Howard J. Shatz. "Financial Futures of the Islamic State of Iraq and the Levant: Findings from a RAND Corporation Workshop." March 29, 2017. https:// www.rand.org/pubs/conf_proceedings/CF361.html.

Clunan, Anne L. "The Fight Against Terrorist Financing." *Political Science Quarterly* 121, no. 4 (2006): 569–596. https://doi.org/10.1002/j.1538-165X.2006.tb00582.x.

Coker, Margaret, and Benoit Faucon. "The Rise and Deadly Fall of Islamic State's Oil Tycoon." *Wall Street Journal*, April 24, 2016. https://www.wsj.com /articles/the-rise-and-deadly-fall-of-islamic-states-oil-tycoon-1461522313.

Collier, Paul. "Economic Causes of Civil Conflict and Their Implications for Policy." World Bank, 2006, 1–26.

Collier, P., A. Hoeffler, and D. Rohner. "Beyond Greed and Grievance: Feasibility and Civil War." *Oxford Economic Papers* 61, no. 1 (March 2008): 1–27. https://doi.org/10.1093/oep/gpn029.

ComplyAdvantage. "Money in Terrorist Hands: What FinTech Firms Should Fear." December 14, 2015. https://complyadvantage.com/blog/money-in-terrorist -hands-what-fintech-firms-should-fear/.

Corkery, Michael. "Once Again, Thieves Enter Swift Financial Networks and Steal." *New York Times*, May 12, 2016. https://www.nytimes.com/2016/05/13 /business/dealbook/swift-global-bank-network-attack.html.

Corley, Christopher L. "The Liberation Tigers of Tamil Eelam (LTTE)." In *Financing Terrorism: Case Studies*, edited by Michael Freeman, 111–142. New York: Routledge, 2012.

Counterterrorism Police. "Multiple Bombings." Code: Severe. Accessed February 10, 2020. https://www.counterterrorism.police.uk/code-severe-podcast/.

Cragin, Kim R., and Sara A. Daly. *Women as Terrorists*. Santa Barbara: Praeger, 2009.

Croissant, Aurel, and Daniel Barlow. "Following the Money Trail: Terrorist Financing and Government Responses in Southeast Asia." *Studies in Conflict and Terrorism* 30 (2007): 131–156.

Cronin, Audrey Kurth. "How Al-Qaida Ends: The Decline and Demise of Terrorist Groups." *International Security* 31, no. 1 (July 2006): 7–48. https://doi.org/10 .1162/isec.2006.31.1.7.

Cuen, Leigh. "New York Woman Charged with Laundering Bitcoin for ISIS." *International Business Times*, December 15, 2017. http://www.ibtimes.com/new-york -woman-charged-laundering-bitcoin-ISIS-2629112.

Daily Sabah. "Turkish Police Discover Around $2M in Cash in Istanbul Office of 2 Daesh-Linked Suspects." April 4, 2018. https://www.dailysabah.com/war-on -terror/2018/04/04/turkish-police-discover-around-2m-in-cash-and-gold-in -istanbul-office-of-2-daesh-linked-suspects.

Darshan-Leitner, Nitsana, and Samuel M. Katz. *Harpoon: Inside the Covert War Against Terrorism's Money Masters*. New York: Hachette, 2017.

Davis, Jessica. "Prevention of Terrorist Financing." In *Handbook of Terrorism Prevention and Preparedness*, edited by Alex P. Schmid 464–494. The Hague: International Centre for Counterterrorism, 2021. https://icct.nl/app/uploads /2021/01/Handbook-ch-14-Davis-FINAL.pdf.

———. "Financing the Toronto 18." In *The Toronto 18*, edited by Kent Roach, Michael Nesbitt, and David Hoffman (forthcoming) Winnipeg: University of Manitoba Press, 2021.

———. "The Future of the Islamic State's Women: Assessing Their Potential Threat." *ICCT Journal*, Policy Brief.

———. "How Terrorists Use the Internet for Weapons and Component Procurement." *GNET*. Accessed February 29, 2020. https://gnet-research.org/2020/02/26/how -terrorists-use-the-internet-for-weapons-and-component-procurement/.

———. "Incel-Related Violence Is Terrorism—and the World Should Start Treating It That Way." *Globe and Mail*, May 20, 2020. https://www.theglobeandmail.com /opinion/article-incel-related-violence-is-terrorism-and-the-world-should-start/.

———. "New Technologies but Old Methods in Terrorism Financing." Royal United Services Institute for Defence and Security Studies, *CRAAFT Research Briefing* no. 2 (July 22, 2020): 7

———. "Rethinking Global Counterterrorist Financing." *Lawfare*, December 6, 2020. https://www.lawfareblog.com/rethinking-global-counterterrorist-financing.

de Goede, Marieke. "The Chain of Security." *Review of International Studies* 44, no. 1 (2018): 24–42.

———. "Risk, Preemption, and Exception in the War on Terrorist Financing." In *Risk and the War on Terror*, edited by Louise Amoore and Marieke de Goede, 113–127. New York: Routledge, 2008.

———. *Speculative Security: The Politics of Pursuing Terrorist Monies*. Minneapolis: University of Minnesota Press, 2012.

———. *Women in Modern Terrorism: From Liberation Wars to Global Jihad and the Islamic State*. Lanham: Rowman and Littlefield, 2017.

Dean, Aimen. "Draining the Ocean to Catch One Type of Fish: Evaluating the Effectiveness of the Global Counter-Terrorism Financing Regime." *Perspectives on Terrorism* 7, no. 4 (2013).

Desmarais, Sonia, Chantal Lavigne, and Karine Bastien. "Identities of 2 Quebec Men Who Fought in Syria Revealed." *CBC News*, December 8, 2016. https://www.cbc.ca/news/canada/montreal/syria-militants-quebec-terrorism-hostages-1.3885740.

Dion-Schwarz, Cynthia, David Manheim, and Patrick Johnston. *Terrorist Use of Cryptocurrencies: Technical and Organizational Barriers and Future Threats*. Santa Monica, CA: RAND Corporation, 2019. https://doi.org/10.7249/RR3026.

Donnelly, Phoebe. "Women in Al-Shabaab Through a New War's Lens." Women in International Security, July 25, 2018. https://www.wiisglobal.org/women-in-al-shabaab-through-a-new-wars-lens/.

Duke, Alan. "Elliot Rodger's Family Struggled with Money, Court Documents Show." CNN, May 27, 2014. https://www.cnn.com/2014/05/27/justice/california-elliot-rodger-wealth/index.html.

Dutton, Jack. "Sharing Financial Intelligence May Reduce Organized Crime, Say British Officials." *National*, July 26, 2019. https://www.thenational.ae/world/europe/sharing-financial-intelligence-may-reduce-organised-crime-say-british-officials-1.891067.

Economist. "Facebook's Planned New Currency May Be Based on a Blockchain." May 30, 2019. https://www.economist.com/finance-and-economics/2019/05/30/facebooks-planned-new-currency-may-be-based-on-a-blockchain.

Egmont, Jon, and Felipe Villamor. "ISIS' Core Helps Fund Militants in the Philippines, Report Says." *New York Times*, June 20, 2017. https://www.nytimes.com/2017/07/20/world/asia/philippines-ISIS-marawi-duterte.html?rref=collection%2Fsectioncollection%2Fasia&_r=0.

Egmont Group. *Annual Report 2016/2017*. 2017. https://egmontgroup.org/en/document-library/10.

Ehrenfeld, Rachel. "Funding Evil: How Terrorism Is Financed and the Nexus of Terrorist and Criminal Organizations." In *Terrornomics*, edited by Sean S. Costigan and David Gold, 27–47. Burlington, VT: Ashgate, 2007.

English, Richard. *Armed Struggle: The History of the IRA*. Oxford, UK: Oxford University Press, 2004.

Ensor, Josie. "Fourth British ISIL Kingpin Unmasked." *Daily Telegraph*, September 26, 2017. https://www.pressreader.com/uk/the-daily-telegraph/20170926/281487866538883.

Epp, Alexander, and Roman Hofner. "The Hate Network: Atomwaffen Division." *Der Spiegel*, September 7, 2018. https://www.spiegel.de/international/the-hate-network-an-inside-look-at-a-global-extremist-group-a-1226861.html.

European Union Agency for Law Enforcement Cooperation (Europol). *European Union Terrorism Situation and Trend Report 2018*. Europol, 2018.

Evans, Martin, and Lexi Finnigan. "British Benefits Payments Used to Fund Paris and Brussels Attack Suspects' Campaign of Terror, Court Hears." *Telegraph*, November 24, 2016. https://www.telegraph.co.uk/news/2016/11/24/man-hat -suspect-brussels-paris-attacks-given-3k-two-men-birmingham/.

Evans, Richard. "Organised Crime and Terrorism Financing in Northern Ireland." *Jane's Intelligence Review* 14, no. 9 (2002): 26–29.

Fanusie, Yaya J. "Jihadists Upping Their Bitcoin Game." *Forbes*, March 29, 2019. https://www.forbes.com/sites/yayafanusie/2019/03/29/jihadists-upping-their -bitcoin-game/#57a0fb5e79bc.

———. "Terrorist Networks Eye Bitcoin as Cryptocurrency's Price Rises." *Cipher Brief*, December 21, 2017. https://www.thecipherbrief.com/terrorist-networks -eye-bitcoin-cryptocurrencys-price-rises#.Wjvb1ZgHnYB.twitter.

Fanusie, Yaya J., and Alex Entz. *Al-Shabaab Financial Assessment*. Center on Sanctions and Illicit Finance, Foundation for Defense of Democracies, June 2017. https://s3.us-east-2.amazonaws.com/defenddemocracy/uploads/documents /CSIF_TFBB_Al-Shabaab_v05_web.pdf.

Farah, Douglas. *Blood from Stones*. New York: Broadway, 2004.

Fearon, James D. "Why Do Some Civil Wars Last So Much Longer Than Others?" *Journal of Peace Research* 41, no. 3 (2004): 275–301. https://doi.org/10.1177 /0022343304043770.

Felbab-Brown, Vanda. *Shooting Up: Counterinsurgency and the War on Drugs*. Washington, DC: Brookings Institution Press, 2009.

———. "Making a Killing: The Nexus of Terrorism and Wildlife Trafficking." *Cipher Brief*, December 7, 2017. https://www.thecipherbrief.com/making -killing-nexus-terrorism-wildlife-trafficking#.WjmbXwdHp9c.twitter.

Feldman, Robert. "Fund Transfers: African Terrorists Blend Old and New—Hawala and Satellite Telecommunications." *Small Wars and Insurgencies* 17, no. 3 (2006): 356–366.

Financial Action Task Force (FATF). *AML/CFT and Public-Private Sector Partnership*. May 20, 2016. https://www.fatf-gafi.org/publications/fatfgeneral/documents /public-private-sector-partnership.html.

———. *Emerging Terrorist Financing Risks*. October 2015. http://www.fatf-gafi .org/media/fatf/documents/reports/Emerging-Terrorist-Financing-Risks.pdf.

———. *Financing of Recruitment for Terrorist Purposes*. January 2018. http:// www.fatf-gafi.org/media/fatf/documents/reports/Financing-Recruitment-for -Terrorism.pdf.

———. *Financing of the Terrorist Organization Islamic State in Iraq and the Levant (ISIL)*. February 2015. http://www.fatf-gafi.org/media/fatf/documents/reports /Financing-of-the-terrorist-organisation-ISIL.pdf.

———. *Money Laundering/Terrorist Financing Risks and Vulnerabilities Associated with Gold*. July 2015. https://www.fatf-gafi.org/media/fatf/documents/reports /ML-TF-risks-vulnerabilities-associated-with-gold.pdf.

Financial Transactions and Reports Analysis Centre of Canada (FINTRAC). "Operational Brief: Risks and Indicators for Dealers in Precious Metals and Stones." July 2019. https://www.fintrac-canafe.gc.ca/intel/operation/dpms -eng.pdf.

———. "Project Protect Public Service Renewal in Action." August 16, 2019. https://www.fintrac-canafe.gc.ca/emplo/psr-eng.

———. "Terrorist Financing Assessment: 2018." 2018.

FitzGerald, Valpy. "Global Financial Information, Compliance Incentives and Terrorist Funding." *European Journal of Political Economy* 20, no. 2 (2004): 387–401. https://doi.org/10.1016/j.ejpoleco.2003.12.008.

Flanigan, Shawn Teresa. "Charity as Resistance: Connections Between Charity, Contentious Politics, and Terror." *Studies in Conflict and Terrorism* 29, no. 7 (2007): 641–655.

Forman, Marcy M. "Combating Terrorist Financing and Other Financial Crimes Through Private Sector Partnerships." *Journal of Money Laundering Control* 9, no. 1 (2006): 112–118.

Foundation for Defense of Democracies. *Al-Shabaab: Financial Assessment.* June 2017. http://www.defenddemocracy.org/content/uploads/documents/CSIF_TFBB _Al-Shabaab_v05_web.pdf.

France24. "Syria: On the Trail of Looted Antiquities." June 26, 2015. https:// www.youtube.com/watch?v=YBmD19v6zUo.

Freeland, Charles. "How Can Sound Customer Due Diligence Rules Help Prevent the Misuse of Financial Institutions in the Financing of Terrorism?" In *Financing Terrorism*, edited by Mark Pieth, 41–48. Dordrecht: Springer Netherlands, 2002. https://doi.org/10.1007/0-306-48044-1_3.

Freeman, Colin. "Islamic State 'Earning Millions by Playing the Stock Market.'" *Telegraph*, March 2, 2016. http://www.telegraph.co.uk/news/worldnews /middleeast/iraq/12180652/Islamic-state-earning-millions-by-playing-the -stock-market.html.

Freeman, Michael. "The Sources of Terrorist Financing: Theory and Typology." *Studies in Conflict and Terrorism* 34, no. 6 (June 2011): 461–475. https://doi .org/10.1080/1057610X.2011.571193.

Freeman, Michael, and Moyara Ruehsen. "Terrorism Financing Methods: An Overview." *Perspectives on Terrorism* 7, no. 4 (2013).

Garowe Online. "Somalia: ISIL-Linked Faction Imposes Tax on Businesses in Bosaso." August 15, 2018. https://www.garoweonline.com/en/news/puntland /somalia-ISIL-linked-faction-impose-taxes-on-businesses-in-bosaso.

Guardian. "Deadly Attack Keeps World on Alert." September 4, 2002. https://www .theguardian.com/world/2002/sep/04/september11.usa.

Germann, Wade A., Eric Hartunian, Richard A. Polen, and Krishnamurti Mortela. "Terrorist Financing in the Philippines." In *Financing Terrorism: Case Studies*, edited by Michael Freeman, 143–164. New York: Routledge, 2012.

Gift of the Givers. "About Us." Accessed June 6, 2020. https://giftofthegivers .org/about-us/.

Giustozzi, Antonio. *Koran, Kalashnikov, and Laptop: The Neo-Taliban Insurgency in Afghanistan.* New York: Columbia University Press, 2008. http://cup.columbia .edu/book/978-0-231-70009-2/koran-kalashnikov-and-laptop.

Glinski, Stefanie. "Afghanistan Forests Are Turning a Profit for the Islamic State." *Foreign Policy*, July 15, 2019. https://foreignpolicy.com/2019/07/15/afghanistans -forests-are-turning-a-profit-for-the-islamic-state/.

Global Witness. "At Any Price We Will Take the Mines: The Islamic State, the Taliban and Afghanistan's White Talc Mountains." May 22, 2018. https://www.global witness.org/en/campaigns/afghanistan/talc-everyday-mineral-funding -afghan-insurgents/.

Graham-Harrison, Emma. "Could ISIS's 'Cyber Caliphate' Unleash a Deadly Attack on Key Targets?" *Guardian*, April 12, 2015. https://www.theguardian.com /world/2015/apr/12/isis-cyber-caliphate-hacking-technology-arms-race.

Guittet, E. P., and J. Jeandesboz. "Security Technologies." In *The Routledge Handbook of New Security Studies*, edited by J. Peter Burgess, 229–239. New York: Routledge, 2010.

Guled, Abdi. "Extremist Group Al-Shabab Sets Up COVID-19 Center in Somalia." *AP News*, June 12, 2020. https://apnews.com/fc7930ffdf0202de626a8fe043c7fb9b.

Gunaratna, Rohan, and Arabinda Acharya. "Terrorist Finance and the Criminal Underground." In *Denial of Sanctuary: Understanding Terrorist Safe Havens*, edited by Michael A. Innes, 97–111. Westport, CT: Praeger, 2007.

Gurulé, Jimmy. "The Demise of the UN Economic Sanctions Regime to Deprive Terrorists of Funding." *Case Western Reserve Journal of International Law* 41, no. 1 (2009): 19–64.

Hall, Richard. "ISIS Suspects Raise Thousands Through Online Crowdfunding Campaign from Syria Camp." *Independent*, July 25, 2019. https://www .independent.co.uk/news/world/middle-east/isis-syria-camp-al-hol-paypal -telegram-online-crowdfunding-a9021006.html.

Hansen-Lewis, Jamie, and Jacob N. Shapiro. "Understanding the Daesh Economy." *Perspectives on Terrorism* 9, no. 4 (2015): 142–155.

Hardouin, Patrick. "Banks Governance and Public-Private Partnership in Preventing and Confronting Organized Crime, Corruption, and Terrorism Financing." *Journal of Financial Crime* 16, no. 3 (2009): 199–209. https://doi.org/10.1108 /13590790910971757.

Harper, Tom. "From London Bridge to Ariana Grande, UK Terror Attacks in 2017 Cost Just £5,000." *Sunday Times*, September 9, 2018. https://www.thetimes .co.uk/article/from-london-bridge-to-ariana-grande-uk-terror-attacks-in-2017 -cost-just-5-000-vck5tdttg.

Hasbi, Ahmad Helmi, and Remy Mahzam. "Cryptocurrencies: Potential for Terror Financing?" CSS Blog Network. May 23, 2018. https://isnblog.ethz.ch/technology /cryptocurrencies-potential-for-terror-financing.

Herhalt, Chris. "Minassian Described Planning and Carrying Out Van Attack in Police Interview." CP24, September 27, 2019. https://www.cp24.com/minassian -described-planning-and-carrying-out-van-attack-in-police-interview-1.4612876.

Hess, Michel. "Substantiating the Nexus Between Diaspora Groups and the Financing of Terrorism." In *Terrornomics*, edited by Sean S. Costigan and David Gold, 49–63. Burlington, VT: Ashgate, 2007.

Hewitt, Christopher. "The Costs of Terrorism: A Cross-National Study of Six Countries." *Terrorism* 11, no. 3 (1988): 169–180. https://doi.org/10.1080/105761088 08435709.

Hiraal Institute. "The AS Finance System." July 2018. https://hiraalinstitute.org/wp -content/uploads/2018/07/AS-Finance-System.pdf.

Hoffman, Bruce, and Jacob Ware. "Assessing the Threat of Incel Violence." *Studies in Conflict and Terrorism* (2020). https://doi.org/10.1080/1057610X.2020 .1751459.

Horgan, John, and Max Taylor. "Playing the 'Green Card': Financing the Provisional IRA—Part 1." *Terrorism and Political Violence* 11, no. 2 (June 1999): 1–38. https://doi.org/10.1080/09546559908427502.

———. "Playing the 'Green Card': Financing the Provisional IRA—Part 2." *Terrorism and Political Violence* 15, no. 2 (June 2003): 1–60. https://doi.org /10.1080/09546550312331293027.

House of Commons. "Report of the Official Account of the Bombings in London on 7th of July 2005." UK Government. https://assets.publishing.service.gov .uk/government/uploads/system/uploads/attachment_data/file/228837/1087.pdf.

Humud, Carla E., Liana Rosen, and Robert Pirog. "Islamic State Financing and U.S. Policy Approaches." Congressional Research Service, April 10, 2015. https:// fas.org/sgp/crs/terror/R43980.pdf.

Hwang, Julie Chernov. "Dakwah Before Jihad: Understanding the Behaviour of Jemaah Islamiyah." *Contemporary Southeast Asia* 41, no. 1 (2019): 14–34.

Hyland, Frank. "The Many Faces of the PKK." *Terrorism Focus* 4, no. 25 (2007). https://jamestown.org/program/the-many-faces-of-the-pkk/.

Immigration and Customs Enforcement. "Human Trafficking vs. Human Smuggling." US Government, 2017. https://www.ice.gov/sites/default/files/documents/Report /2017/CSReport-13-1.pdf.

Irwin, Angela Samantha Maitland, Kim-Kwang Raymond Choo, and Lin Liu. "Modelling of Money Laundering and Terrorism Financing Typologies." *Journal of Money Laundering Control* (2012).

Jakarta Post. "Police Track Foreign Funding of IS-Linked JAD." July 26, 2019. https://www.thejakartapost.com/news/2019/07/26/police-track-foreign-funding -of-is-linked-jad.html.

———. "Police Track Funding of Jamaah Islamiyah Terror Group." July 2, 2019. https://www.thejakartapost.com/news/2019/07/02/police-track-funding-of -jamaah-islamiyah-terror-group.html.

Jamwal, N. S. "Hawala: The Invisible Financing System of Terrorism." *Strategic Analysis* 26, no. 2 (2002): 181–198. https://doi.org/10.1080/09700160208 450038.

Jayasinghe, Uditha, and James Hookway. "U.S., India Warned Sri Lanka Weeks Before Easter Terror Attacks." *Wall Street Journal*, April 23, 2019. https://www .wsj.com/articles/sri-lanka-makes-arrests-in-easter-bombing-attacks-115559 18580.

Jervis, Robert. "Cooperation Under the Security Dilemma." *World Politics* 30, no. 2 (1978): 167–214. https://doi.org/10.2307/2009958.

Johnsson, Michael, and Svante Cornell. "Countering Terrorist Financing: Lessons from Europe Conflict and Security." *Georgetown Journal of International Affairs* 8, no. 1 (2007): 69–78.

Jordan, Jenna. "Attacking the Leader, Missing the Mark: Why Terrorist Groups Survive Decapitation Strikes." *International Security* 38, no. 4 (2014): 7–38. https://doi.org/10.1162/ISEC_a_00157.

Joscelyn, Thomas. "US Designates Members of Rawi Network for Financing Islamic State." *FDD's Long War Journal*, April 16, 2019. https://www.longwarjournal .org/archives/2019/04/us-designates-members-of-rawi-network-for-financing -islamic-state.php.

Kambere, Geoffrey, Play Hock Goh, Pranav Kumar, and Fulgence Msafiri. "Lashkar-e-Taiba (LeT)." In *Financing Terrorism: Case Studies*, edited by Michael Freeman, 75–92. New York: Routledge, 2012.

Katz, Rita, and Michael Kern. "Terrorist 007, Exposed." *Washington Post*, March 26, 2006. http://www.washingtonpost.com/wp-dyn/content/article/2006/03/25 /AR2006032500020.html.

Keatinge, Tom. "Identifying Foreign Terrorist Fighters: The Role of Public-Private Partnerships, Information Sharing and Financial Intelligence." The Hague and London: International Centre for Counterterrorism/Royal United Services Institute, 2015. https://rusi.org/sites/default/files/201506_op_identifying_foreign _terrorist_fighters_0.pdf.

———. "The Role of Finance in Defeating Al Shabaab." London: Royal United Services Institute, 2014, 39.

Keatinge, Tom, and Florence Keen. "Lone-Actor and Small Cell Terrorist Attacks: A New Front in Counter-Terrorist Finance?" Royal United Services Institute Occasional Paper, January 2017.

———. "Social Media and Terrorist Financing: What Are the Vulnerabilities and How Could Public and Private Sectors Collaborate Better?" Global Research

Network on Terrorism and Technology Paper 10, Royal United Services Institute, 2019.

Keatinge, Tom, Florence Keen, and Kayla Izenman. "Fundraising for Right-Wing Extremist Movements: How They Raise Funds and How to Counter It." *RUSI Journal* 164, no. 2 (February 2019): 10–23. https://doi.org/10.1080/03071847.2019.1621479.

Keen, Florence. "Public-Private Collaboration to Counter the Use of the Internet for Terrorist Purposes." London: Global Research Network on Terrorism and Technology, Royal United Services Institute, 2019. https://rusi.org/sites/default/files/20190206_gifct_paper_1_keen_public-private_partnerships_web.pdf.

Kenner, David. "All ISIS Has Left Is Money. Lots of It." *Atlantic*, March 24, 2019. https://www.theatlantic.com/international/archive/2019/03/ISIS-caliphate-money-territory/584911/.

Kenney, Michael. *From Pablo to Osama: Trafficking and Terrorist Networks, Government Bureaucracies, and Competitive Adaptation.* University Park: Pennsylvania State University Press, 2007.

Knutson, Ted. "Terrorists Trying Multiple Times to Raise Funds via Crypto—Without Much Success, Congress Told." *Forbes*, September 7, 2018. https://www.forbes.com/sites/tedknutson/2018/09/07/terrorists-trying-multiple-times-to-raise-funds-via-crypto-without-much-success-congress-told/#3b38cd802c64.

Komar, Rao, Christian Borys, and Eric Woods. "The Blackwater of Jihad." *Foreign Policy*, February 10, 2017. https://foreignpolicy.com/2017/02/10/the-world-first-jihadi-private-military-contractor-syria-russia-malhama-tactical/.

Koseli, Mutlu, Niyazi Ekici, Murat Erkan Eren, and Christopher Bitner. "Use of Kidnapping and Extortion as a Tool for Financing Terrorism: The Case of the PKK." *Behavioral Sciences of Terrorism and Political Aggression* (2020): 1–16.

Kriner, Matthew, and Colin P. Clarke. "How the Boogaloo Bois Went from Meme to Movement." *Slate*, August 19, 2020. https://slate.com/news-and-politics/2020/08/boogaloos-growth-memes-blm.html.

La, John. "Comment les Terroristes du 22 Mars ont Finance les Attentats." *La Libre Belgique.* August 2, 2017. https://www.lalibre.be/belgique/comment-les-terroristes-du-22-mars-ont-finance-les-attentats-5980be80cd70d65d251f4e95.

———. "Forced Remittances in Canada's Tamil Enclaves." *Peace Review* 16, no. 3 (2004): 379–385. https://doi.org/10.1080/1040265042000278630.

Léonard, Sarah, and Christian Kaunert. "Combating the Financing of Terrorism Together? The Influence of the United Nations on the European Union's Financial Sanctions Regime." In *The Influence of International Institutions on the EU: When Multilateralism Hits Brussels*, edited by O. Costa and K. Jørgensen, 96–110. London: Palgrave Macmillan, 2012. http://ebookcentral.proquest.com/lib/oculcarleton-ebooks/detail.action?docID=931704.

Levitt, Matthew. *Hamas: Politics, Charity, and Terrorism in the Service of Jihad.* New Haven, CT: Yale University Press, 2007.

———. "Introduction." In *Neither Remaining nor Expanding*, edited by Matthew Levitt, 1–14. Washington, DC: Washington Institute for Near East Policy, 2017. https://www.washingtoninstitute.org/uploads/Documents/pubs/PolicyFocus155-CT8-7.pdf.

———. "USA Ties Terrorist Attacks in Iraq to Extensive Zarqawi Network." *Jane's Intelligence Review* (2004).

Levitt, Matthew, and Michael Jacobson. "The U.S. Campaign to Squeeze Terrorists' Financing." *Journal of International Affairs* 62, no. 1 (Fall 2008).

Levy, Jack S., and William R. Thompson. *Causes of War*. "Civil War," 186–204. West Sussex, UK: Wiley, 2010.

L'express. "Financement du Terrorisme: 416 Donateurs Identifiés en France en Deux Ans." April 26, 2018. https://www.lexpress.fr/actualite/societe/financement -du-terrorisme-416-donateurs-identifies-en-france-en-deux-ans_2003792.html.

Lia, Brynjar, and Ashild Kjøk. "Islamist Insurgencies, Diasporic Support Networks, and Their Host States: The Case of the Algerian GIA in Europe 1993–2000." 2001/03789. Kjeller: Norwegian Defence Research Establishment, 2001.

Liang, Christina Schori. "The Criminal-Jihadist: Insights into Modern Terrorist Financing." Geneva: Geneva Centre for Security Policy, August 2016.

Looney, Robert. "The Mirage of Terrorist Financing: The Case of Islamic Charities." *Strategic Insights* 5, no. 3 (March 2006).

Lormel, Dennis M. "Lessons Learned from the Paris and Brussels Terrorist Attack." *ACAMS Today*, March 22, 2016. https://www.acamstoday.org/lessons-learned -paris-brussels-attacks/.

Magdy, Sam, and Ashraf Sweilam. "Militants Rob Bank, Attack Church in Egypt's Sinai; 7 Dead." Associated Press, October 16, 2017. https://apnews.com /9b6b816ce2c645dfab8c4460cc84876e.

Mahendrarajah, Shivan. "Conceptual Failure, the Taliban's Parallel Hierarchies, and America's Strategic Defeat in Afghanistan." *Small Wars and Insurgencies* 25, no. 1 (2014): 91–121. https://doi.org/10.1080/09592318.2014.893957.

Malik, Nikita. "How Criminals and Terrorists Use Cryptocurrency: And How to Stop It." *Forbes*, August 31, 2018. https://www.forbes.com/sites/nikitamalik /2018/08/31/how-criminals-and-terrorists-use-cryptocurrency-and-how-to-stop -it/#40b77f693990.

Mansour, Renad, and Hasham al-Hashimi. "ISIS Inc." *Foreign Policy*, January 16, 2018. https://foreignpolicy.com/2018/01/16/isis-inc-islamic-state-iraq-syria/.

Maritime Executive. "Charcoal Smuggling Finances Somali Terrorist Groups." January 16, 2019. https://www.maritime-executive.com/article/charcoal-smuggling -finances-somali-terrorist-groups.

Mashal, Mujib. "Afghan Taliban Awash in Heroin Cash, a Troubling Turn for War." *New York Times*, October 29, 2017. https://www.nytimes.com/2017/10/29 /world/asia/opium-heroin-afghanistan-taliban.html?smid=tw-nytimesworld &smtyp=cur.

Maxwell, Nick J, and David Artingstall. "Information-Sharing Partnerships in the Disruption of Crime." Occasional Paper, October 2017.

Mbodiam, Brice R. "Cameroon: Boko Haram Has Stolen CFA 3bn Worth of Cattle Since 2013." *Business in Cameroon*, September 7, 2018. https://www .businessincameroon.com/breeding/0709-8324-cameroon-boko-haram-has -stolen-cfa3bn-worth-of-cattle-since-2013-world-bank.

McCoy, Olivia. "Is ISIS Being Funded by Anonymous Bitcoin Donations?" *Newsweek*, August 18, 2017. https://www.newsweek.com/barcelona-terror -attack-ISIS-kept-afloat-anonymous-bitcoin-donations-652090.

McGrath, Kevin. *Confronting Al-Qaeda: New Strategies to Combat Terrorism*. Annapolis, MD: Naval Institute Press, 2011.

McGrath, Maggie. "Why It Would Have Been Perfectly Legal for the San Bernardino Shooter to Borrow $28,400 from Prosper." *Forbes*, December 8, 2015. https://www.forbes.com/sites/maggiemcgrath/2015/12/08/why-it-would -have-been-perfectly-legal-for-the-san-bernardino-shooter-to-borrow-28500 -from-prosper/.

McKiernan, David D., Benjamin Bahney, David M. Blum, J. Edward Conway, Brian A. Gordon, Howard J. Shatz, and Colonel Clayton O. Sheffield. *Counterterrorism and Threat Finance Analysis During Wartime.* Lanham, MD: Lexington, 2015.

Meir Amit Intelligence and Terrorism Information Center. "Funding Terrorism: ISIS Raises Funds Through an Affiliated Website, Using Bitcoins." March 7, 2019. https://www.terrorism-info.org.il/app/uploads/2019/03/E_054_19.pdf.

———. "In View of Its Financial Problems, ISIS Is Selling Coins That It Minted at the Time of the Islamic State." Accessed January 12, 2018. http://www.terrorism-info.org.il/app/uploads/2018/01/E_003_18.pdf.

Mémier, Marc. "AQMI et Al-Mourabitoun: Le Dijhad Sahelien Reunifie?" *Etudes de l'Ifri,* January 2017.

Mendick, Robert, Martin Evans, and Victoria Ward. "Exclusive: Manchester Suicide Bomber Used Student Loan and Benefits to Fund Terror Plot." *Telegraph,* May 27, 2017. https://www.telegraph.co.uk/news/2017/05/26/exclusive-manchester-suicide-bomber-used-student-loan-benefits/.

Miguel del Cid Gómez, Juan. "A Financial Profile of the Terrorism of Al-Qaeda and Its Affiliates." *Perspectives on Terrorism* 4, no. 4 (2010).

Mironova, Vera. *From Freedom Fighters to Jihadists: Human Resources of Non-State Armed Groups.* Oxford, UK: Oxford University Press, 2019. https://oxford.universitypressscholarship.com/view/10.1093/oso/9780190939755.001.0001/oso-9780190939755.

Moghadam, Assaf. *Nexus of Global Jihad: Understanding Cooperation Among Terrorist Actors.* New York: Columbia University Press, 2017.

Monnier, Olivier. "Islamic State, al-Qaeda Support Fuels Attacks in West Africa." Bloomberg. Accessed on February 9, 2018. https://www.bloomberg.com/news/articles/2018-02-05/islamic-state-al-qaeda-support-fuels-attacks-in-west-africa.

Moore, Jack, and Gareth Browne. "Qatari Hostage Payments Funded Al Qaeda Group Now Syria's Most Powerful Militant Faction." *National,* April 29, 2018. https://www.thenational.ae/world/mena/qatari-hostage-payments-funded-al-qaeda-group-now-syria-s-most-powerful-militant-faction-1.725873.

Murdoch, Lindsay. "Marawi Uprising Funded by $1.9 Million from Islamic State." *Sydney Morning Herald,* October 25, 2017. http://www.smh.com.au/world/marawi-uprising-funded-by-19-million-from-islamic-state-20171025-gz7s7o.html.

Musharbash, Yassin. "The al-Qaida Guide to Kidnapping." *Spiegel Online,* December 1, 2005. https://www.spiegel.de/international/how-to-the-al-qaida-guide-to-kidnapping-a-387888.html.

Napoleoni, Loretta. "The Evolution of Terrorist Financing Since 9/11: How the New Generation of Jihadists Fund Themselves." In *Terrornomics,* edited by Sean S. Costigan and David Gold, 13–26. Burlington, VT: Ashgate, 2013.

———. "Terrorist Financing: How the New Generation of Jihadists Funds Itself." *RUSI Journal* 151, no. 1 (2006): 60–65. https://doi.org/10.1080/03071840609442004.

National Commission on Terrorist Attacks. *The 9/11 Commission Report: Final Report of the National Commission on Terrorist Attacks upon the United States.* New York: Norton, 2004.

National Consortium for the Study of Terrorism and Responses to Terrorism (START), University of Maryland. 2019. Global Terrorism Database (GTD). https://www.start.umd.edu/gtd.

Nebenzya, Vasily. "Russia Accuses Islamic State of Running Online Casinos." *Moscow Times,* February 9, 2018. https://themoscowtimes.com/news/Russia-accuses-islamic-state-running-online-casinos-60446.

Nesser, Petter. *Islamist Terrorism in Europe*. Oxford, UK: Oxford University Press, 2018.

Neumann, Peter R. "Don't Follow the Money: The Problem with the War on Terrorist Financing." *Foreign Affairs* 96 (2017): 93–102

Oakley, Richard T. "The Abu Sayyaf Group: A Destructive Duality." In *Terrorist Criminal Enterprises: Financing Terrorism Through Organized Crime*, edited by Kimberley L. Thachuk and Rollie Lal, 173–184. Santa Barbara, CA: Praeger, 2018.

Office of the Lead Inspector General. "Operation Inherent Resolve: Operations Pacific Eagle-Philippines, January 1, 2018–March 31, 2018." 2018. https://media.defense .gov/2018/may/14/2001916692/-1/-1/1/fy2018_lig_oco_oir2_q2_mar2018.pdf.

Official of the Northern Ireland Office. "Tackling Terrorist Finance." *Commonwealth Law Bulletin* 18, no. 4 (1992): 1482–1485.

Oftedal, Emilie. "The Financing of Jihadi Terrorist Cells in Europe." Kjeller: Norwegian Defence Research Establishment, 2014. http://www.ffi.no/no/Rapporter /14-02234.pdf.

Olivier, Mathieu. "Nigeria: 'Boko Haram Was Funded and Inspired by Bin Laden'—Zenn." *Africa Report*, May 13, 2020. https://www.theafricareport .com/27750/nigeria-boko-haram-was-funded-and-inspired-by-bin-laden-zenn/.

Ontario Superior Court of Justice. "Reasons for Judgement." *R. v. Mohammad Momin Khawaja*.

Pagan, Hector, Celina Realuyo, Emily Spencer, Bernd Horn, Mark Hanna, Christian Leuprecht, and Mike Rouleau et al. *SOF Role in Combating Transnational Organized Crime*. MacDill Air Force Base, FL: Joint Special Operations University Press, 2016.

Pagliery, Jose, and Charles Riley. "North Korea–Linked 'Lazarus' Hackers Hit a Fourth Bank in Philippines." CNN, May 27, 2016. https://money.cnn.com /2016/05/26/technology/swift-bank-hack-philippines-lazarus/.

Parker, Marc, and Max Taylor. "Financial Intelligence: A Price Worth Paying?" *Studies in Conflict and Terrorism* 33, no. 11 (2010): 949–959. https://doi.org /10.1080/1057610X.2010.514574.

Passas, Nikos. "Fighting Terror with Error: The Counter-Productive Regulation of Informal Value Transfers." *Crime, Law, and Social Change* 45, no. 4 (2006): 315–336. https://doi.org/10.1007/s10611-006-9041-5.

Passas, Nikos, and Kimberly Jones. "Commodities and Terrorist Financing: Focus on Diamonds." *European Journal on Criminal Policy and Research* 12, no. 1 (2006): 1–33. https://doi.org/10.1007/s10610-006-9006-3.

PayPal. "What Is a PayPal Money Pool?" Accessed May 14, 2020. https://www .paypal.com/ca/smarthelp/article/money-pools-overview-and-frequently-asked -questions-faq3566.

Pek, Ahmet, and Behsat Ekici. "Narcoterrorism in Turkey: The Financing of the PKK-KONGRA GEL from Illicit Drug Business." In *Understanding and Responding to the Terrorism Phenomenon: A Multi-Dimensional Perspective*, edited by O. Nikbay and S. Hancerli, 140–152. Amsterdam: IOS Press, 2007.

Peled, Miko. *Injustice: The Story of the Holy Land Foundation Five*. Charlottesville, VA: Just World, 2018.

Petrich, Katharine. "Al-Shabaab's Mata Hari Network." *War on the Rocks*, August 14, 2018. https://warontherocks.com/2018/08/al-shabaabs-mata-hari-network/.

Philippone, Doug. "Hezbollah: The Organization and Its Finances." In *Financing Terrorism: Case Studies*, edited by Michael Freeman, 49–62. New York: Routledge, 2012.

Phillips, Brian J. "What Is a Terrorist Group? Conceptual Issues and Empirical Implications." *Terrorism and Political Violence* 27, no. 2 (March 2015): 225–242. https://doi.org/10.1080/09546553.2013.800048.

Phillips, Michael M. "U.S. Attacks Taliban's Source of Funds in Afghanistan." *Wall Street Journal*, May 30, 2018. https://www.wsj.com/articles/in-afghanistan-u -s-attacks-talibans-source-of-funds-1527672601?mod=e2tw.

Pieth, Mark. "Editorial: The Financing of Terrorism—Criminal and Regulatory Reform." In *Financing Terrorism*, edited by Mark Pieth, 1–3. Dordrecht: Springer, 2002. https://doi.org/10.1007/0-306-48044-1_1.

Prothero, Mitch. "Inside the World of ISIS Investigations in Europe." *Buzzfeed News*, August 21, 2016. https://www.buzzfeednews.com/article/mitchprothero /why-europe-cant-find-the-jihadis-in-its-midst.

———. "Russia Did Pay Extremists to Attack US Soldiers, Taliban Sources Say." *Business Insider*. Accessed July 2, 2020. https://www.businessinsider.com/russia -did-pay-extremists-attack-american-soldiers-taliban-sources-say-2020-7.

R. v. Amara, No. 2025/07 (Superior Court of Justice, January 18, 2010).

R. v. Esseghaier, No. CR-13-10000655-0000 (Superior Court of Justice, September 23, 2015).

Rabasa, Angel, Peter Chalk, Kim Cragin, Sara A. Daly, Heather S. Gregg, Theodore W. Karasik, Kevin A. O'Brien, William Rosenau. "The Convergence of Terrorism, Insurgency, and Crime." In *Beyond al-Qaeda, Part 2: The Outer Rings of the Terrorist Universe*, 101–160. Santa Monica, CA: RAND Corporation, 2006.

Raphaeli, Nimrod. "Financing of Terrorism: Sources, Methods, and Channels." *Terrorism and Political Violence* 15, no. 4 (October 2003): 59–82. https://doi .org/10.1080/09546550390449881.

Rasmussen, Sune Engel. "Kidnapped Professors Beg Trump to Negotiate Release in Taliban Video." *Guardian*, January 11, 2017. http://web.archive.org/web /20170711160512/https://www.theguardian.com/world/2017/jan/11/kevin-king -timothy-john-weeks-taliban-kidnapping-afghanistan.

Raymond, Nate. "Lebanese Bank to Pay U.S. $102 Million in Money-Laundering Case." Reuters, June 25, 2013. https://www.reuters.com/article/us-lebanesebank -settlement-idUSBRE95O17P20130625.

Reese, Justin Y. "Financing the Taliban." In *Financing Terrorism: Case Studies*, edited by Michael Freeman, 93–110. New York: Routledge, 2012.

Reinares, Fernando. *Al-Qaeda's Revenge: The 2004 Madrid Train Bombings.* Woodrow Wilson Center, New York: Columbia University Press, 2017.

Revkin, Mara Redlich. "What Explains Taxation by Resource-Rich Rebels? Evidence from the Islamic State in Syria." *Journal of Politics* 82, no. 2 (2020): 757–764. https://doi.org/10.1086/706597.

RFI Afrique. "Niger: Multiplication des enlèvements dans les régions du lac Tchad et de Maradi." September 7, 2018. https://www.rfi.fr/fr/afrique/20180907-niger -multiplication-enlevements-lac-tchad-maradi.

Rider, Barry A. K. "The Weapons of War: The Use of Anti-Money Laundering Laws Against Terrorist and Criminal Enterprises—Part 1." *Journal of International Banking Regulations* 4, no. 1 (2002): 13–31.

Ridley, Nicholas. *Terrorist Financing: The Failure of Counter Measures*. Cheltenham, UK: Edward Elgar, 2012.

Ridley, Nicholas, and Dean C. Alexander. "Combating Terrorist Financing in the First Decade of the Twenty-First Century." *Journal of Money Laundering Control* 15, no. 1 (2011): 38–57. https://doi.org/10.1108/13685201211194727.

Rodger, James. "Dental Student Abdurahman Kaabar Jailed over 'Breathtaking' Spread of Terror Material." *Birmingham Mail*, January 11, 2019. https://www.birminghammail.co.uk/news/midlands-news/dental-student-abdurahman-kaabar-jailed-15665131.

Roethke, Theodore. "American Law and the Problem of Coerced Provision of Support to a Terrorist Organization as Grounds for Removal." *Political and Civil Rights Law Review* 17 (2007): 173–214

Rollins, John, and Seth Rosen. *International Terrorism and Transnational Crime: Security Threats, U.S. Policy, and Considerations for Change.* 7-5700 R41004. Washington, DC: Congressional Research Service, January 5, 2010.

Rollins, John, and Liana Sun Wyler. "Terrorism and Transnational Crime: Foreign Policy Issues for Congress." Congressional Research Service, June 11, 2014. https://fas.org/sgp/crs/terror/R41004.pdf.

Roston, Aram. "How the US Funds the Taliban." *Nation*, November 30, 2009. https://www.thenation.com/article/archive/how-us-funds-taliban/.

Ruda, Bennett. "Hezbollah: One Man's Narco-Terrorist Is Another Man's Freedom Fighter." *Jewish Press*, July 10, 2018. http://www.jewishpress.com/indepth/opinions/hezbollah-one-mans-narco-terrorist-is-another-mans-freedom-fighter/2018/07/10/?utm_content=buffer75af1&utm_medium=social&utm_source=twitter.com&utm_campaign=buffer.

Rudaw. "ISIS Burns Crop Fields in Makhmour After Farmers Refuse to Pay Tax." May 14, 2019. http://www.rudaw.net/english/middleeast/iraq/140520191.

Rudner, Martin. "Using Financial Intelligence Against the Funding of Terrorism." *International Journal of Intelligence and CounterIntelligence* 19, no. 1 (January 2006): 32–58. https://doi.org/10.1080/08850600500332359.

Ruehsen, Moyara. "Partiya Karkeren Kurdistan (PKK)." In *Financing Terrorism: Case Studies*, edited by Michael Freeman, 63–74. New York: Routledge, 2012.

Sageman, Marc. *Understanding Terror Networks*. Philadelphia: University of Pennsylvania Press, 2004.

Sahara Reporters. "Lai Mohammed Lied: UN Report Reveals FG Made 'Large Ransom Payment' to Boko Haram for Dapchi Girls." August 16, 2018. http://saharareporters.com/2018/08/16/lai-mohammed-lied-%E2%80%94-un-report-reveals-fg-made-%E2%80%98large-ransom-payment%E2%80%99-boko-haram-dapchi.

Sandler, Todd. "Collective Action and Transnational Terrorism." *World Economy* 26, no. 6 (2003): 779–802. https://doi.org/10.1111/1467-9701.00548.

Savage, Charlie, Mujib Mashal, Rukmini Callimachi, Eric Schmitt, and Adam Goldman. "Russian Bounty Suspicions Were Supported by Financial Data." *New York Times*, June 30, 2020. https://www.nytimes.com/2020/06/30/us/politics/russian-bounties-afghanistan-intelligence.html.

Schindler, Hans-Jakob. "The United Nations' View on al-Qaeda's Financing Today." In *How al-Qaeda Survived Drones, Uprisings, and the Islamic State*, 87–92. Washington, DC: Washington Institute for Near East Policy, June 2017. http://www.washingtoninstitute.org/uploads/Documents/pubs/PolicyFocus153-Zelin.pdf.

Schuurman, Bart, Edwin Bakker, Paul Gill, and Noémie Bouhana. "Lone Actor Terrorist Attack Planning and Preparation: A Data-Driven Analysis." *Journal of Forensic Sciences* 63, no. 4 (August 2018): 1191–1200. https://doi.org/10.1111/1556-4029.13676.

Schuurman, Bart, Lasse Lindekilde, Stefan Malthaner, Francis O'Connor, Paul Gill, and Noémie Bouhana. "End of the Lone Wolf: The Typology That Should Not

Have Been." *Studies in Conflict and Terrorism* 42, no. 8 (2019): 771–778. https://doi.org/10.1080/1057610X.2017.1419554.

Sciolino, Iaine. "Bombings in Madrid: The Attack; 10 Bombs Shatter Trains in Madrid, Killing 192." *New York Times*, March 12, 2004. http://www.nytimes.com /2004/03/12/world/bombings-in-madrid-the-attack-10-bombs-shatter-trains-in -madrid-killing-192.html.

Security Intelligence Review Committee. *SIRC Annual Report 2016–2017: Accelerating Accountability.* September 18, 2017. http://www.sirc-csars.gc.ca/anrran /2016-2017/index-eng.html#section_2_1.

Seierstad, Åsne. *One of Us: The Story of a Massacre in Norway—and Its Aftermath,* translated by Sarah Death. New York: Farrar, Straus & Giroux, 2016.

Shabelle Media Network. "Somalia: UK Government Admits Funding ISIL and Al Shabaab." *All Africa*, December 4, 2016. http://allafrica.com/stories /201612040148.html.

Shapiro, Jacob N. "Terrorist Organizations' Vulnerabilities and Inefficiencies." In *Terrorism Financing and State Response: A Comparative Perspective,* edited by Jeanne K. Giraldo and Harold A. Trinkunas, 56–71. Palo Alto, CA: Stanford University Press, 2007.

Shelley, Louise I. *Dark Commerce.* Princeton, NJ: Princeton University Press, 2018.
———. *Dirty Entanglements: Corruption, Crime, and Terrorism.* Cambridge, UK: Cambridge University Press, 2014.

Shortland, Anja. *Kidnap: Inside the Ransom Business.* Oxford, UK: Oxford University Press, 2019.

Silke, Andrew. "In Defense of the Realm: Financing Loyalist Terrorism in Northern Ireland—Part One: Extortion and Blackmail." *Studies in Conflict and Terrorism* 21, no. 4 (1998): 331–361. https://doi.org/10.1080/10576109808436073.

Soufan Center. "Intel Brief: Unraveling the Rawi Terrorist Financing Network." April 25, 2019. http://www.soufangroup.com/intelbrief-unraveling-the-rawi -terrorist-financing-network/.

Straits Times. "416 Who Gave Money to ISIS Identified in France, Says Top Anti-Terror Prosecutor." April 26, 2018. https://www.straitstimes.com/world /europe/416-ISIS-donors-identified-in-france-says-top-anti-terror-prosecutor.

Stubly, Peter. "Wife of Suspected ISIS Terrorist 'Used Payday Loans' to Fund His Bomb-Making Purchases on eBay." *Mirror*, December 2, 2015. http://web .archive.org/web/20170724183612/http://www.mirror.co.uk/news/uk-news /wife-suspected-ISIS-terrorist-used-6938824.

Talley, Ian, and Bradley Hope. "Accused Terrorists Use Loopholes to Tap Frozen Funds." *Wall Street Journal*, June 19, 2019. https://www.wsj.com/articles /accused-terrorists-use-loopholes-to-tap-frozen-funds-11560977005.

Taylor, Matthew. "Norway Gunman Claims He Had Nine-Year Plan to Finance Attacks." *Guardian*, July 25, 2011. https://www.theguardian.com/world/2011 /jul/25/norway-gunman-attack-funding-claim.

Teotonio, Isabel, and Bob Mitchell. "Toronto 18 Member Pleads Guilty." *Toronto Star*, January 20, 2010. https://www.thestar.com/news/gta/2010/01/20/toronto _18_member_pleads_guilty.html.

Thachuk, Kimberley L. "The Gangsterization of Terrorism." In *Terrorist Criminal Enterprises: Financing Terrorism Through Organized Crime,* edited by Kimberley L. Thachuk and Rollie Lal, 11–26. Santa Barbara, CA: Praeger, 2018.

Thachuk, Kimberley L., and Rollie Lal. "An Introduction to Terrorist Criminal Enterprises." In *Terrorist Criminal Enterprises: Financing Terrorism Through Organized Crime,* edited by Kimberley L. Thachuk and Rollie Lal, 1–10. Santa Barbara: Praeger, 2018.

Times of Israel. "Arab Israeli Man, Turkish Citizen Arrested for Helping to Fund Hamas." February 12, 2018. https://www.timesofisrael.com/liveblog_entry /arab-israeli-man-turkish-citizen-arrested-for-helping-to-fund-hamas/.

Toledo, Drei, and Mimi Fabe. "Surge in Remittances Preceded IS Attack on Marawi City." *Gulf Times*, January 4, 2018. http://www.gulf-times.com/story/577027.

TracFin, Tendances et Analyse. "Des Risques de Blanchiment de Capitaux de Financement du Terrorisme en 2016." 2016. https://www.economie.gouv.fr /files/rapport-analyse-tracfin-2016.pdf.

Treicher, Ron. "When Transaction Laundering Finances Terror." *Finextra*, January 17, 2017.

Treverton, Gregory F., Carl F. Matthies, Karla J. Cunningham, Jeremiah Goulka, Greg Ridgeway, and Anny Wong. "Film Piracy and Its Connection to Organized Crime and Terrorism." February 17, 2009. https://www.rand.org/pubs /research_briefs/RB9417.html.

Tritten, Travis J. "The Dark Side of Bitcoin: Terror Financing and Sanctions Evasion." *Washington Examiner*, January 16, 2018. http://www.washingtonexaminer.com /the-dark-side-of-bitcoin-terror-financing-and-sanctions-evasion/article /2646118.

UN Security Council. "'Abd al-Rahman bin 'Umayr al-Nu'aymi," Pub. L. No. 2161. UN Security Council Al Qaeda Sanctions List. 2014. https://www.un .org/securitycouncil/sanctions/1267/aq_sanctions_list/summaries/individual/% 27abd-al-rahman-bin-%27umayr-al-nu%27aymi.

———. "Benevolence International Foundation." UN Security Council Al Qaeda Sanctions List. Accessed May 27, 2020. https://www.un.org/securitycouncil /sanctions/1267/aq_sanctions_list/summaries/entity/benevolence-international -foundation.

———. "Hajjaj bin Fahd Al Ajmi," UN Security Council Al Qaeda Sanctions List. December 11, 2017. https://www.un.org/securitycouncil/sanctions/1267/aq _sanctions_list/summaries/individual/hajjaj-bin-fahd-al-ajmi.

———. "Hanifa Money Exchange Office (Branch Located in Albu Kamal, Syrian Arab Republic)." UN Security Council Al Qaeda Sanctions List. July 20, 2017. https://www.un.org/securitycouncil/sanctions/1267/aq_sanctions_list/summaries /entity/hanifa-money-exchange-office-%28branch-located-in.

———. "Monitoring Team Report." S/2014/815. November 14, 2014.

———. "Monitoring Team Report." S/2015/441. June 16, 2015.

———. "Monitoring Team Report." S/2015/891. November 19, 2015.

———. "Monitoring Team Report." S/2016/629. July 19, 2016.

———. "Monitoring Team Report." S/2017/35. January 13, 2017.

———. "Narrative Summary of Reasons for Listing: Hajjaj bin Fahd al Ajmi." August 15, 2014. https://www.un.org/sc/suborg/en/sanctions/1267/aq_sanctions _list/summaries/individual/hajjaj-bin-fahd-al-ajmi.

———. "Narrative Summary of Reasons for Listing: Sa'd bin Sa'd Muhammad Shariyan al-Kabi." September 21, 2015. https://www.un.org/sc/suborg/en /sanctions/1267/aq_sanctions_list/summaries/individual/sa'd-bin-sa'd-muhammad -shariyan-al-ka'bi.

———. "Twentieth Report of the Analytical Support and Sanctions Monitoring Team." S/2017/573. August 2017.

———. "Twenty-Second Report of the Analytic Support and Sanctions Monitoring Team." S/2018/705. July 27, 2018. http://undocs.org/S/2018/705.

United States of America v. Abdulrahman El Bahnasawy. Criminal Complaint.

United States of America, Plaintiff, v. 155 Virtual Currency Assets, Defendants. Civil Action No. 20-cv-2228 (n.d.).

US Department of Justice. "Global Disruption of Three Terror Finance Cyber-Enabled Campaigns." August 13, 2020. https://www.justice.gov/opa/pr/global-disruption-three-terror-finance-cyber-enabled-campaigns.

US Department of State. *International Narcotics Control Strategy Report*, vol. 2: *Money Laundering and Financial Crimes*. 2005. https://2009-2017.state.gov/documents/organization/51081.pdf.

US Department of the Treasury. "Counter Terrorism Designations: Fawaz al-Rawi Designation." December 13, 2016. https://www.treasury.gov/resource-center/sanctions/OFAC-Enforcement/Pages/20161213.aspx.

———. "Fact Sheet: Designation of Iranian Entities and Individuals for Proliferation Activities and Support for Terrorism." 2007. https://www.treasury.gov/press-center/press-releases/Pages/hp644.aspx.

———. "Memorandum for Department of Defense Lead Inspector General." 2016. https://www.treasury.gov/about/organizational-structure/ig/Audit Reports and Testimonies/OIG-CA-17-001.pdf.

———. "Remarks of Under Secretary for Terrorism and Financial Intelligence David Cohen Before the Center for a New American Security on 'Confronting New Threats in Terrorist Financing.'" March 4, 2014. https://www.treasury.gov/press-center/press-releases/Pages/jl2308.aspx.

———. "Shutting Down the Terrorist Financial Network, December 4, 2001." Press Release, December 4, 2001. https://www.treasury.gov/press-center/press-releases/Pages/po841.aspx.

———. "Treasury Designates Iranian Commercial Airline Linked to Iran's Support for Terrorism." Press Release, October 12, 2011. https://www.treasury.gov/press-center/press-releases/Pages/tg1322.aspx.

———. "Treasury Designates Key Nodes of ISIS's Financial Network Stretching Across the Middle East, Europe, and East Africa." Press Release, April 15, 2019. https://home.treasury.gov/news/press-releases/sm657.

———. "Treasury Identifies Kassem Rmeiti & Co. for Exchange and Halawi Exchange Co. as Financial Institutions of 'Primary Money Laundering Concern.'" Press Release, April 23, 2013. https://www.treasury.gov/press-center/press-releases/pages/jl1908.aspx.

———. "Treasury Sanctions East African Facilitator of Intricate ISIS Financial Network." Press Release, September 7, 2018. https://home.treasury.gov/news/press-releases/sm476.

US House of Representatives, Subcommittee on National Security and Foreign Affairs, and John F. Tierney. *Warlord, Inc.: Extortion and Corruption Along the U.S. Supply Chain in Afghanistan*. Washington, DC: US House of Representatives, 2010. http://media.washingtonpost.com/wp-srv/world/documents/warlords.pdf.

Vidino, Lorenzo, Jon Lewis, and Andrew Mines. "Dollars for Daesh: The Small Financial Footprint of the Islamic State's American Supporters." *CTC Sentinel* 13, no. 3 (March 2020). https://ctc.usma.edu/wp-content/uploads/2020/03/CTC-SENTINEL-032020.pdf.

Vilkko, Valter. *Al-Shabaab: From External Support to Internal Extraction—A Minor Field Study on the Financial Support from the Somali Diaspora to al-Shabaab*. Uppsala: Uppsala Universitet, 2011.

Viswanatha, Aruna, and Brett Wolf. "HSBC to Pay $1.9 Billion U.S. Fine in Money-Laundering Case." Reuters, December 11, 2012. https://www.reuters.com/article/us-hsbc-probe/hsbc-to-pay-1-9-billion-U-S-fine-in-money-laundering-case-idUSBRE8BA05M20121211.

Vittori, Jodi. *Terrorist Financing and Resourcing.* New York: Palgrave Macmillan, 2011.

Vlcek, William. "Hitting the Right Target: EU and Security Council Pursuit of Terrorist Financing." *Critical Studies on Terrorism* 2, no. 2 (2009): 275–291. https://doi.org/10.1080/17539150903010780.

Waldie, Paul. "How a Desmarais Investment Got Entangled in an Alleged Terror-Financing Scheme in Syria." *Globe and Mail*, June 23, 2018. https://www .theglobeandmail.com/business/article-how-a-desmarais-investment-got -entangled-in-an-alleged-terror/.

Warner, Michael. "Wanted: A Definition of 'Intelligence': Understanding Our Craft." Central Intelligence Agency. *Studies in Intelligence* 46, no. 3 (2002). https://www.cia.gov/library/center-for-the-study-of-intelligence/csi-publications /csi-studies/studies/vol46no3/article02.html.

Warrick, Joby. "Hacked Messages Show Qatar Appearing to Pay Hundreds of Millions to Free Hostages." *Washington Post*, April 28, 2018. https://www.washingtonpost .com/world/national-security/hacked-messages-show-qatar-appearing-to-pay -hundreds-of-millions-to-free-hostages/2018/04/27/46759ce2-3f41-11e8-974f -aacd97698cef_story.html?noredirect=on&utm_term=.332a42658e6a.

———. "Retreating ISIS Army Smuggled a Fortune in Cash and Gold out of Iraq and Syria." *Washington Post*, December 21, 2018. https://www.washingtonpost .com/world/national-security/retreating-ISIS-army-smuggled-a-fortune-in -cash-and-gold-out-of-iraq-and-syria/2018/12/21/95087ffc-054b-11e9-9122 -82e98f91ee6f_story.html?noredirect=on&utm_term=.ce84b851a617.

Weinstein, Jeremy M. *Inside Rebellion: The Politics of Insurgent Violence.* Cambridge, UK: Cambridge University Press, 2006.

West, Leah, and Michael Nesbitt. "Proscribing Far Right Terrorism: Canada's New Terrorist Listing of Two Far Right Extremist Groups." *Intrepid*, July 4, 2019. https://www.intrepidpodcast.com/blog/2019/7/4/proscribing-far-right-terrorism -canadas-new-terrorist-listing-of-two-far-right-extremist-groups.

Whitcomb, Dan. "Two Women Convicted in U.S. of Financing Somali Group al Shabaab." Reuters, October 25, 2016. https://www.reuters.com/article/us-crime -alshabaab-idUSKCN12P2U0.

Willgress, Lydia. "Teenager Who Spent Student Loan Trying to Join ISIL and Used a 'Step-by-Step Guide to Terrorism' Is Jailed." *Telegraph*, July 28, 2016. https://www.telegraph.co.uk/news/2016/07/28/teenager-who-spent-student-loan -trying-to-join-isis-and-used-a-s/.

Williams, Phil. *Criminals, Militias, and Insurgents: Organized Crime in Iraq.* Carlisle, PA: Army War College Press, 2009. https://purl.fdlp.gov/GPO /LPS116438.

———. "Warning Indicators, Terrorist Finances, and Terrorist Adaptation." *Strategic Insights* 6, no. 1 (January 2005): 2–16.

Wilson, Tom, and Dan Williams. "Hamas Shifts Tactics in Bitcoin Fundraising, Highlighting Crypto Risks: Research." Reuters, April 26, 2019. https:// www.reuters.com/article/us-crypto-currencies-hamas-idUSKCN1S20FA.

Winer, Jonathan M. "Globalization, Terrorist Finance, and Global Conflict: Time for a White List?" In *Financing Terrorism*, edited by Mark Pieth, 5–40. Dordrecht: Springer, 2002. https://doi.org/10.1007/0-306-48044-1_2.

Winer, Jonathan M., and Trifin J. Roule. "Fighting Terrorist Finance." *Survival* 44, no. 3 (2002): 87–104.

Wittig, Timothy S. "Financing Terrorism Along Chechnya-Georgia Border, 1999–2002." *Global Crime* 10, no. 3 (2009).

————. *Understanding Terrorist Finance*. London: Palgrave Macmillan, 2011. https://doi.org/10.1057/9780230316935.

Yuen, Stacey. "It's Not Just Russia—Terror Financiers Are Also Using Social Media Propaganda." CNBC, December 19, 2017. https://www.cnbc.com/2017/12/18 /social-media-propaganda-terror-financiers-operate-on-internet.html.

Zabyelina, Yuliya. "The 'Capone Discovery': Extortion as a Method of Terrorism Financing." *Studies in Conflict and Terrorism* (2019): 1–16. https://doi .org/10.1080/1057610X.2019.1678860.

————. "The Industry of Terror: Criminal Financing of the North Caucasus Insurgency." In *Terrorist Criminal Enterprises*, edited by Kimberley L. Thachuk and Rollie Lal, 63–78. Santa Barbara: Praeger, 2018.

Zarate, Juan. *Treasury's War: The Unleashing of a New Era of Financial Warfare*. London: Hachette, 2013.

Zehorai, Itai. "The Richest Terror Organizations in the World." *Forbes*, January 24, 2018. https://www.forbes.com/sites/forbesinternational/2018/01/24/the-richest -terror-organizations-in-the-world/#3f96867f7fd1.

Zelin, Aaron Y, and Katherine Bauer. "The Development of Tunisia's Domestic Counter-Terrorism Finance Capability." *CTC Sentinel* 12, no. 8 (2019): 28–36.

Index

drug trafficking, 84; organizational use of funds, 122–123; "riding shotgun," 63–64, 80; state sponsorship to obtain, 14

seed money: bank robberies providing, 105; LTTE business investments, 53; operational expenses, 129–130; terrorist patrons, 39–40, 120; wealthy donors, 23–24

self-financing, 31–33, 41–42, 129–130, 215(fig.)

Shahnaz, Zoobia, 101

Shahzad, Faisal, 164

Shining Path (Peru): drug trafficking, 82

shoplifting, 105

slavery, 87

small-scale attacks, 200–201

smuggling: cash couriers and smugglers, 158–159; drug trafficking, 81–85; goods and people, 85–88; operational financing, 91(fig.); organizational financing, 90(fig.); women's roles in, 183. *See also* drug trafficking

social media: charitable sector exploitation, 49–50; financial intelligence gathering, 199–200; financial technology and, 221–223; fundraising and movement, 166; identity-based support networks, 28

social network analysis, 198–199

social services, 123–126

Somalia: charcoal exports, 86; charitable sector exploitation, 49; diaspora financing, 67–68; external funding for, 28; financial technologies, 165–166; hawala links to al-Qaeda, 163; ISIL control of banks, 104; maritime piracy, 80; women in terrorist organizations, 183

source data, 6–8

South Africa: facilitating ransoming of individuals, 77–78

South America, 82–83, 89

South Korea: kidnappings for ransom, 74

Soviet Union: state-sponsored terrorism, 15

Spain: drug trade financing terrorist attacks, 85

Sri Lanka: self-funded attacks, 32. *See also* Liberation Tigers of Tamil Eelam

state-sponsored terrorism: financial facilitators moving and obscuring funds, 186–187; main methods of fund-raising, 215(fig.); money management, 141; money movement through the formal sector, 156–157; motives for funding, 18–20; organizational versus operational funding, 21–22; terrorist groups' obligations, 20–21; use of cash couriers, 159

storage of funds: financing mechanisms, methods, and use, 217(fig.), 220–221(table); organizational and operational, 149(fig.); Ponzi scheme targeting Hizballah, 198; purpose and mechanisms, 213–218; strategies and goals, 143–148. *See also* banks; hawala

Stormfront, 167

Strasbourg plot (2000), 188

student loan fraud, 100–101

subeconomies: kidnappings for ransom, 77

Sudan: state-sponsored terrorism, 15

Sunder, Shad, 22

SunTrust Bank, Florida, 157–158

support networks: charitable sector, 45–46; donor categories, 13; financial, 155; financial crime, 101; funding sources, 13–15, 22, 214, 215(fig.), 220(table); identity-based networks, 25–30, 33–34; main methods of fund-raising, 215(fig.); the role of corruption, 127; territorial control and, 69; women creating, 183–184

surveillance, financial, 199. *See also* intelligence gathering

SWIFT banking hack, 224

Switzerland: LTTE business investments, 54

Sydney/Melbourne plot (2005), 31, 100, 142–143, 185

synagogue bombing (Tunisia), 117

Syria: identity-based support networks, 27; state-sponsored terrorism, 15

Tajheez al-Ghazi (fitting or arming a soldier), 29

Taliban: business investments, 54; competition for control of resources,

About the Book

Terrorists need money . . . to recruit and train people, to buy weapons, to maintain safe houses, to carry out attacks. Which raises the question: how do they procure and protect funds to finance their operations? In *Illicit Money*, Jessica Davis thoroughly answers that question.

Davis explores the full spectrum of terrorist finance, drawing on extensive case studies to dissect how individuals, cells, and organizations raise and manage, as well as hide, funds. In her concluding chapters, she considers both opportunities and challenges related to countering these illicit activities.

Jessica Davis is president and principal consultant at Insight Threat Intelligence, Ottawa. She previously served as senior strategic analyst at the Canadian Security Intelligence Service (CSIS).